CHINESE COOKERY

by Rose Cheng & Michele Morris

CONTENTS

ANOTHER BEST-SELLING VOLUME FROM H.P. BOOKS
Publisher: Helen Fisher; Editor: Carlene Tejada; Art Director: Don Burton; Book Design and Assembly: Ken Heiden; Typography: Cindy Coatsworth, Joanne Nociti, Michelle Claridge; Calligraphy: Francesca Haigh; Food Stylist: Janet Pittman
Photography: George deGennaro Studios
Technical Consultant: David Wong

Published by H.P. Books, P.O. Box 5367, Tucson, AZ 85703
602/888-2150
ISBN 0-89586-088-0; ISBN 0-89586-087-2 (cloth)
Library of Congress Catalog Card No. 81-80800
©1981 Fisher Publishing, Inc. Printed in U.S.A.

Cover photo: Shrimp with Snow Peas, page 54.

CENTURIES OF CHINESE CUISINE

"Have you eaten?" is the common greeting between friends in China. The most populous country in the world, China has always faced the problem of supplying enough food for its people. Eating is therefore a serious business and one of the joys of life.

From the Chinese peasant who knows good Chinese cabbage when he tastes it, to the diplomat who savors his roast duck, all Chinese are food connoisseurs. Each insists on the freshest, most tender meats and vegetables available. The exception is in northern China's cold climate where fresh foods are sometimes scarce. Cooks there often depend on dried foods such as mushrooms, shrimp and tiger lily buds for adding seasoning and texture.

Chinese cooking may be one of the world's most diverse and exotic cuisines, yet China's population has survived on a monotonous diet. If you lived in China, perhaps as much as three-quarters of your food would be rice or other grains and the remaining one-quarter would be mostly vegetables. You would eat three meals a day and snack frequently. In southern China, breakfast might be rice porridge and a steamed dumpling such as Shao Mai, pages 32 and 33, or Steamed Shrimp Dumplings, pages 34 and 35. Some Cantonese don't eat breakfast or lunch, but go to the teahouse for brunch, or *dim sum.* If you lived in northern China, you would begin your day with a bowl of noodles or Northern-Style Pancakes, page 152, Yu T'iau, page 154, and Soybean Milk, pages 186 and 187. Everywhere in China, both lunch and dinner include soup, vegetables and a little meat or fish.

You would probably not find milk, butter or cheese because cows are scarce. Meat, especially beef, has always been in short supply. Farmlands are used to raise food for people rather than fodder for animals. Because pigs and chickens are scavengers, pork and poultry appear more frequently on menus than beef. In general, protein in your diet would consist mainly of bean curd, freshwater fish or seafood. But it would be prepared with such thought and artistry that you would delight in every bite!

Food, according to the Chinese, should be a total experience designed to please all your senses. Cooks plan menus in the same manner artists block out a painting. The goal is to create a meal of variety and contrast. A cold dish may be served beside a hot one, sweets appear with pickled vegetables, and bland dishes act as a foil for spicy ones. Certain foods are combined because their fragrances produce an unforgettable aroma or because their colors resemble an artist's palette. White rice and green broccoli might be accented by a skillfully carved tomato rose. Texture contrast is important. Crunchy water chestnuts may be in the same dish with creamy bean curd. Crisp cabbage is often presented in a smooth sauce.

Chinese cooks create their masterpieces in simple kitchens that have not changed much over the years. The cooking apparatus in a typical kitchen is a large steel wok heated with gas. This wok can be used for stir-frying, steaming or deep-frying. A large electric rice cooker to steam and keep warm vast quantities of rice is a common fixture in Chinese homes. Most kitchens do not have ovens, leaving the roasting of meats to restaurant kitchens. We have included recipes that call for roasting poultry and meat so Westerners with ovens can sample these delicacies.

At the Table

In restaurants and many homes, you are greeted at the table with hot scented towels for your face and hands. There is no one main dish. Instead, three or four dishes of the same importance are served together. Meals are always family-style which means dishes of food are placed on the table so you can help yourself. To begin, cup a small porcelain bowl of rice in one hand. With chopsticks, transfer morsels of meat or vegetable slices from the serving dishes to your rice. Then, raising the bowl halfway between the table and your mouth, scoop up the food with your chopsticks. Knives or forks are not necessary because food is chopped into bite-size pieces before cooking.

Celebrations

Festivals revolve around food. When a child is born, the proud father presents boiled eggs, dyed red, to friends and relatives. Red symbolizes happiness and good luck. Birthday dinners often include a bowl of noodles because they are a symbol of long life. When a young couple announce their engagement, special sweet cakes are distributed to friends.

Chinese New Year, the most important festival of all, begins at four or five o'clock in the morning. Tables are laden with rice, vegetables, tea, wine and oranges. Red paper banners with the Chinese characters for happiness, wealth and good fortune are hung from the doors. Many sweets are eaten during the celebration. Steamed Layer Cakes or Steamed Cake, page 179, Sesame Bows, page 184, and Open Mouth Laughs, page 185, are only a few.

A colorful custom during the festivities is burning paper horses to worship the kitchen god. On the 24th day of the 12th lunar month, each kitchen god is supposed to report the behavior of his family to the Jade Emperor in the heavens. The family will be blessed or punished accordingly. The kitchen god returns to his family on the 4th day of the new year to resume his duty as their protector. So on the two days when the kitchen god is traveling between heaven and earth, the Chinese burn paper representing paper money to help him on his journeys. They also prepare sweets as a bribe so the Jade Emperor will receive only good reports of the family.

The Moon Festival is celebrated on the 15th day of the eighth lunar month. In Chinese mythology, the moon is a female element. Pomegranates, symbolizing fertility, and other fruits are eaten. At night, friends and relatives gather to watch the moon and to eat moon cakes. Cantonese Moon Cakes, pages 180 and 181, contain whole egg yolks representing the moon.

Moon cakes are the ancestors of fortune cookies. According to legend, moon cakes were responsible for freeing China from hated Tartar rule in the Fourteenth Century. Because everyone would be eating moon cakes at the same time, secret messages instructing the people to overthrow the Tartars were baked inside the cakes. The plan worked, the Tartars were vanquished and the Chinese ruler returned to his throne.

Rose Cheng, pictured above, was born in Nanking, China, and raised in Taipei, Taiwan. She has attended cooking classes since she was 15 years old and has been carefully taught the major cuisines of China by leading chefs. A resident of the United States since 1973 and now living in Tucson, Arizona, Rose teaches Chinese cooking at various cooking schools and at the University of Arizona.

Michele Morris has a degree in creative writing from the University of Arizona. While living in Taipei, she was editor-in-chief of an English language trade weekly and studied both the language and cooking of China. She is currently living in New York City and is on the staff of a travel magazine.

CUISINES OF CHINA

The four major styles of cooking which influence Chinese cuisine are Mandarin, from the city of Peking in northern China; Cantonese, named for a southern seaport; Szechuan, representing cooking of the central plains; and Shanghai, from the melting-pot seaport in the east.

Mandarin is China's classic cuisine. Mandarin recipes are given first in each recipe section. Cantonese recipes, most familiar to the western world, follow the Mandarin recipes. Szechuan is growing in popularity and these recipes are given next. Shanghai recipes, with their western influence, are given last.

MANDARIN

Peking, Chinese for *northern capital*, was the location of the Imperial Palace for many centuries. It became the gourmet center of China. Chefs from all over the country were recruited to serve their specialties to the court. The word *Mandarin* originally meant a *high-placed government official*. It has evolved to mean *aristocratic* or *of high rank*. Mandarin-style cooking is therefore the gourmet cuisine of China.

Peking is a walled city standing on a high plain. Summers are warm, but fierce northern winds and snowfalls are common in winter. For centuries, northern China has suffered from lack of rain. Rice—which needs to grow in wet fields—has never been a leading crop. Wheat and millet are the area's food staples. Wheat-flour dumplings, noodles and pancakes are served instead of rice.

Northern cooks are particularly skillful with pancakes. These are not breakfast pancakes to be topped with fruit or syrup. Chinese pancakes take the place of bread and are served with stir-fried dishes. Delicate Mandarin Pancakes, page 153, are similar to Mexican flour tortillas. Green Onion Pancakes, page 163, are filled with green onions and then fried.

Peking once had a reputation for lavish banquets. Mandarin cooking today features light, elegant and mildly seasoned foods. Soy sauce, garlic, sesame oil and green onions are used generously. Restaurants are famous for Peking Duck, page 71. The long cooking process requires an oven so Peking Duck is not usually made in Chinese homes.

Mongolian Fire Pot, page 114, comes from the Mongols in the cold mountain region. Fuel is scarce in northern China and the idea is to huddle around the fire pot warming your hands while a tureen full of broth is heating. Paper-thin slices of pork, beef or lamb are dipped into the bubbling broth until cooked and then dipped into spicy sauces. After the meal, the flavorful broth is poured into bowls and served as soup.

Soybeans are an important crop of northern China, particularly in Manchuria. Milk is extracted from soybean paste and used to make bean curd. Buddist vegetarians jokingly refer to bean curd as "meat without bones" because of its high protein content. Bean curd can be cooked in a variety of ways. It easily absorbs the flavors of sauces and seasonings, resulting in a range of very tasty dishes.

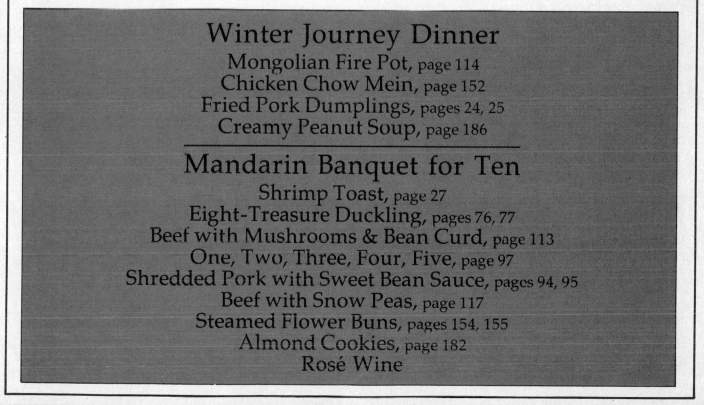

Winter Journey Dinner
Mongolian Fire Pot, page 114
Chicken Chow Mein, page 152
Fried Pork Dumplings, pages 24, 25
Creamy Peanut Soup, page 186

Mandarin Banquet for Ten
Shrimp Toast, page 27
Eight-Treasure Duckling, pages 76, 77
Beef with Mushrooms & Bean Curd, page 113
One, Two, Three, Four, Five, page 97
Shredded Pork with Sweet Bean Sauce, pages 94, 95
Beef with Snow Peas, page 117
Steamed Flower Buns, pages 154, 155
Almond Cookies, page 182
Rosé Wine

CANTONESE

The old and famous seaport of Canton lies near the mouth of the Chu River, also called the Pearl River, in southern China. Not far from Canton, the island of Hong Kong lies in the open sea. Being near the sea and far from the ruling influence of Peking, the Cantonese were the first to make contact with the western world. Corn, tomatoes and peanuts were imported from Europe, while Cantonese laborers and chow mein were exported—particularly to the west coast of North America. The Cantonese were the first to establish Chinese restaurants outside China.

Chop Suey is not an authentic Chinese dish. It was created from leftovers by the Cantonese chef of a wealthy American household in San Francisco. When questioned by his employer as to the name of this delicious new dish, the chef—not wanting to admit he had resorted to leftovers—quickly replied, "Chop suey," which is Cantonese for *mixed up.*

Mountains, forests and jungles cover much of southern China which also has a relatively long coastline. The region is warm most of the year and winters are mild, so the growing season is year round. Ample supplies of fruits and vegetables are grown as well as feed for chicken and pigs. Fishermen bring in an exotic array of seafood including shrimp, lobster, oysters, scallops, abalone, squid and sometimes shark fin or jellyfish. With all this diversity, pungent seasonings are not needed to stimulate palates bored with the same daily fare. Chicken broth, rice wine, sugar and fresh ginger root are the most common seasonings.

Rice is the staple food. In fact, it's so basic that the Chinese word for food, *fan,* is also the word for rice.

The Cantonese love small appetizers and have created a teatime cuisine called *dim sum.* These are the delightful Steamed Shrimp Dumplings, pages 34 and 35, Shao Mai, pages 32 and 33, and other small treats that are served in tea houses from mid-morning to mid-afternoon.

Buddhist vegetarianism and the Taoist philosophy of enjoying foods in their natural states have flourished in this region. Cooking is more casual than in other regions, resulting in coarser chopping and cutting. Many foods are quickly stir-fried, leaving ingredients crisp, tender and colorful.

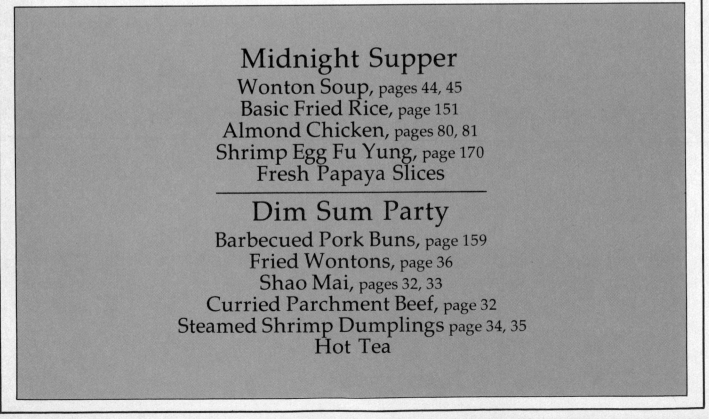

Midnight Supper
Wonton Soup, pages 44, 45
Basic Fried Rice, page 151
Almond Chicken, pages 80, 81
Shrimp Egg Fu Yung, page 170
Fresh Papaya Slices

Dim Sum Party
Barbecued Pork Buns, page 159
Fried Wontons, page 36
Shao Mai, pages 32, 33
Curried Parchment Beef, page 32
Steamed Shrimp Dumplings page 34, 35
Hot Tea

SZECHUAN

Tea and silk have made the province of Szechuan famous. The food of the area is just beginning to make a name for itself. The province of Hunan, which borders Szechuan, has had a strong influence on the cuisine of the area.

Szechuan includes plains, valleys and the deltas of the mighty Yangtze River in central China. Protected from cold winter winds and summer typhoons by tall mountain ranges, the climate is hot and humid. Wheat is grown in winter and rice is cultivated in summer, so both noodles and rice are common.

Spicy food is daily fare in tropical climates because it induces perspiration which has a cooling effect. Food in central China is decidedly hot. If you're a novice at eating spicy foods, your first taste of Szechuan cooking may be your last! If you reach for a glass of water to douse the flaming sensation, the fire soars higher. It's easy to understand why the Chinese drink quenching beer with this fiery cuisine.

Favorite seasonings are hot peppers, garlic, ginger, vinegar, sesame oil and green onions. A classic Szechuan dish is Hot & Sour Soup, page 49, seasoned with vinegar and pepper.

At first glance, some Szechuan recipes seem to break all rules. One dish might contain as many as five different spices. But the various flavors and sensations—sweet, sour, hot, spicy and the ability to cause slight numbness—can be tasted or felt simultaneously after the initial hot taste mellows. Szechuan food is not meant to be gulped. Savor it slowly so you can appreciate all its nuances.

Szechuan cooks have developed many cold dishes that can be cooked ahead of time. This makes life in a hot climate a little easier. Cold Noodles With Hot Sauce, page 161, and Szechuan Cucumber Slices, page 36, are popular in hot weather. Twice-Cooked Pork, page 108, is partially cooked and cooled so it can be sliced and stir-fried just before serving.

Autumn Festival Dinner
Sizzling Rice Soup page 48
Pearl Balls, page 37
Twice-Cooked Pork, page 108
Mongolian Beef, page 116
Cucumber Slices with Dried Shrimp, page 142
Mango Pudding, page 182

Spicy Szechuan Supper
Hot & Sour Soup, page 49
Sesame Seed Beef, page 125
Princess Shrimp, page 63
Szechuan Cucumber Slices, page 36
Sweet Almond Jelly, page 187

SHANGHAI

Once a small fishing village, Shanghai is now the largest city in China and an industrial and commercial center. It is situated near the mouth of the Yangtze River so the city has access to the farmlands of central China. Boats sail down the river hauling tea, silks, soybeans and cotton to Shanghai for export.

At one time, Shanghai had a bustling international settlement where foreigners established factories, banks and trading centers. It wasn't long before Shanghai developed a reputation for a cosmopolitan cuisine. Visitors to the city, both from within China and from other countries, brought their recipes and cooking secrets. Adventurous Shanghai cooks tried recipes, borrowed ideas and often created their own versions of the originals.

Western influences on Shanghai cooking are obvious in the use of tomato sauce and creamed sauce. The brown sauce of Shanghai is similar to gravy, but not as heavy.

Shanghai cooks use an assortment of soy sauces including dark and light soy sauces and those based on fish and mushrooms. Sugar is a popular seasoning. Milk and milk products, which almost never appear in the cuisines of other regions, occasionally appear in Shanghai recipes. The region's seacoast contributes delicate seafood dishes such as Golden Shrimp Balls, page 39, and Fish Ball Soup, page 50.

Meat is often braised or stewed so it has a much richer flavor than meat from other areas of China. *Red cooking* is a characteristic technique in Shanghai cuisine. The name comes from the rich red-brown gravy resulting from stewing pork or beef in soy sauce. The meat is turned frequently while cooking so it is evenly seasoned and colored.

Meat is often chopped very fine before cooking as in the famous Lion's Head Casserole, page 109. Chopped meat is pressed into large meatballs which are fried until golden, then braised in soy sauce. When arranged on a platter with Chinese cabbage, meatballs resemble a lion's head and the cabbage its mane. A popular quick and easy dish is Ground Beef with Sweet Corn, page 130.

Anniversary Celebration
Parchment Chicken Shanghai-Style, page 39
Cold Meat Platter, page 130
Braised Fish with Tomato Sauce, page 69
Orange Sherbet

Holiday Brunch
Golden Shrimp Balls, page 39
Fifteen-Minute Chicken, page 91
Ground Beef with Sweet Corn, page 130
Steamed Rice, page 151
Fresh Pineapple & Watermelon Slices

GETTING READY

Cooking Preparations

As you become familiar with Chinese recipes, you'll realize that 90 percent of the preparation time is getting foods ready to cook.

The Chinese do not use knives and forks at the table so all necessary cutting is done ahead of time, usually before cooking. Razor-sharp cleavers are used to cut ingredients into bite-size pieces that can be picked up with chopsticks. All food pieces are cut into similar sizes and shapes so they will cook uniformly.

Sauces are prepared and meats are marinated before cooking begins. Because cooking time is usually very brief, all the necessary ingredients must be within arm's reach before you begin to stir-fry or deep-fry.

Chinese Cleavers

Two Chinese cleavers, along with a thick chopping block, are indispensable. You'll use them to chop meats and vegetables, to crush garlic cloves with their broad edges and to tenderize meat with their dull edges. You can even use a cleaver to transport ingredients from the chopping block to the wok.

Chinese cleavers have blades about 8 inches long and 3 inches wide. They come in two weights—each used for a different purpose. Use the thicker, heavier cleaver, or chopping cleaver, for cutting through meats and chicken with bones. A thinner, lighter cleaver, or slicing cleaver, is best for slicing meats and chopping vegetables. Always use each cleaver for its particular function. If you use a slicing cleaver to chop through bones, you'll destroy its fine edge. And the chopping cleaver is too clumsy and heavy for slicing meats and delicate vegetables.

How to Use a Cleaver—Close your left hand in a loose fist and place it on top of the food to be cut. Hold the cleaver by its handle in your right hand. Position the knuckles of your fist against the side of the blade and move them in the same direction you move the blade as you chop. Never lift the cleaver above your knuckles and they will guide the blade and keep your fingers safe.

Cutting Methods

Slicing can be straight, diagonal or at an angle. Straight slicing is for soft vegetables such as mushrooms. Diagonal or angle-slice celery and meats to reduce the fibrous texture. Angle-slicing is also used for firm vegetables to create more surface area and reduce cooking time.

Shredding is similar to the julienne technique. Cut the food into long strips about 2 inches wide and then chop it into matchsticks.

Slice beef at an angle to increase surface area for cooking.

Shred by slicing into strips, then cutting into matchsticks.

Dicing is used for vegetables such as onions and green peppers. First cut the vegetables into strips and then slice vertically through the strips. Size of the dice can vary according to the dish. Chinese cooks like to see uniform food pieces in the same dish. If the recipe calls for peas and diced vegetables, cut the vegetables the same size as a pea. If a vegetable in the dish is to be cut in 1-inch pieces, cut the other vegetables the same size.

Chopping is the coarsest cut. Whole chickens are chopped into 2-inch pieces. Vegetables can be chopped into 1/2-inch to 1-inch pieces.

Mincing is chopping very fine. The size of the pieces should be about 1/16 inch square. Garlic and fresh ginger root are frequently minced.

Chop shrimp and pork fat to a fine paste.

Chop green pepper, dice carrot and mince ham.

Cut vegetable slices, paper-thin pork slices and ginger root coins for stir-frying.

Shred or chop fresh ginger root. Mince with a cleaver or on the coarse side of your grater.

UTENSILS

The Wok

Although the wok is centuries old, it is a beautifully designed and sophisticated utensil. Its round shape makes it perfect for stir-frying, deep-frying or steaming. All recipes in this book were tested in a standard wok 14 inches in diameter.

The most efficient wok is made of steel. It is about 14 inches in diameter and has a slightly flat bottom so it can be used on either a gas stove or an electric stove. Some woks have two metal handles, others have one long wooden handle.

A domed lid to cover your wok is helpful for cooking dishes requiring long steaming.

How to Season a New Wok

● Fill your new wok 2/3 full of water. Bring it to a boil over high heat. Let it boil 7 to 8 minutes. Turn off the heat and let the wok cool.
● Pour the water from the cooled wok. Wash the wok thoroughly with hot water and a mild detergent. Rinse and dry it well with paper towels.
● Rub the inside of the wok with 2 tablespoons of vegetable oil. Do not use corn oil as it has a lower burning point than other vegetable oils. Place the wok over high heat. Rotate and tilt the wok from side to side frequently to distribute excess oil.
● After 5 to 6 minutes, turn off the heat and set the wok aside to cool. Wipe excess oil from the cooled wok with a paper towel.
● Your wok is now seasoned and ready to use. After using your wok, wash it gently with a mild detergent. Then rinse and dry it thoroughly. To be sure the wok is dry and will not rust, place it briefly over high heat. During the first 2 weeks, rub 1 or 2 drops of vegetable oil over the inside of the wok before putting it away. With good care your wok will give you many years of use.

Wok Spatula & Ladle

The wok spatula is a long-handle tool used for tossing, mixing and stirring food in a wok. Many wok sets include a spatula. It is shaped to scoop and lift food from the sides and bottom of the wok. A regular spatula or wooden spoon is not as efficient for stir-frying.

A ladle is not usually included in a wok set. If you prepare Chinese meals frquently, a ladle will be helpful. Use it for dishing cooked food from the wok as well as for serving soups. A ladle can also be used to push food around in the wok when stir-frying.

Slotted Spoon

When deep-frying, a long-handle slotted spoon is helpful for lowering food into the oil and for removing the cooked food from the oil and draining it over the wok.

Deep-Fry Thermometer

A thermometer is essential for measuring oil temperature for deep-frying. Ensure best results by making sure oil is at the specified temperature.

Steamers

Bamboo steamers or steamer trays are used singly or stacked in tiers and placed over boiling water in a wok. The sloping sides of the wok support the bottom steamer so it is not sitting in the boiling water. The steamer bottoms are loosely woven to let steam rise to the next tray. A lid on the top steamer prevents steam from escaping.

Food to be cooked can be placed directly in the steamer as when steaming buns. Or it can be placed in a baking dish and then in the steamer, as when steaming chicken. When steaming in a baking dish, place the baking dish on a rack in the bottom of the wok or pot. The rack should fit in the wok or pot so it is at least 2 inches above the boiling water.

Bamboo steamers range from tiny 4-inch dim sum steamers to 16-inch poultry steamers. The most practical size has a 12-inch diameter.

After each use, rinse bamboo steamers and lid. Shake off excess water and air-dry them. If necessary, wash steamers with a mild detergent.

Metal steamers are used in place of a wok and bamboo steamer trays. Each metal steamer set consists of a lid, two steamer tiers or trays and a tightly fitting pot to hold water for steaming.

COOKING METHODS

Chinese cooks are experts in three cooking methods: stir-frying, deep-frying and steaming. Special procedures are necessary to obtain best results in each method.

Stir-Frying

The most common cooking method is stir-frying. The Chinese word *chow* literally means *toss-cooking* and that's exactly what happens. Food is lifted up from the surface of the wok and dropped back in with a tossing movement of the spatula. You can stir-fry in a few tablespoons of oil or in a cup of oil. Stir-frying refers to the action—not to the amount of oil.

It is important to heat the wok before adding the oil. Then heat the oil before adding food. If you miss these basic steps, the stir-fried vegetables will not be crisp-tender and the finished dish will be far from perfect.

Foods are stir-fried in appropriate order so nothing will be overcooked or underdone. Long-cooking vegetables such as carrots are added before quick-cooking ones such as bean sprouts. Have all ingredients prepared and within reach before you heat the oil. Once you begin stir-frying, you will not have time to cut and chop.

Deep-Frying

Oil for deep-frying must be at the temperature specified in the recipe. If oil is not hot enough, the food will absorb it and be soggy and greasy. If oil is too hot, food will brown quickly but will not be cooked inside.

Using a deep-frying thermometer is the most accurate method for determining oil temperature. Chinese cooks have a seemingly less scientific method: Drop a small dry rice noodle or a piece of Crisp Rice, page 151, into the hot oil. If the noodle or rice puffs in a few seconds, the oil is ready. At this point, the surface of hot oil will have a shimmering quality.

Oil level should not be over half the depth of the wok or it might splash out.

Do not deep-fry food in oil that is hotter than the specified temperature. If oil is too hot, turn off the heat and let the oil cool.

Dry food thoroughly before lowering it into hot oil. Oil and water don't mix! When a drop of water touches hot oil, the oil will bounce away, spattering over your arm or into your face.

Do not drop food into hot oil. Gently lower food into hot oil with a spatula, strainer or long-handle tongs so there is no splashing. Turn food in hot oil with a spatula or chopsticks. Remove food with a slotted spoon or strainer, drain it over the wok and place it on paper towels.

Deep-fry in a flat-bottom wok or in a heavy deep pot. A curve-bottom wok containing hot oil is dangerous—if it tips, you're likely to be caught in the hot oil spill.

Recycling Oil

Oil used to deep-fry can be recycled many times. Let it cool in the wok, then strain it into a large pitcher, pour it into a bottle or jar with a tight-fitting lid and refrigerate it.

To remove any odor from recycled oil, heat it to 375°F (190°C). Deep-fry 2 or 3 slices of ginger root until golden. Discard the ginger, strain the oil if necessary and refrigerate it.

Don't be alarmed if cold oil solidifies. Let it stand 20 to 30 minutes at room temperature and it will become fluid. If oil becomes dark, do not use it. Dark color indicates oil has deteriorated and may be rancid.

Steaming

Use enough water in the bottom of the wok to come at least 2 inches below the first steamer tier. Bring water to a rolling boil. Place the steamer tray over the rapidly boiling water and steam over high heat according to the recipe directions. If steaming time is long, do not let the water boil away. Add more boiling water to maintain the water level.

While food is steaming, do not lift the lid from the steamer tray. If steam escapes from the tray, the cooking process will stop.

At the end of the steaming time, carefully remove the wok or pot from the heat. Let it cool slightly. Then stand well back and slowly remove the lid from the wok or steamer tray. Steam causes bad burns.

CHINESE INGREDIENTS

Chinese Ingredients

All the food items listed below are available in most Chinese or Oriental grocery stores. Some Chinese foods are available through mail order. Look for advertisements in food magazines.

Supermarkets carry more Chinese ingredients than you may realize. They all sell soy sauce and boast a shelf of commonly used canned Chinese foods such as water chestnuts and sliced bamboo shoots. Many supermarkets carry fresh foods such as Chinese cabbage, ginger root, bean sprouts and Chinese parsley, or *cilantro*. In the gourmet or international foods sections you may discover noodles, rice wine or rice wine vinegar and various spices and flavorings.

Health food stores, food co-ops and gourmet shops often stock Chinese foods but they may be scattered throughout the store. Check spices and condiments, canned goods, rice and grains and frozen food sections.

If you still haven't found what you're looking for, ask the manager to order it for you.

Agar Agar—Dried seaweed; often used like gelatin. It is sold in strips or sticks and must be soaked in cold water to soften.

Almonds, Blanched—Almond halves with skins removed. They add texture, flavor and nutrition to many traditional dishes.

Bamboo Shoots—Ivory-colored shoots from young bamboo plants. They are sold canned whole, sliced or in chunks. Rinse them with cold water before using. To store, refrigerate them in cold water in a covered container; change the water daily.

Bean Curd (Dofu or Tofu)—High-protein, low-calorie and no-cholesterol food made from milk which is obtained from pureed soybeans. It has a smooth texture and bland flavor so it combines well with other foods and is often used in stir-fried dishes and soups. Although bean curd can be bought in 3-inch squares, directions for making your own are on page 169. To store 2 or 3 days, refrigerate in cold water in a covered container; change the water daily.

Bean Noodles (Bean Threads or Cellophane Noodles)—Dry thin transparent noodles made from mung beans. They must be soaked in hot water before using.

Bean Sprouts—Grown from mung beans. The crunchy white sprout has a green cap and small tail. Sprouts should be eaten fresh or cooked less than 1 minute to preserve crispness. Refrigerate in cold water in a covered container. Use as soon as possible. Canned bean sprouts do not have the desired flavor and texture.

Chili Oil—Oil flavored with hot red peppers. You can buy it or make your own, page 85.

Chinese Cabbage (Napa Cabbage)—Tall, tightly packed fresh cabbage with wide white stalks and light green crinkled leaves.

Chinese Egg Noodles—Thin flat noodles made with flour and eggs. They are springier than other noodles because the dough is handled more, releasing gluten in the flour. They are available fresh or frozen.

Chinese Sausage (La Ch'ang)—Hard and spicy pork sausage which may be frozen. It is cured and needs no cooking.

Chinese Turnip (Daikon)—A fresh white vegetable shaped like a large sweet potato. It has a subtle flavor but gives off a strong odor while cooking. Frequently used in soups.

Chinese Parsley (Cilantro, Fresh Coriander)—A fresh bright green herb with a pungent flavor. It's often used as a garnish.

Dried Bean Curd—Bean curd that has been pressed for a long time and cooked with seasonings such as star anise.

Dried Black Mushrooms—Strong-flavored dried mushrooms. They must be soaked and the tough stems removed before using. Store them in a covered container in a dry cool place.

Dried Orange Peel—Tangerine peel cut into pieces about 2'' x 1'' and dried. You can buy it or prepare it yourself. Dry tangerine peel in the hot sun for several days until it is brittle. Or use your food dryer. One piece is enough to add sweet flavor to a stewed meat dish. Store in a covered container in a cool dry place.

Dried Red Chilies—Very hot, orange-red peppers that have been dried. They are popular in Szechuan cooking. The seeds are especially spicy.

Store dried peppers in a covered container at room temperature.

Dried Seaweed (Laver)—Thin square sheets of dark seaweed. It is very nutritious and high in iodine.

Dried Shrimp—Small shrimp that have been shelled, salted and sun-dried. They add a pungent or sharp flavor to vegetable dishes. Soak them before using. Store dried shrimp in a tightly covered container in a cool dry place.

Dry Sherry—Used in marinades to season and tenderize meat and fish. Dry sherry is not as salty as cooking sherry. It is preferred for Chinese cooking because soy sauce and other ingredients are salty.

Duck Sauce—Spicy sweet sauce used as a condiment with duck and meats. The recipe is on page 71. Sweet bean sauce or hoisin sauce may be substituted.

Egg Roll Skins—Paper-thin pastry wrappers made with high-gluten flour and water. Look for them in refrigerator or frozen food sections in some supermarkets, gourmet shops and Oriental food stores.

Five-Spice Powder—A blend of star anise, cinnamon, cloves, fennel and Szechuan peppercorns. Allspice is sometimes substituted, but the flavor is different. Store it in a covered container in a dry cool place.

Ginger Root—A gnarled root which adds distinctive spicy flavor to many Chinese dishes. It is sold fresh in some supermarkets. To use, remove the tan skin with a paring knife and cut the white portion into slices 1/8 inch thick and 1 inch in diameter—roughly the size of a quarter. Powdered ginger can be substituted but is not as flavorful. Substitute 1/2 teaspoon powdered ginger for 1 teaspoon minced fresh ginger or for 2 slices fresh ginger. Unpeeled fresh ginger root will keep very well in the vegetable crisper of your refrigerator or it can be wrapped and frozen. Break off pieces as you need them.

Hoisin Sauce—Thick reddish-brown sauce made from soybeans and spices. It is spicy and mildly sweet. Once the can is opened, refrigerate the contents in a covered container.

Hot Bean Sauce—Thick reddish sauce made from beans, hot peppers and spices. It is salty, spicy and hot. Once the can is opened, refrigerate the sauce in a covered container. As a substitute, use 1 tablespoon Hot Chili Sauce, page 143, mixed with 1/2 teaspoon salt for 1 tablespoon hot bean sauce.

Hot Mustard Powder—Very spicy powder made from ground mustard seeds. Store in a covered container in a cool dry place.

Lichees—Walnut-size fruit with reddish skin and sweet white pulp. Available fresh or canned.

Maltose—Natural sugar made from wheat sprouts. Used frequently in Chinese cooking.

Oyster Sauce—Rich brown sauce made from oysters. Often used as an alternative to soy sauce. Once the bottle is opened, refrigerate the sauce in a covered container.

Pickled Cucumbers—Canned pickles made from cucumbers. They are salty but sweet. Often served for breakfast and used in soup.

Plum Sauce—sweet spicy sauce used for dipping. It is available in cans or bottles.

Red Bean Paste (Sweet Bean Paste)—Thick paste made from red beans. It is used as a filling for sweet pastries. Once the can is opened, refrigerate the contents in a covered container. One 18-1/3-ounce can equals 2 cups. One 4-ounce can equals 1/4 cup.

Red Dates (Jujube Nuts)—Small dried dates used to sweeten soups, meats and pastries. They must be soaked or boiled in hot water before using.

Rice

The Chinese use long-grain or short-grain white rice to make the steamed rice which is served with all their meals. To make a perfect pot of steamed rice, use a saucepan with a tight-fitting lid. The saucepan should be large enough to let the rice expand during cooking but not so large that the rice becomes a crust on the bottom of the pan. See Steamed Rice, page 151.

Leftover steamed rice is the basis for fried rice. Cold day-old rice works best. Fried rice is a marvelous way to combine small amounts of leftover meats and vegetables. But it doesn't have to be made with leftovers. See Basic Fried Rice, page 151, and Yangchou Fried Rice, page 165.

Sweet rice, or glutinous rice, is a short-grain, plump, milk-white, pearly rice. It must be soaked before cooking. Cooked sweet rice is sticky and is often used as a basis for desserts, pastries and stuffings. See Coconut Rice Balls, page 188, and Sweet Rice Omelet, pages 176 and 177.

Rice Noodles—Dried thin noodles made from rice flour. If they are to be used in soups or stir-fried dishes, they must be soaked. Deep-fried rice noodles will puff and become crunchy. Store them at room temperature or in a cool dry place.

Rice Vinegar—Mild vinegar made from fermented rice. White vinegar or cider vinegar may be substituted.

Rice Wine—Made from fermented rice. It has a higher alcohol content than grape wine. Dry white wine may be substituted.

Rock Sugar—Crystals of pure cooked sugar. Not as sweet as granulated sugar.

Salty Black Beans (Fermented Black Beans)—Small black beans preserved in salt and packed in packages. They are not appealing in appearance or aroma, but add delightful flavor to many dishes. The beans must be rinsed in warm water and drained, then chopped or minced before using. Once the can has been opened, store the beans in a tightly covered container at room temperature.

Sesame Oil—Savory golden brown oil made from toasted sesame seeds. Use it sparingly as a flavoring. Sesame oil burns easily so do not use it to stir-fry or deep-fry. Store it in a cool place or in the refrigerator.

Sesame Seed Paste—Thick brown-black paste made from ground sesame seeds. Creamy peanut butter may be substituted.

Sesame Seeds—Small, flat, oval seeds from the sesame plant. Hulled seeds are cream-colored. Unhulled seeds are often black, depending on the variety. Toasting sesame seeds brings out their nutty flavor.

Sha Cha Sauce—Spicy sauce often used as a dipping sauce or as a marinade. As a substitute, use 3 tablespoons Hot Chili Sauce, page 98, mixed with 1/2 teaspoon minced garlic for 3 tablespoons sha cha sauce. Hoisin sauce may also be substituted. Once the can is opened, refrigerate the sauce in a covered container.

Snow Peas—Flat green pea pods. They are tender but crisp and slightly sweet. Their strings must be removed before cooking. Cook snow peas very quickly so they retain their color and crispness.

Soy Sauce—See above.

Star Anise—Small, hard, star-shaped fruit with a licorice flavor. It is used to flavor meat and poultry, especially when stewed. Store in a tightly covered container at room temperature.

Straw Mushrooms—Small brownish-black mushrooms with a high-domed cap. They are available canned. Some may have a covering or skin which does not have to be removed.

Sweet Bean Sauce—Made from soybeans. It's a canned salty condiment most often used to flavor pork. Once the can is opened, refrigerate the contents in a covered container.

Soy Sauce

Most soy sauces are made from soybeans, flour, salt and water. Although there are many different kinds and grades, the most common are black soy sauce and thin soy sauce. Mushroom soy sauce, fish soy sauce and other variations are regional versions to be used for certain local dishes.

Black or dark soy sauce contains caramel and sugar so it has a slightly sweet taste and is darker and thicker than thin soy sauce.

Thin or light soy sauce is saltier than black soy sauce. Because of its saltiness, you don't need to add extra salt when you use it.

Most supermarkets do not carry either black or thin soy sauce. They are available in Oriental food stores. The saltiness of the soy sauce you buy in supermarkets depends on the particular brand.

Keep opened bottles of soy sauce tightly closed and refrigerated to help retain the flavor. Because soy sauce can lose its flavor fairly quickly, it's best to buy it in small bottles unless you use it on a daily basis.

Sweet Cucumbers—Canned shredded cucumbers in syrup. The can may also contain pieces of carrot and papaya. Do not drain off the syrup before using. Once the can is opened, refrigerate cucumbers and syrup in a covered container.

Sweet Rice (Glutinous Rice)—Short-grain rice that becomes sticky when cooked. It must be soaked for 1 to 2 hours before cooking. Sweet rice is used in stuffing, dumplings and pastries.

Sweet Rice Powder—Made from sweet rice. Desserts made with sweet rice powder instead of flour have a sticky consistency and may resemble undercooked dough. Store it in a dry place.

Szechuan Peppercorns (Flower Peppercorns, Brown Peppercorns)—Dried reddish berries that resemble miniature flowers. They are fragrant and mildly hot. Use them sparingly. Store them in a tightly covered container in a cool dry place.

Tea—See page 20.

Tiger Lily Buds (Golden Needles)—Pale golden brown dried buds with a delicate flavor. They must be soaked before using. Add them to soups and stir-fried dishes for flavor and texture.

Water Chestnuts—Walnut-size vegetables grown in lakes. Peel before using. Canned water chestnuts are peeled. To store, refrigerate them in cold water in a covered container. Change the water daily and use the water chestnuts as soon as possible.

Wheat Starch—A powdery substance used to make light translucent skins for dainty pastries such as Steamed Shrimp Dumplings, pages 34 and 35. Store wheat starch the same way you store flour.

Wonton Skins—Small pastry wrappers made with flour, eggs and water. They are available in packages and are frequently sold frozen.

Wood Ears—A dried fungus. They must be soaked and their hard stems removed before using. Sometimes baking soda is added to the soak water to hasten the softening process. They will expand several times their size during soaking. Wood ears have almost no flavor but add needed crunchy texture to some stir-fried dishes. They absorb flavor from other seasonings.

Garnishes

Garnishes for Chinese food can be very simple. Prepare garnishes ahead of time so when food is taken from the wok, it can be quickly arranged on a platter with the garnishes. Serve the garnished dish immediately so it can be enjoyed while still hot. Two or three green onion brushes are attractive on a large platter of food, page 68. One radish or tomato rose provides a colorful dramatic accent, page 148.

Tea

If you enjoy Chinese food, you should drink Chinese tea with it. Tea is grown in the warm hills of southeastern China and in Taiwan. Each province in the area is known for its special tea. There is a tea to suit every mood and occasion.

Like wines, teas can be divided into three groups. Red or black tea has a full robust flavor. The red-black color of red tea is a result of full fermentation during processing. Pu Erh tea is a popular red tea. Green tea, like white wine, is lighter and more subtle. It has not undergone any fermentation. Green tea leaves are steamed soon after they are picked so the leaves will retain their color. Loong Jan Tea, or Dragon Well Tea, has a fresh pure taste. It comes from the province of Chinkiang. Su Hsien Tea, or Water Nymph Tea, is from Kwangtung. It is mild, smooth and lightly scented. Shao Mai Tea, or Eyebrows of Longevity Tea, has a clear natural flavor.

Oolong tea and jasmine tea have characteristics of both red and green teas. They are semi-fermented. The most famous semi-fermented tea is Tung Ting. It is grown in Taiwan and has a full aromatic and vigorous flavor.

To make onion brushes, shred ends of green onions. Let stand in ice water.

To make vegetable roses, use a small sharp knife to cut vegetables in spirals.

Know Your Ingredients,
pages 18 and 19

1 bean noodles	**9** seaweed	**17** daikon
2 rice noodles	**10** Szechuan peppercorns	**18** dried black mushrooms
3 water chestnuts	**11** red dates	**19** red bean paste
4 agar agar	**12** black dates	**20** bean sprouts
5 sesame seeds	**13** bamboo shoots	**21** tiger lily buds
6 black sesame seeds	**14** Chinese cabbage	**22** dried shrimp
7 wood ears	**15** ginger root	**23** round wonton skins
8 star anise	**16** hoisin sauce	

APPETIZERS & DIM SUM

Dim sum is Cantonese for *heart's delight* because these treats and snacks served in tea houses are meant to be enjoyed whenever your heart desires. Mouth-watering bite-size dumplings stuffed with pork, shrimp or sweet bean paste are deep-fried, baked or steamed and served with spicy dips. Dim sum can also be vegetables, steamed buns or cakes, marinated cold meats, or chow mein and other noodle dishes.

There is a tea house to suit every budget—from ornate buildings with shiny red pillars and pointed yellow roofs to palm-thatched roadside stands. In Hong Kong, some tea houses are huge houseboats carved to look like glittering green dragons floating in the bay.

Tea houses are usually open from eleven o'clock in the morning until two in the afternoon. During these hours, everyone throngs to the tea houses: Businessmen sip tea behind newspapers, students stuff themselves on dumplings and shoppers stop for a quick snack.

When entering a tea house, your first impression is absolute chaos. Dishes clatter as waiters hurry to clear off tables. Waitresses, pushing carts laden with dim sum, sing out the names of dim sum treats. After being served a pot of tea, you beckon to the waitress and help yourself to a delicacy from her cart. When you want more tea, just raise the lid of your teapot and a pot of fresh tea will appear like magic! After your lunch, the bill is tabulated according to the number of empty dishes piled on the table.

Dim sum restaurants can be found in many cities outside China, especially in areas with large Chinese populations.

Although it is the Cantonese who are world-famous for their dim sum, all regions in China specialize in snack foods. Spring Rolls are Shanghai delicacies served at New Year festivals. Favorite snacks in the province of Szechuan are noodles and pickled vegetables. In Peking, boiled meat dumplings and beer are popular.

Mandarin Egg Rolls

Mandarin

Dried bean curds are a product of soy milk. You can buy them in Oriental food stores.

Marinade:
   1 teaspoon rice wine or dry sherry
   1 teaspoon minced fresh ginger root
   1/2 teaspoon salt
   2 teaspoons cornstarch

1 cup shredded pork loin, page 11
6 dried black mushrooms
2 cups hot water
1-1/2 lbs. fresh bean sprouts
6 cups boiling water
6 cups cold water
5 tablespoons vegetable oil
1 garlic clove, crushed
6 dried bean curds, page 15,
   shredded, page 11
3 tablespoons soy sauce
1-1/2 teaspoons salt
2 tablespoons sesame oil
1 tablespoon cornstarch, if needed
15 egg roll skins
6 cups oil for deep-frying
Sweet & Sour Sauce, page 64
Hot Mustard Sauce, see below

Mix marinade ingredients in a medium bowl. Add pork; mix well. Let stand 20 minutes. Soak dried black mushrooms in 2 cups hot water until soft, 15 to 20 minutes. Blanch bean sprouts by submerging in 6 cups boiling water; drain. Plunge into 6 cups cold water. Drain mushrooms and remove hard stems. Shred mushrooms with a cleaver, page 11. Heat 5 tablespoons oil in a wok over high heat 1 minute. Stir-fry garlic until golden, 30 seconds. Add marinated pork. Stir-fry 1 or 2 minutes until pork is no longer pink. Add shredded mushrooms and dried bean curds. Stir-fry 1 minute. Reduce heat to medium. Stir in soy sauce and salt. Remove wok from heat and let cool. Add blanched bean sprouts and sesame oil; mix well. If mixture is too watery, stir in a little cornstarch. Place 1 egg roll skin on a flat surface with corners at top, bottom, left and right. Place 3 tablespoons filling just below center of skin. Fold bottom corner over filling. Roll once and fold left and right corners over filling; continue rolling toward top corner. Press firmly to close. Egg roll should be about 4 inches long. Repeat with remaining egg roll skins and filling. Heat 6 cups oil in a wok over high heat to 350°F (175°C). Reduce heat to medium. Carefully lower several egg rolls into hot oil with a slotted metal spoon. Deep-fry 2 minutes or until golden brown. Turn each egg roll and fry other side 2 minutes. Remove with slotted spoon, draining well over wok. Repeat with remaining egg rolls. Serve hot with Sweet & Sour Sauce and Hot Mustard Sauce for dipping. Makes 6 servings.

Hot Mustard Sauce   Photo on page 121.

Dip Mandarin Egg Rolls, above, in this tangy sauce or use it to top cold vegetables.

5 tablespoons hot mustard powder
5 tablespoons water
1 teaspoon rice vinegar or
   white vinegar
2 teaspoons sesame oil

Combine mustard powder and water in a small bowl, mixing well to dissolve any lumps. Let stand 1 minute. Add vinegar and sesame oil; mix well. Sauce may be covered and refrigerated up to 1 week. Makes 1/3 cup.

Fried Pork Dumplings

Mandarin

The bottoms of these dumplings are brown and crunchy, while the tops are light and moist.

Dough:
    2-1/2 cups all-purpose flour
    2/3 cup boiling water
    1/3 cup cold water

Filling:
    3/4 lb. Chinese cabbage
    4 cups water
    Cold water
    3/4 lb. ground pork
    1 teaspoon rice wine or dry sherry
    1 teaspoon minced fresh ginger root
    1/2 cup minced green onions
    3 tablespoons soy sauce
    1-1/4 teaspoons salt
    1 tablespoon lard or vegetable oil
    1 teaspoon sesame oil

About 6 tablespoons vegetable oil
1-1/3 cups water
Sesame Soy Dip, page 26
Chinese parsley, if desired

To prepare dough, place flour in a large bowl. Make a well in the center. Slowly add boiling water, mixing with a fork or chopsticks. Add cold water; mix dough until smooth. Cover bowl with a damp cloth towel and let stand 15 minutes while preparing filling. To blanch cabbage, bring 4 cups water to a boil in a wok or large pot; add cabbage. Cook 1 minute; drain. Quickly plunge cabbage into cold water. Drain well, squeezing to remove excess water. Chop blanched cabbage very fine. Combine ground pork, wine, ginger root, green onions, soy sauce, salt, lard or vegetable oil and sesame oil in a large bowl; mix well. Add chopped cabbage to pork mixture. Mix 2 to 3 minutes to combine thoroughly; set aside. Place dough on a floured surface and knead until smooth. Divide dough into 4 portions. Use your hands to shape each piece into a roll 12 inches long. Chop roll into 12 equal pieces with a cleaver. Roll each piece between your palms into a small ball, then pat flat. Use a rolling pin to roll out each piece to a circle 2-1/2 inches in diameter. Cup a circle in the palm of your hand. Place 1 tablespoon pork filling in center. Fold circle over filling to make a half circle and pinch once at the top. Make 2 or 3 pleats on each side and pinch together to seal. Dumpling should resemble a small crescent. Heat a 12-inch skillet over high heat 30 seconds to 1 minute. Add 2 tablespoons oil; heat 30 seconds. Carefully place half the dumplings pleated-side up around edge of skillet without overlapping and then in center of skillet. Fry until bottoms are golden, about 1 minute. Add 2/3 cup water. Cover and cook until 1 to 2 tablespoons water remain. Add 1 tablespoon oil to skillet. Cook covered over low heat 1 to 2 minutes. Remove from heat. Place a large plate over skillet and invert quickly. Remove skillet. Repeat with remaining dumplings, vegetable oil and water. Arrange dumplings on a platter. Garnish with Chinese parsley, if desired. Serve hot with Sesame Soy Dip. Makes 48 dumplings.

How to Make Fried Pork Dumplings

1/After heating oil in skillet, arrange dumplings so they brown evenly.

2/When dumplings are golden on one side, remove from skillet and serve golden-side up.

Bacon Rolls

Mandarin

Ginger root adds tantalizing flavor to chicken livers rolled up in bacon.

12 bacon slices
6 chicken livers
2 cups boiling water
Marinade:
  2 teaspoons rice wine or dry sherry
  1 teaspoon sugar
  2 tablespoons soy sauce
  1/4 teaspoon pepper
4-1/2 teaspoons shredded fresh
  ginger root, page 12
6 green onions,
  chopped in 1-inch pieces
1 tablespoon honey

Cut bacon slices in half to make 24 pieces. Cut each chicken liver into 4 pieces. Place chicken livers in a small saucepan with 2 cups boiling water. Boil 1 minute. Remove with a small strainer; drain on paper towels. Combine marinade ingredients in a medium bowl. Add ginger root, green onions and boiled chicken livers; mix well. Let stand 2 hours. Place 1 piece each of chicken liver, ginger root and green onion at one end of a piece of bacon. Roll up and secure with a wooden pick. Repeat to make 24 rolls. Place on a baking sheet. Preheat broiler 5 minutes. Combine honey and 1 tablespoon leftover marinade in a small bowl; mix well. Place bacon rolls on baking sheet under broiler 3 minutes. Remove from broiler and brush honey mixture on each bacon roll. Turn each roll over and broil other side 3 minutes. Serve hot. Makes 24 appetizers.

Boiled Pork Dumplings

Mandarin

Try these dumplings with Szechuan Cucumber Slices, page 36.

Dough:
   2-1/2 cups all-purpose flour
   1 teaspoon salt
   1 cup water

Filling:
   3/4 lb. Chinese cabbage
   About 4 cups boiling water
   4 cups cold water
   3/4 lb. ground pork
   1 teaspoon rice wine or dry sherry
   1 teaspoon minced fresh ginger root
   1/2 cup minced green onions
   3 tablespoons soy sauce
   1-1/4 teaspoons salt
   1 tablespoon lard or vegetable oil
   3 tablespoons sesame oil

8 cups boiling water
1 cup cold water

Dipping sauce:
   3 tablespoons soy sauce
   1 teaspoon rice vinegar or
      white vinegar
   1 teaspoon minced garlic or
   1 teaspoon Chili Oil, page 85

To prepare dough, place flour and salt in a large bowl. Slowly stir in water with chopsticks or a wooden spoon. Knead dough until smooth. Cover with a damp cloth towel and let stand 15 minutes. To blanch cabbage, place in a medium saucepan with 4 cups boiling water. Cook 1 minute. Remove cabbage and plunge into 4 cups cold water. Drain well, squeezing to remove excess water. Chop cabbage very fine. Combine ground pork, wine, ginger root, green onions, soy sauce, salt, lard or vegetable oil and sesame oil in a large bowl; mix well. Add chopped cabbage to meat mixture. Mix 2 to 3 minutes to combine thoroughly; set aside. Dust pastry board with flour and knead dough again until very smooth. Use your hands to shape dough into a long roll 1 inch in diameter. Chop into 50 small equal pieces with a cleaver. Roll each piece into a small ball, then pat flat. Use a rolling pin to roll out each piece to a circle 1-1/2 inches in diameter. Edges of the circles should be thinner than the centers. Cup 1 circle in the palm of your hand. Place 1/2 tablespoon pork filling in the center. Fold dough over filling to make a half circle and pinch once in the center of the edge. Crimp edges together to seal. Dumpling should resemble a small crescent. Repeat with remaining dough circles and filling. Place half the dumplings, one at a time, in a large pot containing 8 cups boiling water. Stir carefully with a large spoon to prevent dumplings from sticking to bottom of pot. Cover and bring water to a boil over high heat. Add 2/3 cup cold water to boiling water and bring to a second boil. Add 1/3 cup cold water to boiling water and bring to a third boil. Remove dumplings with a strainer. Drain well, place on a platter and serve hot. Mix ingredients for dipping sauce in a small dish and serve with dumplings. Makes 50 dumplings.

Sesame Soy Dip

When you serve Fried Pork Dumplings, page 24, put a small bowl of this dip on the table.

1/4 cup light soy sauce
2 teaspoons sesame oil
2 tablespoons rice vinegar or
   white vinegar

Combine all ingredients in a small bowl; mix well. Makes about 1/4 cup.

Shrimp Toast

Mandarin

Cornstarch helps shrimp paste adhere to the bread during deep-frying.

1/2 lb. fresh shrimp
2 oz. pork fat
1 egg white
1/2 teaspoon rice wine or dry sherry
1/2 teaspoon salt
1/2 teaspoon minced fresh ginger root
1 tablespoon cornstarch
5 slices white bread
1 teaspoon black sesame seeds or
poppy seeds
1 tablespoon minced ham, if desired
6 cups oil for deep-frying
Peppersalt, page 88, if desired

Shell and devein shrimp, page 59. Rinse and pat dry with a paper towel. Flatten each shrimp with the broad side of a cleaver to make chopping easier. Use cleaver to finely chop shrimp and pork fat. Combine chopped pork fat and shrimp; chop to a fine paste. Place shrimp paste in a medium bowl. Use a spoon or your hands to mix shrimp paste with egg white, wine, salt, ginger root and cornstarch; set aside. Remove crusts from bread. Cut each slice into 4 squares. Mound 1 rounded teaspoon shrimp paste on each square of bread and press gently. Garnish with sesame seeds, poppy seeds and minced ham, if desired. Heat 6 cups oil in a wok over high heat to 350°F (175°C). Reduce heat to medium. Carefully lower bread squares shrimp-side down into hot oil with a slotted metal spoon. Deep-fry 4 or 5 at a time until edges of bread turn golden, about 1 minute. Turn each bread square and cook other side 30 seconds. Remove from oil with slotted spoon; drain on paper towels. Repeat with remaining bread squares. Serve hot. Sprinkle with Peppersalt, if desired. Makes 20 appetizers.

Deep-Fried Scallops

Cantonese

It's important to have the oil at the right temperature; see page 14.

1/2 lb. fresh scallops

Marinade:
2 teaspoons rice wine or dry sherry
1/4 teaspoon salt
1/4 teaspoon pepper

1/3 cup cornstarch
1/4 teaspoon salt
1 egg, beaten
1/2 cup fine breadcrumbs
8 cups oil for deep-frying

Wash scallops; pat dry with a paper towel. Mix marinade ingredients in a medium bowl. Add scallops; mix well. Let stand about 15 minutes. Combine cornstarch and salt in a small plastic bag. Add several scallops at a time and shake well to coat. Dip coated scallops in beaten egg, then in breadcrumbs. Heat oil in a wok over high heat to 350°F (175°C). Reduce heat to medium. Carefully lower scallops into hot oil with a slotted metal spoon. Deep-fry several at a time until golden brown, about 2 minutes. Remove from oil with slotted spoon. Drain on paper towels. Serve hot. Makes 4 servings.

Steamed Pork Dumplings

Cantonese

Dried black mushrooms need to be softened. Do not soak fresh mushrooms.

Dough:
2-1/2 cups all-purpose flour
1/4 teaspoon salt
1/2 teaspoon sesame oil
2/3 cup boiling water
1/3 cup cold water

Filling:
1 lb. ground pork
5 dried black mushrooms or
   1/3 lb. fresh mushrooms
2 cups hot water to soften dried
   black mushrooms
4 cups water
1 lb. Chinese cabbage or
   other cabbage
1 teaspoon minced fresh ginger root
2 tablespoons minced green onion
2 tablespoons soy sauce
1-1/2 teaspoons salt
2 tablespoons sesame oil

6 cups boiling water
Sesame Soy Dip, page 26

To prepare dough, place flour, salt and sesame oil in a large bowl. Add boiling water; mix well with chopsticks or a wooden spoon. Add cold water. Knead dough until thoroughly mixed. Cover with a cloth towel and let stand about 15 minutes. Place ground pork in a large bowl. If using dried black mushrooms, soak them in 2 cups hot water until soft, 15 to 20 minutes, then drain and remove hard stems. Chop softened black mushrooms or fresh mushrooms into small pieces. Add to pork. To blanch cabbage, bring 4 cups water to a boil in a wok or large pot. Add cabbage. Cook 30 seconds; drain. Quickly plunge cabbage into cold water. Drain and pat dry with a paper towel. Chop cabbage into very fine pieces. Squeeze out excess water. Add chopped cabbage and remaining filling ingredients to pork and mushrooms; mix well and set aside. Knead dough on a lightly floured surface until very smooth. Shape into a long roll 1-inch in diameter. Chop into 36 to 40 equal pieces. Flatten each piece with the palm of your hand and use a rolling pin to roll out to a circle 3 inches in diameter. Place 1 to 2 teaspoons filling in center. Fold dough over filling to make a half circle. Pleat edges and pinch together to seal. Arrange as many dumplings on a damp cloth in a steamer as will fit without touching each other. Cover steamer. Pour 4 cups boiling water into a wok or large pot. Place steamer over boiling water. Steam over high heat 10 to 12 minutes, adding more boiling water as needed. Let cool slightly before removing dumplings. Serve hot with Sesame Soy Dip. Makes 36 to 40 appetizers.

How to Brew a Pot of Tea

Start by boiling fresh cold water. Hot tap water results in tea with a flat flavor. Scald the inside of a clean China teapot with some of the boiling water. Measure the tea leaves into the hot teapot—about 1 teaspoon of leaves for each cup of water to be used. Pour boiling water over the tea leaves, cover the pot and let the tea steep for 3 minutes. You can refill the teapot once without adding more leaves if you steep it 4 minutes instead of 3. Then discard the twice-used tea leaves and use fresh leaves to make a third pot of tea.

How to Serve Tea—Chinese cups do not have handles. Hot tea is poured from a teapot into fragile cups made from thin china. The cup is held on the flat fingers of one hand acting as a saucer and supported with the fingertips of the other hand. Sugar and milk or cream are never added to Chinese tea.

How to Store Tea—Because tea leaves are dried, they will absorb moisture and lose their fresh flavor when exposed to the air. Store tea in a tightly covered container in a dry, cool place.

For dim sum, serve tea and such delicacies as, clockwise from the top, Fried Wontons, page 36; Tomato Sauce, page 69; Pork & Vegetable Buns, page 156; Shao Mai, page 32, and Steamed Shrimp Dumplings, page 34.

Stuffed Chicken Wings

Cantonese

When deep-frying, a spatula or spoon with a long handle is safer than a utensil with a short handle.

12 chicken wings
1 tablespoon cornstarch
2/3 lb. fresh shrimp
1 oz. pork fat

Marinade:
   1 teaspoon rice wine or dry sherry
   1/2 teaspoon minced fresh
     ginger root
   1/2 teaspoon salt
   1/4 teaspoon pepper
   1/2 teaspoon sesame oil
   1 tablespoon cornstarch
   1 egg white

3 tablespoons crushed blanched
  almonds
6 cups oil for deep-frying

Remove middle bone from chicken wings to make a pocket for stuffing. Sprinkle each wing with a little cornstarch. Shell and devein shrimp, page 59; rinse. Use a cleaver to chop shrimp and pork fat into small pieces. Combine chopped pork fat and shrimp; mix well. Chop mixture to a fine paste. Combine marinade ingredients in a medium bowl. Add shrimp mixture; mix well. Let stand 10 minutes. Divide shrimp mixture into 12 portions. Place 1 portion in the pocket of each chicken wing. Dip a teaspoon in water and smooth the filling. Dip the filled end of the chicken wing into almonds to coat. Heat oil in a wok over high heat to 350°F (175°C). Reduce heat to medium. Carefully lower stuffed chicken wings into hot oil with a slotted metal spoon. Deep-fry several at a time about 5 minutes until golden brown, turning once. Remove from oil with slotted spoon; drain on paper towels. Serve hot. Makes 12 appetizers.

Deep-Fried Shrimp

Cantonese

Serve these crisp shrimp with Hot Mustard Sauce, page 23, or Sweet & Sour Sauce, page 64.

1/2 lb. fresh shrimp
Marinade:
   2 teaspoons rice wine or dry sherry
   1/4 teaspoon salt
Batter:
   1/4 cup all-purpose flour
   1/3 cup ice water
   1/4 cup cornstarch
   1 egg yolk
   1/4 teaspoon salt
   1/4 teaspoon sugar
   1 teaspoon shortening
   1/2 teaspoon baking powder
8 cups oil for deep-frying

Shell and devein shrimp, page 59. Rinse and pat dry with a paper towel. Mix marinade ingredients in a medium bowl. Add shrimp; mix well. Let stand 20 minutes. Mix batter ingredients in a medium bowl. Heat 8 cups oil in a wok over high heat to 350°F (175°C). Reduce heat to medium. Dip shrimp one at a time into batter to coat. Carefully lower shrimp into hot oil with a slotted metal spoon. Deep-fry several at a time until golden, about 1 minute. Turn each shrimp and fry other side about 30 seconds. Remove from oil with slotted spoon. Drain on paper towels. Repeat with remaining shrimp. Serve warm. Makes about 12 appetizers.

How to Make Stuffed Chicken Wings

1/Use a cleaver to cut off largest wing section.

2/Hit the second joint with the back edge of the cleaver to separate the bones.

3/Grasp exposed end of bone with your fingers and pull out to make a pocket for filling.

4/Place filling in the pocket of each wing. Smooth with a teaspoon and dip into crushed almonds.

Curried Parchment Beef

Cantonese

This crisp appetizer will delight any curry lover.

1/2 lb. beef flank steak

Marinade:
  1 teaspoon rice wine or dry sherry
  1 teaspoon cornstarch
  1/2 teaspoon sugar
  1/8 teaspoon baking soda
  1/2 teaspoon salt
  2 teaspoons curry powder
  2 teaspoons sesame oil
  1-1/2 teaspoons minced onion
  1 tablespoon soy sauce
  1 tablespoon vegetable oil
  1 egg, separated

10 egg roll skins
6 cups oil for deep-frying

Slice flank steak across the grain into thin strips. Combine marinade ingredients in a medium bowl. Add beef slices; mix well. Let stand 30 minutes. Place egg roll skins on a flat surface with corners at top, bottom, left and right. Place 1 tablespoon beef mixture near the bottom corner and spread it diagonally. Fold bottom corner over filling and roll toward top corner, stopping a third of the way from top corner. Fold left and right corners over filling. Moisten inside of each corner with egg yolk and press to seal. Egg roll should resemble a small envelope. Heat 6 cups oil in a wok over high heat to 350°F (175°C). Reduce heat to medium. Carefully lower egg rolls into hot oil with a slotted metal spoon. Deep-fry 2 or 3 at a time in hot oil until golden, about 1 minute on each side. Remove from oil with slotted spoon. Drain on paper towels. Makes 10 large appetizers.

Shao Mai   Photo on page 29.

Cantonese

Shao Mai *means* cooked to sell. *They are sold by housewives on the streets of Canton.*

4 dried black mushrooms
2 cups hot water
10 oz. pork loin
1 oz. pork fat
1/2 (4-oz.) can bamboo shoots or
  water chestnuts, drained

Marinade:
  1/2 teaspoon rice wine or dry sherry
  1 teaspoon sesame oil
  1 teaspoon salt
  1/4 teaspoon sugar
  1/4 teaspoon pepper
  1 tablespoon cornstarch
  1 egg, beaten

30 round or square wonton skins
1/2 carrot, chopped in 1/8-inch pieces
About 30 fresh Chinese parsley leaves,
  chopped
4 to 6 cups boiling water

Soak dried mushrooms in 2 cups hot water until soft, 15 to 20 minutes. Drain, remove hard stems and chop mushrooms very fine with a cleaver. Finely dice pork loin, pork fat and bamboo shoots or water chestnuts. Combine marinade ingredients in a medium bowl. Add diced mushrooms, pork loin, pork fat and bamboo shoots or water chestnuts. Stir about 5 minutes to mix well. If using square wonton skins, trim corners and edges to make circles. Divide pork mixture into 3 equal sections. Divide each section into 10 equal portions. Place 1 portion in center of each circle. Pleat skin around filling to make a little pouch, leaving top open. Dip a teaspoon in water and smooth filling. Sprinkle carrot and Chinese parsley leaves on filling. Arrange as many dumplings on a damp cloth in a steamer as will fit without touching each other. Cover steamer. Pour 4 to 6 cups boiling water into a wok or large pot. Place steamer over boiling water. Steam over high heat 6 to 8 minutes. Repeat with remaining dumplings. Makes 30 appetizers.

Sweet Fried Cashews

Cantonese

Honey brings out the rich flavor of cashews.

6 tablespoons sugar
6 tablespoons honey
1-2/3 cups water
1-1/2 cups raw cashews
6 cups oil for deep-frying

Mix sugar, honey and water in a small saucepan. Bring to a boil over medium heat. Add cashews; mix well to coat with sauce. Cook 5 minutes. Remove cashews from saucepan with a slotted spoon and drain on paper towels. Heat oil in a wok over high heat to 325°F (165°C). Reduce heat to low. Carefully lower cashews into hot oil with a slotted metal spoon. Deep-fry 5 to 6 minutes until golden brown. Remove cashews with slotted spoon. Drain on paper towels. Cashews will become crunchy as they cool. Serve at room temperature. Makes 1-1/2 cups.

Variation

Sweet Fried Walnuts: Substitute 1-1/2 cups walnut halves for the cashews.

How to Make Shao Mai

1/If you're using square wonton skins, trim corners to give them a round shape.

2/Pleat wonton skin around filling, leaving top open.

Steamed Shrimp Dumplings   Photo on page 29.

Cantonese

When dumplings are steamed, their skins become transparent so you can see the shrimp filling.

1 cup wheat starch, page 21
1/4 teaspoon salt
1 cup boiling water
2 teaspoons lard or shortening
2/3 lb. fresh shrimp
Marinade:
  3/4 teaspoon salt
  1/4 teaspoon sugar
  1/2 teaspoon sesame oil
  1 tablespoon cornstarch
  1/4 teaspoon pepper
  1/2 egg white
2 oz. pork fat
1/3 cup chopped whole bamboo shoots
About 6 cups boiling water

Place wheat starch and salt in a large bowl. Make a well in the center and pour in boiling water, stirring quickly with spoon or chopsticks until dry ingredients stick together. Cover with a clean cloth towel and let stand 15 minutes. Add lard or shortening; knead dough 3 to 4 minutes. Shell and devein shrimp, page 59; rinse. Chop shrimp into 1/2-inch pieces with a cleaver. Combine marinade ingredients in a medium bowl. Add shrimp; mix well. Let stand 20 minutes. Use a cleaver to chop pork fat. Add chopped pork fat and bamboo shoots to marinated shrimp; mix well. Refrigerate until ready to use. On a floured surface, use your hands to shape dough into a long roll 1 inch in diameter. Chop into thirty-six 1/2-inch pieces with a cleaver. Roll each piece into a ball and place on chopping board. Lightly oil the broad side of cleaver. Press oiled side of cleaver on each ball to make a thin circle. Rotate blade to make a 3-inch circle. Repeat with remaining balls, lightly oiling cleaver before pressing each ball. If you don't have a cleaver, pat out the dough in the palm of your hand or roll out with a rolling pin. Place 2 teaspoons shrimp filling in center of a circle, being sure to include at least 1 piece of shrimp. Fold dough over filling to make a half circle. Pleat one side and pinch to seal. Repeat with remaining circles and filling. Arrange as many dumplings on a damp cloth in a steamer as will fit without touching each other. Cover steamer. Pour 4 cups boiling water into a wok or large pot. Place steamer over boiling water. Steam 7 minutes over high heat. Let cool slightly before removing dumplings. Serve hot. Makes 36 appetizers.

Ginger Sauce

Dip Steamed Shrimp Dumplings, pages 34 and 35, in this delectable sauce.

5 slices fresh ginger root, page 16
3 tablespoons soy sauce
1 tablespoon rice vinegar or
  white vinegar
1/4 teaspoon sugar

Mince ginger root with a cleaver. Combine minced ginger root, soy sauce, vinegar and sugar in a small bowl; mix well. Let stand 5 to 10 minutes before serving. Makes about 1/4 cup.

How to Make Steamed Shrimp Dumplings

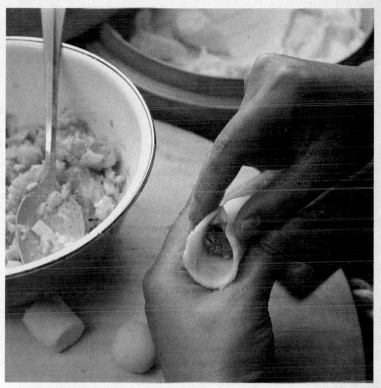

1/Flatten each dough ball by pressing with an oiled cleaver, rotating cleaver to make a circle as you press.

2/Fold dough over filling, pleating one side and pinching edges to seal.

Barbecued Pork

Cantonese

Pork strips are seasoned in a pungent marinade, then basted with a honey mixture while roasting.

1-1/2 lbs. pork shoulder or pork butt

Marinade:
  2 tablespoons rice wine or dry sherry
  **2 thin slices fresh ginger root,
      page 16**
  1 tablespoon oyster sauce
  **1/2 teaspoon five-spice powder ·or
      1/4 teaspoon ground allspice**
  4-1/2 teaspoons soy sauce
  1 tablespoon sugar
  2 tablespoons hoisin sauce
  2 tablespoons ketchup
  **1-1/2 teaspoons bean sauce,
      if desired**
  1/2 teaspoon ground cinnamon
1 tablespoon honey
1 sliced peeled cucumber, if desired

Cut pork into three 5" x 2" strips. Place strips flat in a shallow baking dish. Combine marinade ingredients in a small bowl; mix well. Pour over pork strips. Let pork marinate at least 6 hours in refrigerator. Drain, reserving marinade. Mix honey and 3 tablespoons reserved marinade in a small bowl; set aside. Preheat oven to 350°F (175°C). Fill a shallow roasting pan with water and place in bottom of oven. Carefully place pork strips on a roasting rack above roasting pan so all sides are exposed to heat. If you don't have a roasting rack, insert the curved end of an S-shaped hook, paper clip or drapery hook in pork strips and hang them from the top shelf. Roast 30 minutes. Baste pork strips with honey mixture. Roast 15 minutes and baste again. Roast 10 minutes longer or until pork strips are crisp and golden brown. Remove from oven and let cool. Cut pork strips diagonally into 1/4-inch slices. Arrange in overlapping layers on a platter. Garnish with cucumber slices, if desired. Serve at room temperature. Makes 6 servings.

Fried Wontons   Photo on page 29.

Cantonese

Enjoy them with Sweet & Sour Sauce, page 64, Hot Mustard Sauce, page 23, or Tomato Sauce, page 69.

1/4 lb. fresh shrimp
5 whole water chestnuts, minced
1/2 teaspoon rice wine or dry sherry
1 egg white
1/8 teaspoon salt
1/8 teaspoon pepper
20 wonton skins
1 egg yolk, slightly beaten
6 cups oil for deep-frying

Shell and devein shrimp, page 59. Rinse and pat dry with a paper towel. Use a cleaver to chop shrimp into a fine paste. Place in a small bowl with water chestnuts, wine, a fourth of the egg white, salt and pepper. Place 1 wonton skin on a flat surface with corners at top, bottom, left and right. Place 1/2 teaspoon shrimp mixture near bottom corner. Fold the corner over filling and press sides to seal. Dab egg yolk on one side of filling. Fold left and right sides under filling, leaving corners free. Press to seal. Repeat with remaining wonton skins and filling. Heat 6 cups oil in a wok over high heat to 350°F (175°C). Reduce heat to medium. Carefully lower wontons into hot oil with a slotted metal spoon. Deep-fry several at a time 1 minute. Turn each wonton and deep-fry other side 1 minute or until golden brown. Remove from oil with slotted spoon. Drain on paper towels. Serve hot. Makes 20 appetizers.

Szechuan Cucumber Slices

Szechuan

Spicy cucumbers are a delicious cold appetizer and especially good with Boiled Pork Dumplings, page 26.

3 large cucumbers, unpeeled
4-1/2 teaspoons salt
3 to 4 garlic cloves, sliced
4 dried hot red peppers, chopped
1/3 cup sesame oil
1/2 cup rice vinegar or white vinegar
1/3 cup sugar

Wash cucumbers, cut in half lengthwise and remove seeds. Cut cucumber halves into 1/2-inch slices. Place in a medium bowl. Sprinkle with salt and let stand about 4 hours. Squeeze liquid from cucumbers. Place cucumbers, garlic and red peppers in a serving dish. Heat sesame oil in a small saucepan over high heat until oil begins to smoke. Pour over cucumber slices. Heat vinegar in a small saucepan over high heat until it boils. Pour over cucumber slices. Add sugar; mix well. Cover and let stand about 4 hours before serving. May be refrigerated up to 1 week. Serve cold. Makes 1-1/2 to 2 cups.

How to Make Fried Wontons

1/Fold corner over filling and press each side to seal. Dab egg yolk on one side of filling.

2/Fold sides under filling, leaving corners free. Press to seal.

Pearl Balls

Szechuan

Meatballs are rolled in glutinous rice because white rice won't stick to the meatball.

2 tablespoons dried shrimp, chopped
1 cup hot water
1 lb. ground pork
2 tablespoons cold water
2 tablespoons chopped green onion
1 teaspoon minced fresh ginger root
1 teaspoon rice wine or dry sherry
1 tablespoon soy sauce
1/2 teaspoon salt
2 teaspoons cornstarch
1 egg
**2 tablespoons chopped water
  chestnuts, if desired**
1 cup sweet rice, page 17
2 cups cold water
1 teaspoon cornstarch
About 8 cups boiling water

Soak dried shrimp in 1 cup hot water 10 to 15 minutes. Coarsely chop ground pork with a cleaver. Add 2 tablespoons cold water. Chop pork again to a fine paste. Drain shrimp well; discard water. In a medium bowl, combine softened dried shrimp, green onion, ginger root, wine, soy sauce, salt, cornstarch, egg and water chestnuts, if desired. Mix with a wooden spoon or your hand until the mixture is sticky; set aside. Rinse glutinous rice. Combine rice and 2 cups cold water in a medium bowl. Let soak 30 minutes. Divide pork mixture into 4 equal sections. Divide each section into 6 portions. Shape each portion into a ball. Sprinkle cornstarch on a baking sheet or in a shallow dish. Drain rice and spread on baking sheet on top of cornstarch. Roll each pork ball in rice to coat thoroughly. Again shape rice-covered pork into a ball. Carefully place pork balls on a damp cloth in a steamer, leaving about 2 inches between each ball. Cover steamer. Pour 4 cups boiling water into a wok or large pot. Place steamer over boiling water. Steam 25 to 30 minutes over high heat, adding more boiling water as needed. Remove from heat. Let cool a few minutes before removing pork balls. Serve hot. Makes 24 appetizers.

Hot & Sour Chinese Cabbage

Szechuan

Squeeze all the water from the cabbage so it won't cause the vinegar to splatter.

2 lbs. Chinese cabbage
2 tablespoons salt
4-1/2 teaspoons minced garlic
6 dried hot red peppers,
    broken in 1/2-inch squares
1/3 cup rice vinegar or white vinegar
1/2 cup sugar

Cut cabbage into 3" x 1/2" pieces. Mix cabbage pieces and salt in a large bowl. Let stand 4 hours. Drain cabbage and squeeze to remove water; discard water. Return cabbage to bowl. Add garlic and red peppers. Bring vinegar to a boil in a small saucepan. Pour over cabbage mixture. Add sugar; mix well. Cover and let stand 4 hours. Serve cold as a relish. May be refrigerated up to 1 week. Makes 6 to 8 servings.

Spring Rolls

Shanghai

Spring rolls are eaten on Chinese New Year.

Marinade:
  1 teaspoon rice wine or dry sherry
  1/4 teaspoon salt
  1 teaspoon cornstarch
1/3 lb. ground pork
4 dried black mushrooms
2 cups hot water
4 cups shredded cabbage, page 11
1/2 cup shredded fresh carrots,
    page 11
3 cups boiling water
6 tablespoons vegetable oil
1/2 cup shredded bamboo shoots,
    page 11
1 teaspoon salt
1-1/2 teaspoons sugar
1/4 teaspoon pepper
3 tablespoons soy sauce
3 tablespoons cornstarch
1 tablespoon sesame oil
12 egg roll skins
2 tablespoons all-purpose flour
3 tablespoons water
6 cups oil for deep-frying
Sauces for dipping such as
    soy sauce, Sweet & Sour Sauce,
    page 64, Hot Mustard Sauce,
    page 23, or Hot Chili Sauce,
    page 143

Combine marinade ingredients in a medium bowl. Add ground pork; mix well. Let stand 10 minutes. Soak dried mushrooms in 2 cups hot water until soft, 15 to 20 minutes. Drain and remove hard stems. Shred mushrooms with a cleaver, page 11. Place cabbage and carrots in 3 cups boiling water in a medium saucepan. Boil 2 minutes. Drain and cover with cold water. Let cool. Drain and squeeze vegetables to remove excess water. Heat 6 tablespoons oil in a wok over medium heat 30 seconds. Add marinated pork. Stir-fry 2 minutes until pork is no longer pink. Remove pork with slotted spoon and set aside. Combine vegetable mixture and bamboo shoots in wok. Stir-fry until soft, about 5 minutes. Add salt, sugar, pepper, soy sauce, cornstarch and cooked pork to vegetables; mix well. Remove from heat. Add sesame oil; mix well. Place 1 egg roll skin on a flat surface with corners at top, bottom, left and right. Combine flour and water in a small cup. Place 1/2 cup of pork filling just below the center of egg roll skin. Fold bottom corner over filling. Roll once and fold left and right corners over filling. Continue rolling toward top corner. Dab a little flour and water mixture under the top corner. Press firmly to seal. Repeat with remaining egg roll skins and filling. Heat 6 cups oil in a clean wok over high heat to 350°F (175°C). Reduce heat to medium. Carefully lower several egg rolls into hot oil with a slotted metal spoon. Deep-fry several at a time 2 minutes. Turn each egg roll and deep-fry other side 2 minutes. Egg roll skins should be golden brown. Remove with slotted spoon, draining well over wok. Repeat with remaining egg rolls. Serve hot. Makes 12 large appetizers.

Parchment Chicken Shanghai-Style

Shanghai

The parchment is really crisp-fried egg roll skins. Serve with Hot Mustard Sauce, page 23.

1/3 lb. chicken breasts, boned, skinned

Marinade:
  1/2 teaspoon rice wine or dry sherry
  2 slices fresh ginger root, page 16
  3 green onions, chopped in 1-inch lengths
  1/4 teaspoon salt
  1 teaspoon soy sauce
  1/2 teaspoon sugar
  1 egg white

10 egg roll skins
1 egg yolk, slightly beaten
6 cups oil for deep-frying

Slice chicken breasts into thin strips. Combine marinade ingredients in a medium bowl. Add chicken strips; mix well. Let stand 1 hour. Remove and discard ginger slices. Place egg roll skins on a flat surface with corners at top, bottom, left and right. Place 1 tablespoon marinated chicken near bottom corner and spread it toward bottom corner. Fold corner over filling and roll toward top corner, stopping a third of the way from top corner. Fold left and right corners over filling. Dab egg yolk on one side of filling. Press to seal. Fold top corner down, moisten inside of corner with egg yolk and press to seal. Egg roll should resemble a small envelope. Heat 6 cups oil in a wok over high heat to 350°F (175°C). Reduce heat to medium. Carefully lower egg rolls into hot oil with a slotted metal spoon. Deep-fry 2 or 3 egg rolls at a time in hot oil until golden, 1 minute on each side. Remove from oil with slotted spoon. Drain on paper towels. Makes 10 large appetizers.

Golden Shrimp Balls

Shanghai

A crisp outer layer masks the succulent shrimp filling.

1/2 lb. fresh shrimp
2 oz. pork fat
1/2 teaspoon salt
1 teaspoon rice wine or dry sherry
1 teaspoon sesame oil
1 teaspoon cornstarch
1 egg white
1 cup fine breadcrumbs
6 cups oil for deep-frying

Shell and devein shrimp, page 59. Rinse and pat dry with a paper towel. Flatten each shrimp with the broad side of a cleaver to make chopping easier. Finely chop shrimp and pork fat with a cleaver. Combine chopped pork fat and shrimp. Chop mixture to a fine paste. Using a spoon or your hands, thoroughly mix shrimp paste with salt, wine, sesame oil, cornstarch and egg white. Roll mixture in the palms of your hands into 1-inch balls. Put breadcrumbs in a shallow dish. Roll shrimp balls in breadcrumbs to coat thoroughly. Heat 6 cups oil in a wok over high heat to 350°F (175°C). Reduce heat to medium. Carefully lower shrimp balls into hot oil with a slotted metal spoon. Deep-fry 4 or 5 at a time until golden, about 3 minutes. Remove from oil with slotted spoon. Drain on paper towels. Repeat with remaining shrimp balls. Serve hot. Makes about 20 appetizers.

SOUPS

The miracle of a Chinese soup is that it appears light and mild and then surprises you with its glorious flavor. Chinese cooks use chicken broth as a base for most soups. Pork broth is sometimes used. Beef broth is never used because its flavor is too pronounced.

Make your own chicken broth by simmering a whole chicken, two slices of ginger and a green onion in two to three quarts of water for two hours. Skim off the fat as it rises to the surface so the broth will have its traditional lightness. Strain the cooled broth and refrigerate it for a few days or freeze it for several months.

Some canned broth and bouillon are salty. If you use them, you may want to reduce the amount of salt called for in the recipe.

Soup is not considered an appetizer in China. A tureen of soup is placed in the center of the table with the other dishes so you may help yourself at any time during the meal. Water is not served at the table, so in addition to providing delightful flavor and nourishment, soup quenches your thirst. Several soups may be placed on the table at a banquet. At home, one soup is the rule.

Sizzling Rice Soup is a Szechuan specialty. It's also a conversation stopper. When you bring it to the table your guests will sit up and take notice! Place the bowl containing the deep-fried rice squares in the center of the table. As you pour the hot broth over the rice squares, the rice sizzles and pops, sounding a little bit like a Chinese New Year's celebration! Suggest that everyone stand back because a few pieces of hot rice might pop out of the bowl.

Egg Drop Soup is an example of a soup with a pork broth base. After the broth has simmered, beaten eggs are added and the broth is stirred in one direction only so the eggs form threads.

At banquets or as an evening snack, a sweet nut soup is sometimes served. These soups are easy to make and an exotic experience. Creamy Almond Soup is on page 186 and Sweet Peanut Soup is on page 187.

Oxtail Soup   Photo on page 43.

Mandarin

Use stew meat if you can't find an oxtail.

2 lbs. oxtail
8 cups water
2-1/2 cups diced tomatoes
1 tablespoon rice wine or dry sherry
2 tablespoons all-purpose flour
6 tablespoons vegetable oil
1 cup diced onion
1/2 cup sliced carrot
3 tablespoons ketchup
2 tablespoons soy sauce
1 teaspoon salt
1 tablespoon chopped fresh parsley,
  if desired

Use a sharp cleaver to cut through oxtail cartilege and divide into small sections. Bring 8 cups water to a boil in a medium saucepan. Add oxtail sections, 1 cup tomatoes and wine. Cover and simmer 3 hours over low heat until meat is tender. Heat a small skillet over medium heat 30 seconds to 1 minute. Add flour and stir-fry until golden brown. Remove from skillet; set aside. Heat 1/4 cup oil in skillet over medium heat 1 minute. Add onion; stir-fry 1 minute. Add carrot and remaining tomatoes. Stir-fry 2 minutes. Add 1 cup oxtail. Simmer over low heat until carrot slices are tender. Heat 2 tablespoons oil in a wok over medium heat 30 seconds. Add cooked flour; stir fry 2 seconds. Add 2 cups oxtail broth to cooked flour; mix thoroughly to make a paste. Stir in ketchup, soy sauce and salt. Add stewed vegetables. Cook over low heat 3 minutes. Add cooked oxtail; stir to mix. Bring to a boil. Serve hot in a tureen or serving bowl. Sprinkle with parsley, if desired. Makes 4 servings.

Bean Curd with Spinach Soup

Mandarin

Delicious and nutritious. Bean curd and spinach are full of protein and vitamins.

1/2 lb. fresh spinach, rinsed
3 (3-inch) squares Bean Curd,
  page 169
1 oz. pork fat
4 cups water
1 cup chicken broth
1 teaspoon salt
1 teaspoon sesame oil

Cut spinach into 2-inch pieces. Cut bean curd into 1-inch squares. Chop pork fat into small pieces. Place in a medium saucepan over medium heat and stir-fry until browned. Remove rendered fat and reserve for another use. Add 4 cups water, chicken broth and salt to browned pork. Bring to a boil and add bean curd. Boil 1 minute. Add spinach. Boil 10 seconds and remove from heat. Stir in sesame oil. Serve hot. Makes 4 servings.

Egg Drop Soup

Mandarin

Beaten eggs cook as they are stirred into hot pork broth.

1 (1-1/2-lb.) pork bone
6 to 8 cups boiling water
1 slice fresh ginger root, page 16
1 teaspoon rice wine or dry sherry
1/2 teaspoon salt
1 teaspoon water
1 teaspoon cornstarch
2 eggs
1 tablespoon chopped green onion
1/4 teaspoon pepper
2 tablespoons chopped ham
1 teaspoon sesame oil
Fresh snow peas, if desired

Place pork bone in a large pot with 6 to 8 cups boiling water. Add ginger root and wine. Reduce heat to low. Cover and simmer 2 hours. Remove bone and discard. Add salt to broth. Combine water and cornstarch in a small bowl to make a paste. Stir cornstarch paste into broth. Bring to a boil over high heat. Beat eggs well and pour into broth. Remove from heat. Quickly stir in one direction only to form egg threads. Remove from heat. Add green onion, pepper, ham and sesame oil. Garnish with snow peas if desired. Serve immediately. Makes 4 to 6 servings.

Velvet Corn Soup

Cantonese

Stir this soup in one direction only so the threads of egg white won't break.

4 oz. chicken breasts, skinned, boned
3 egg whites
1 cup chicken broth
5 cups water
1 (12-oz.) can cream-style corn
2 teaspoons salt
1/4 cup cornstarch
1/4 cup water
1 tablespoon chopped green onion
1 tablespoon chopped ham, if desired

Mince chicken and place in a small bowl. Add egg whites; mix thoroughly. Combine chicken broth and 5 cups water in a medium saucepan. Bring to a boil over medium heat. Add corn and salt. Bring to a second boil. Dissolve cornstarch in 1/4 cup water to make a paste. Add cornstarch paste to corn mixture. Continue to boil until soup thickens. Reduce heat to low. Stirring in 1 direction only, mix in chicken and egg white mixture. Cook 1 minute. Pour soup into a tureen or large serving bowl. Garnish with chopped green onion and chopped ham, if desired. Serve hot. Makes 6 servings.

Pictured from the top are Velvet Corn Soup, Egg Drop Soup and Oxtail Soup, page 41.

Wonton Soup

Cantonese

Filled wontons will float when they're cooked.

Filling:
   1/4 lb. fresh shrimp
   1/4 lb. finely ground pork
   1/2 teaspoon minced fresh
     ginger root
   1/2 teaspoon salt
   1 tablespoon soy sauce
   1 egg
   1/2 tablespoon sesame oil
   1/2 teaspoon sugar
   1 teaspoon rice wine or dry sherry
   2 tablespoons minced green onion

30 wonton skins
1 egg yolk, slightly beaten
8 cups water
1 cup cold water
4 dried black mushrooms or
   1/2 lb. fresh mushrooms
2 cups hot water to soak
   black mushrooms
1 cup chicken broth
5 cups water
1/3 cup shredded bamboo shoots,
   page 11
1/2 teaspoon sesame oil
1 teaspoon salt
1/2 teaspoon pepper

Shell and devein shrimp, page 59. Rinse and pat dry with paper towel. Use a cleaver to chop shrimp into a fine paste. Combine shrimp paste with remaining filling ingredients in a large bowl; mix well. Place 1 wonton skin on a flat surface with corners at top, bottom, left and right. Place about 1 teaspoon filling in bottom corner of a wonton skin. Fold corner over filling and roll up, stopping 1 inch from top corner. Press down on each side of filling to seal. Dab egg yolk on one side of filling. Fold sides under filling, leaving corners free. Press to seal. Repeat with remaining wonton skins and filling. Any remaining filling may be frozen. As each wonton is assembled, place on a large plate under a dry towel. Bring 8 cups water to a boil in a large saucepan. Carefully lower each wonton into boiling water with a slotted metal spoon. Stir gently to prevent wontons from sticking to bottom of pot. Bring to a second boil. Add 1 cup cold water and bring to a third boil. Wontons will float when done. Carefully remove each wonton with slotted spoon and set aside. Discard water. If using dried black mushrooms, soak them in 2 cups hot water until soft, 15 to 20 minutes. Drain and remove hard stems. Shred softened black mushrooms or fresh mushrooms with cleaver, page 11. Pour chicken broth and 5 cups water into saucepan. Bring to a boil over high heat. Add bamboo shoots and shredded mushrooms. Reduce heat to medium and cook 5 minutes. Add sesame oil, salt and pepper. Carefully lower cooked wontons into soup and serve at once. Makes 4 to 6 servings.

中國菜

When sealing wontons, a mixture of 1 tablespoon of water and 2 tablespoons of all-purpose flour can be substituted for the beaten egg yolk.

How to Make Wonton Soup

 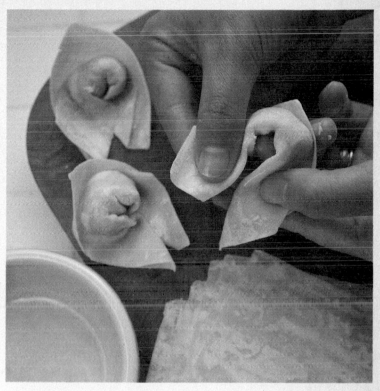

1/Fold corner over filling and continue rolling almost to opposite corner. Dab egg yolk on one side of filling.

2/Fold sides under filling, leaving corners free. Press to seal.

Abalone-Chicken Soup

Cantonese

Baking soda is used to tenderize the abalone.

10 cups water (2-1/2 qts.)
1 lb. chicken thighs
1 tablespoon rice wine or dry sherry
2 slices fresh ginger root, page 16
2 green onions,
  chopped in 4-inch pieces
1-1/2 teaspoons salt
1 (4-oz.) can abalone, drained
1/2 teaspoon baking soda
1-1/2 teaspoons sesame oil

Bring 10 cups water to a boil in a large saucepan over high heat. Chop each chicken thigh into two 1-1/2- to 2-inch lengths with a sharp cleaver. Add chicken pieces, wine, ginger root, green onions and salt to boiling water. Reduce heat to low, cover and simmer 1 hour. Cut abalone into 1/4-inch slices. Combine baking soda and sesame oil in a small bowl. Add sliced abalone; mix well and let stand 20 minutes. turn heat under soup to high. Add abalone. Cook 3 to 4 minutes. Serve hot. Makes 6 to 8 servings.

Chicken-Cucumber Soup

Cantonese

Steaming makes chicken extra tender and juicy.

1 (2-lb.) chicken
6 cups water
1/2 tablespoon rice wine or dry sherry
2 green onions
2 slices fresh ginger root, page 16
1/4 teaspoon salt
About 8 cups boiling water
1 (4-oz.) can pickled cucumbers

Chop chicken into 2-inch pieces with a sharp cleaver. Place in a large casserole or baking dish. Add 6 cups water, wine, green onions, ginger root and salt. Pour 4 cups boiling water into a wok or large pot. Place casserole or baking dish on a steamer rack over boiling water. Cover wok and steam over high heat 30 minutes, adding more water as needed. Add pickled cucumbers and their juice to chicken. Steam 10 minutes longer. Remove wok from heat. Let cool slightly before removing casserole from steamer. Serve hot. Makes 6 servings.

Bean Curd & Oyster Soup

Cantonese

If you can't find fresh oysters, substitute one 4-ounce can of oysters.

1/2 lb. fresh oysters
Marinade:
  2 green onions, mashed with cleaver
  2 slices fresh ginger root, page 16, mashed with cleaver
  1 tablespoon rice wine or dry sherry
  2 tablespoons cornstarch
  1/4 teaspoon sugar
1 (3-inch) square Bean Curd, page 169
5 cups water
1/2 cup chicken broth
1-1/2 teaspoons salt
1-1/2 tablespoons minced fresh ginger root
1/4 teaspoon pepper
1 teaspoon sesame oil

Rinse oysters well with cold water. Combine marinade ingredients in a medium bowl. Add oysters; mix well. Let stand 20 minutes. Dice bean curd into 3/4-inch cubes. Combine 5 cups water, chicken broth, salt, ginger root and bean curd in a large saucepan. Bring to a boil over medium heat. Add oysters one by one to soup and bring to a second boil. Stir in pepper and sesame oil. Serve hot. Makes 6 servings.

Tomato Egg-Flower Soup

Cantonese

This soup is as delicious as its name is imaginative. The flowers are really swirled eggs.

1 cup chicken broth
5 cups water
1 teaspoon salt
3 tablespoons fresh or frozen peas
1 large tomato, diced
1-1/2 (3-inch) squares Bean Curd,
  page 169, diced in 1/2-inch cubes
1 teaspoon cornstarch
2 tablespoons water
2 eggs
1/2 teaspoon sesame oil
2 tablespoons chopped green onion
1/2 teaspoon pepper

Bring chicken broth, water, salt and peas to a boil in a large saucepan. Add tomato and bean curd. Cook 5 minutes over medium heat. Mix cornstarch with 2 tablespoons water. Stir into soup. Beat eggs slightly in a small bowl. Slowly pour beaten eggs onto surface of soup. Stir soup in one direction until it swirls. Eggs will form threads. Quickly turn off heat and add sesame oil, green onion and pepper. Serve at once. Makes 4 to 6 servings.

Mustard Green Soup

Szechuan

Make this tasty soup in 30 minutes or less.

1/4 lb. pork butt
Marinade:
  1 teaspoon soy sauce
  1 teaspoon vegetable oil
  1/4 teaspoon pepper

1/2 cup chicken broth
4 cups water
1/2 cup shredded fresh
  mustard greens, page 11
1/2 cup shredded canned
  bamboo shoots, drained, page 11
1/2 teaspoon salt
1 teaspoon sesame oil
1 tablespoon chopped green onion

Slice pork into thin strips. Shred strips with a cleaver, page 11. Combine marinade ingredients in a small bowl. Add pork shreds; mix well. Let stand 15 minutes. Combine chicken broth and 4 cups water in a medium saucepan. Bring to a boil over high heat; reduce heat to medium. Add mustard greens and bamboo shoots. Boil 5 minutes. Add pork shreds with marinade. Cook 2 minutes longer. Stir in salt, sesame oil and green onion. Serve immediately. Makes 4 servings.

Sizzling Rice Soup

Szechuan

Hot soup poured over deep-fried rice squares makes them sizzle and pop.

1/4 cup shredded chicken or pork butt
1/2 teaspoon rice wine or dry sherry
1/2 teaspoon cornstarch
1/4 cup small fresh shrimp
1/2 teaspoon rice wine or dry sherry
1/2 teaspoon cornstarch
4 cups oil for deep-frying
1 tablespoon vegetable oil
1 cup chicken broth
4 cups water
1-1/2 teaspoons salt
1/4 cup sliced bamboo shoots
1/4 cup thinly sliced carrot
1/4 cup sliced mushrooms
2 tablespoons frozen peas
1/4 teaspoon white pepper
1 teaspoon sesame oil
5 or 6 (2-inch) squares Crisp Rice,
    page 151

Combine chicken or pork, 1/2 teaspoon wine and 1/2 teaspoon cornstarch in a small bowl; mix well. Let stand 20 minutes. Shell and devein shrimp, page 59; rinse. Combine shrimp, 1/2 teaspoon wine and 1/2 teaspoon cornstarch in a small bowl; mix well. Let stand 20 minutes. Heat 4 cups oil in a wok over high heat to 400°F (205°C). While oil for deep-frying is heating, heat 1 tablespoon oil in medium saucepan over medium heat 1 minute. Add chicken broth, 4 cups water and salt. Bring to a boil. Add bamboo shoots, carrot, mushrooms and peas. Cook 2 to 3 minutes. Add chicken and shrimp. Cook 2 minutes. Stir in white pepper and sesame oil. Test oil for deep-frying by dropping in a small piece of crisp rice. The oil is hot enough if rice puffs out in 3 seconds. Carefully lower rice squares in hot oil and deep-fry over high heat until rice puffs out and turns golden. Quickly remove rice squares from oil with a slotted spoon, draining well over wok. Place in a tureen or large bowl. At the table, pour hot soup over hot rice squares. The rice will sizzle and pop. Makes 4 servings.

How to Make Sizzling Rice Soup

1/Remove deep-fried rice squares from hot oil and drain over wok. Place in a tureen or bowl.

2/Carefully pour hot soup over hot rice squares and serve soup immediately.

Hot & Sour Soup

Szechuan

Wood ears and lily buds add little flavor, but their texture is important.

3 dried wood ears
20 dried tiger lily buds
3 cups hot water
1/4 lb. pork butt
Marinade:
   1/2 teaspoon rice wine or dry sherry
   1/2 teaspoon cornstarch
   1 teaspoon sesame oil
1-1/2 cups chicken broth
5 cups water
1 teaspoon salt
2 oz. fresh mushrooms, sliced, or
   1/2 (4-oz.) can drained sliced
   mushrooms
1/4 cup sliced water chestnuts
1/4 cup shredded bamboo shoots,
   page 11
2 tablespoons shredded fresh carrot,
   page 11
1 (3-inch) square Bean Curd,
   page 169, thinly sliced
2 tablespoons Worcestershire sauce
1 teaspoon vinegar, if desired
5 tablespoons cornstarch
5 tablespoons water
1 egg beaten
1/2 teaspoon black pepper
1/2 teaspoon white pepper
1 tablespoon sesame oil

Soak wood ears and lily buds in 3 cups hot water 15 minutes to soften. Remove stems from softened wood ears. Shred wood ears with a cleaver, page 11. Slice pork into thin strips. Use a cleaver to chop strips into shreds, page 11. Combine marinade ingredients in a small bowl. Add pork shreds; mix well. Let stand 15 minutes. Combine chicken broth and 5 cups water and salt in a medium saucepan. Bring to a boil over high heat; reduce heat to medium. Add mushrooms, water chestnuts, bamboo shoots, carrot, wood ears and lily buds to broth. Simmer 3 to 4 minutes. Add pork shreds with marinade and bean curd. Bring to a boil. Add Worcestershire sauce and vinegar, if desired. Dissolve cornstarch in 5 tablespoons water to make a paste. Slowly stir into soup. Cook over medium heat until soup thickens slightly. Stir egg into soup. Add black pepper, white pepper and sesame oil. Serve hot. Makes 4 servings.

中國菜

To cut wood ears into long shreds, roll up softened wood ears and slice the roll.

Fish Ball Soup

Shanghai

The fresher the fish—the better the soup will be.

1/2 lb. fresh fish, boned
1/2 teaspoon rice wine or dry sherry
1 teaspoon salt
1 tablespoon chopped shallots
4-1/2 teaspoons chopped water
   chestnuts
4-1/2 teaspoons cornstarch
5 cups boiling water
3 cups cold water
1 cup chicken broth
1-1/2 teaspoons salt
6 oz. fresh spinach,
   cut in 2-inch lengths
1 teaspoon sesame oil
1/4 teaspoon pepper

Place fish skin-side down on a chopping board. Finely chop fish with a cleaver without cutting through skin. Scrape fish into a medium bowl; discard skin. Add wine, salt, shallots, water chestnuts and cornstarch. Use chop sticks or a wooden spoon to stir mixture about 5 minutes until fish is very sticky. Use a teaspoon dipped in cold water to make small balls from the fish mixture. Place fish balls in 5 cups boiling water over medium heat. Bring fish broth to a second boil. Remove fish balls with a slotted spoon and place in 3 cups cold water to cool 1 minute. Remove with slotted spoon and set aside. Add chicken broth and salt to fish broth. Bring to a third boil. Add spinach, wait a few seconds and carefully lower fish balls back into broth with slotted spoon. Add sesame oil and pepper; stir once. Serve hot. Makes 4 servings.

Watercress with Fish Broth

Shanghai

Bone fish with the skin on so the meat won't fall apart.

4 to 6 oz. fresh fish, boned, skinned
Marinade:
   1/2 teaspoon rice wine or dry sherry
   1/4 teaspoon salt
   1 teaspoon cornstarch
   1/2 teaspoon sesame oil

2/3 cup chicken broth
5 cups water
1-1/2 teaspoons salt
6 oz. watercress, cut in 1-inch lengths
1/4 teaspoon pepper
1 teaspoon sesame oil

Cut fish into paper-thin slices with a cleaver. Combine marinade ingredients in a medium bowl. Add fish; mix well. Let stand 20 minutes. Combine chicken broth, 5 cups water and salt in a medium saucepan. Bring to a boil over medium heat. Add fish slices and watercress. Bring to a second boil. Add pepper. Remove from heat. Stir in sesame oil. Serve hot. Makes 6 servings.

Bean Noodle Soup

Shanghai

You can make this tasty soup in minutes. It's full of protein because the noodles are made from soybeans.

2 oz. bean noodles
3 cups hot water
2/3 cup chicken broth
4 cups water
1-1/4 teaspoons salt
1/4 lb. ground or shredded pork,
  page 11
1 tablespoon chopped green
  onion
1/4 teaspoon pepper
1 teaspoon sesame oil

Soak bean noodles in 3 cups hot water about 15 minutes to soften. Drain softened noodles and chop into 4-inch lengths. Combine chicken broth, 4 cups water and salt in a medium sauccpan. Bring to a boil over high heat. Add bean noodles. Cook 1 minute over medium heat. Add pork. Cook 1 minute longer. Add green onion and turn off heat. Stir in pepper and sesame oil. Serve hot. Makes 4 servings.

Asparagus Soup

Shanghai

Introduce your next Chinese meal with this light refreshing soup.

1 (16-oz.) can white asparagus,
  drained
5 cups water
1 cup chicken broth
1 teaspoon salt
1/4 teaspoon pepper
1 teaspoon sesame oil

Chop each asparagus stalk into 2-inch pieces with a cleaver. Bring water and chicken broth to a boil in a large saucepan over high heat. Add chopped asparagus and salt. Bring to a second boil. Stir in pepper and sesame oil. Serve hot. Makes 6 servings.

FISH & SEAFOOD

China's many miles of sea coast, rivers and lakes provide enough fish or seafood so that one or the other appears frequently at meals. Seafood, especially shrimp, is a constant source of dining enjoyment in the large seaports of Taiwan, Hong Kong, Shanghai and Canton.

The island of Taiwan, also known as Formosa, is noted not only for its abundance of seafood but for its variety of fresh-water fish. In many fish shops you can see glass tanks as large as station wagons displaying live fish. It's from these tanks you'll choose the fish you want for dinner.

Hong Kong, which was built at the end of the Kowloon peninsula, is surrounded by a bountiful supply of seafood from the warm waters of the South China Sea. It's also one of the most colorful and exotic harbors of the world. Every day, Chinese fishing boats, called *junks*, spread their wing-like sails and glide into the harbor with shrimp, squid, oysters, turbot, scallops and lobsters. Huge fish markets crowd the areas surrounding the docks.

A busy boat village, called Aberdeen, has grown up in a small nearby harbor. For the boat people, or families who live and work on their junks, there are floating schools, clinics and stores. *Sampans*, small boats with one long paddle in the rear, are skulled about the harbor by peasant women. Sampans are used much like taxis and delivery trucks to ferry people and produce around the floating village. Aberdeen has several floating restaurants. With their bright red pillars and curved yellow roofs, these restaurants resemble Chinese palaces.

Away from the seacoast, fresh-water fish are often part of the daily fare. Carp farms, where fish are raised in shallow pools, are common because carp thrive in the muddy waters of the Yellow River.

Shanghai is famous for Smoked Fish. Fish is not actually smoked but the result tastes smoky. Carp slices are deep-fried then cooked in a sauce based on ginger and five-spice powder.

Stir-Fried Squid with Cauliflower

Mandarin

Frozen squid can be found in the frozen food section of many supermarkets.

1 lb. fresh or thawed frozen squid
Marinade:
  2 teaspoons rice wine or dry sherry
  1 tablespoon sesame oil
  1 teaspoon cornstarch
  1 teaspoon minced fresh ginger root
Seasoning sauce:
  1 teaspoon salt
  1 tablespoon soy sauce
  1/2 teaspoon sugar
  1/4 teaspoon pepper
  1/2 teaspoon sesame oil
  1/2 teaspoon cornstarch
  1/2 cup water

1/2 cup vegetable oil
2 garlic cloves, minced
2 green onions, shredded, page 11
1 lb. cauliflower,
  broken in small pieces

Remove head and tail from squid; discard. Rinse off any ink. Remove skin and rinse squid again. Pat dry with a paper towel. Cut squid into 3 strips. Use a cleaver to score inside surface with crisscross diagonal cuts without cutting through. Cut squid into 2" x 1-1/2" pieces. Combine marinade ingredients in a medium bowl. Add squid; mix well. Let stand 15 minutes. Combine ingredients for seasoning sauce in a small bowl; mix well and set aside. Heat oil in a wok over medium heat 1 minute. Stir-fry half the garlic until golden, 30 seconds. Add squid and green onions. Stir-fry 1 minute. Remove squid with a slotted spoon, draining well over wok; set aside. Stir-fry remaining minced garlic until golden. Add cauliflower. Stir-fry 1 minute. Add seasoning sauce to vegetables. Cover and simmer until sauce is reduced to about 1/4 cup. Add cooked squid. Mix well and serve hot. Makes 4 servings.

Braised Fish with Bean Curd

Mandarin

You can use eight fresh mushrooms instead of four dried black mushrooms, but don't soak them.

1 (1-1/2-lb.) whole fresh fish such as
  trout, carp, whitefish or perch
4 dried black mushrooms
2 cups hot water
5 tablespoons lard or vegetable oil
5 slices fresh ginger root, page 16
3 green onions,
  chopped in 2-inch lengths
1 garlic clove, crushed
2 teaspoons rice wine or dry sherry
3 tablespoons soy sauce
1/2 teaspoon salt
1/2 teaspoon sugar
1/4 cup chicken broth
2 cups boiling water
2 (3-inch) squares Bean Curd,
  page 169
1 tablespoon sesame oil
1/2 teaspoon pepper

Clean fish and pat dry with a paper towel. Score fish several times on each side in a crisscross pattern for faster cooking and easier serving; see scoring fish on page 67. Soak mushrooms in 2 cups hot water until soft, 15 to 30 minutes. Drain and remove hard stems. Chop mushrooms into thin slices with a cleaver. Heat lard or oil in a large skillet over medium heat 1 minute. Stir-fry ginger root and green onions 30 seconds. Remove and discard ginger root. Carefully place whole fish in skillet. If fish is too long, cut in 2 pieces. Cover and cook until bottom of fish is golden brown. Turn fish carefully and cook until other side is golden brown. Add garlic, wine, sliced mushrooms, soy sauce, salt, sugar, chicken broth and 2 cups boiling water. Cover and cook over low heat 5 minutes. Dice bean curd into 1-inch cubes. Add to skillet. Cover and cook 15 minutes. Stir in sesame oil and pepper. Place on a platter and serve immediately. Makes 4 servings.

Shrimp with Snow Peas

Cantonese

Oyster sauce is the secret to the delectable flavor.

2/3 lb. fresh shrimp

Marinade:
 **1-1/2 teaspoons rice wine or
  dry sherry**
 1/2 teaspoon salt
 **1/2 teaspoon minced fresh
  ginger root**
 1-1/2 teaspoons cornstarch
 1 teaspoon sesame oil

Seasoning sauce:
 1 tablespoon chicken broth
 3 tablespoons water
 1/2 teaspoon cornstarch
 3 tablespoons oyster sauce

1/2 cup vegetable oil
1 garlic clove, crushed
1/4 teaspoon salt
1/2 lb. fresh snow peas

Shell and devein shrimp, page 59. Rinse and pat dry with a paper towel. Combine marinade ingredients in a medium bowl. Add shrimp; mix well. Let stand 30 minutes. Pat dry with a paper towel. Combine ingredients for seasoning sauce in a small bowl; mix well. Heat oil in a wok 30 seconds over high heat. Stir-fry garlic until golden, 30 seconds. Add shrimp. Stir-fry about 30 seconds until shrimp are pink. Remove from wok with a slotted spoon, draining well over wok. Add salt and snow peas to oil in wok. Stir-fry over high heat 30 seconds. Add seasoning sauce. Stir-fry until sauce thickens slightly. Add cooked shrimp. Stir-fry to coat shrimp with sauce. Serve hot. Makes 4 servings.

Shrimp with Lobster Sauce

Cantonese

The elegant sauce is called Lobster Sauce *because it tastes as if it contains lobster.*

1 lb. fresh shrimp

Marinade:
 2 teaspoons rice wine or dry sherry
 1 teaspoon cornstarch
 1/8 teaspoon black pepper
 **1/2 teaspoon minced fresh
  ginger root**

1/2 onion
1/2 green pepper
6 tablespoons vegetable oil
1 tablespoon minced garlic
**2 tablespoons salty black beans,
 rinsed, chopped**

Lobster Sauce:
 1/4 cup chicken broth
 1/4 cup water
 1 teaspoon cornstarch
 4-1/2 teaspoons oyster sauce

2 egg whites

Shell and devein shrimp, page 59. Rinse and pat dry with a paper towel. Combine marinade ingredients in a medium bowl. Add shrimp; mix well. Let stand 30 minutes. Chop onion and green pepper into 3/4-inch squares. Pat marinated shrimp dry with a paper towel. Heat oil in a wok over high heat 1 minute. Stir-fry marinated shrimp 1 minute or until pink. Remove shrimp with a slotted spoon, draining well over wok; set aside. Add garlic and black beans to oil in wok. Stir-fry 1 minute. Add diced onion and green pepper. Stir-fry 1 minute. Mix ingredients for lobster sauce in a small bowl. Add to wok and bring to a boil. When sauce has thickened, stir in cooked shrimp. Beat egg whites in a small bowl and pour in a slow stream into wok. Quickly remove from heat and mix well. Serve immediately. Makes 4 to 6 servings.

Shrimp Legs with Seaweed

Cantonese

Stuffed shrimp are wrapped in seaweed to look like legs in trousers.

**24 fresh large shrimp or prawns
   with shells (about 1 lb.)**

Marinade:
   1 teaspoon rice wine or dry sherry
   1/2 teaspoon salt
   1 teaspoon minced fresh ginger root

1 oz. pork fat
**5 oz. small fresh or
   frozen shelled shrimp**
**1/2 (4-oz.) can whole or
   sliced water chestnuts, drained**
1 tablespoon rice wine or dry sherry
4-1/2 teaspoons chopped green onion
1/2 teaspoon salt
1/2 teaspoon sugar
1/4 teaspoon pepper
1/2 teaspoon sesame oil
2 teaspoons cornstarch
6 sheets of seaweed
1 tablespoon all-purpose flour
1/2 tablespoon water
6 cups oil for deep-frying
About 1 cup Chinese parsley
3 Tomato Roses, page 21
1 tablespoon Peppersalt, page 88

Leaving tails intact, shell and devein 24 large shrimp or prawns, page 59; rinse. Combine marinade ingredients in a medium bowl. Add cleaned large shrimp or prawns; mix well. Let stand 15 minutes. Chop pork fat with a cleaver. Use the point of a paring knife to devein 5 ounces small shrimp. Add to chopped pork fat and water chestnuts. Chop with a cleaver to a fine paste. Add wine, green onion, salt, sugar, pepper, sesame oil and cornstarch. Cut seaweed into 3-1/2" x 2-1/2" pieces. Pat marinated large shrimp or prawns dry with a paper towel. Place 1 shrimp or prawn in the middle of each piece of seaweed, letting tail extend just over the edge. Top with 1 tablespoon shrimp paste. Fold one end of seaweed over shrimp and roll up. Mix flour and 1/2 tablespoon water to make a paste. Use your fingers to seal edges of seaweed packets with flour and water paste. Heat 6 cups oil in a wok over high heat to 350°F (175°C). Carefully lower packets into hot oil with a slotted metal spoon. Deep-fry several packets at a time over medium heat 2 to 3 minutes, pressing tails into oil, until shrimp are pink. Remove from oil with slotted spoon. Drain on paper towels. Arrange around edge of a large platter. Garnish with Chinese parsely and Tomato Roses. Sprinkle with Peppersalt and serve hot. Seaweed wrapping may be eaten. Makes 4 to 6 servings.

How to Make Shrimp Legs with Seaweed

1/Wrap each shrimp or prawn and filling in a piece of seaweed, letting tail hang out.

2/After shrimp legs are deep-fried and drained, arrange them on a large platter with garnishes.

Butterfly Shrimp

Cantonese

Deep-fried breaded shrimp unfold to resemble golden butterflies.

1 lb. fresh prawns or large shrimp

Marinade:
    1-1/2 teaspoons minced fresh ginger root
    1-1/2 teaspoons rice wine or dry sherry
    1/4 teaspoon pepper
    1 teaspoon salt

4 to 5 tablespoons cornstarch
1 egg, beaten
1 cup fine breadcrumbs
6 cups oil for deep-frying
4 lettuce leaves, if desired
1 sliced tomato, if desired

Shell and devein prawns or shrimp, page 59. Rinse and pat dry with a paper towel. Make a deep vertical cut along back of each, so it opens to resemble a butterfly. Using the broad side of a cleaver, pound lightly to tenderize. Combine marinade ingredients in a medium bowl. Add prawns or shrimp; mix well. Let stand 30 minutes. Place cornstarch in a saucer. Pat marinated prawns or shrimp dry with a paper towel. Coat with cornstarch. Dip in beaten egg and then in breadcrumbs. Set aside on waxed paper. Heat 6 cups oil in a wok over high heat to 350°F (175°C). Reduce heat to medium. Carefully lower coated prawns or shrimp into hot oil with a slotted metal spoon. Deep-fry several at a time 2 minutes or until golden brown, turning once. Remove with slotted spoon. Drain well on paper towels. Arrange on a plate garnished with lettuce leaves and tomato slices, if desired. Serve hot. Makes 4 servings.

Sweet & Sour Shrimp

Cantonese

Pineapple and deep-fried shrimp are stirred into tangy sauce.

1 lb. fresh shrimp

Marinade:
  1 teaspoon rice wine or dry sherry
  1/2 teaspoon salt
  1/2 teaspoon minced fresh
    ginger root
  1 teaspoon sesame oil
  1 egg white

2 tablespoons cornstarch
6 cups oil for deep-frying
1 green pepper,
  chopped in 1-inch squares
1 tomato, chopped
2/3 cup Sweet & Sour Sauce,
  page 64
1/3 cup water
2 tablespoons chicken broth
1/3 cup diced pineapple

Shell and devein shrimp, page 59. Rinse and pat dry with a paper towel. Combine marinade ingredients and shrimp in a medium bowl; mix well. Let stand 30 minutes. Place cornstarch in a saucer. Pat marinated shrimp dry with a paper towel and coat with cornstarch. Heat 6 cups oil in a wok over high heat to 350°F (175°C). Reduce heat to medium. Carefully lower shrimp into hot oil with a slotted metal spoon. Deep-fry several at a time until pink, about 15 seconds. Remove shrimp with slotted spoon. Drain well on paper towels. Remove oil except 2 tablespoons from wok. Heat wok 1 minute over medium heat. Add green pepper and tomato. Stir-fry about 1 minute. Add Sweet & Sour Sauce, 1/3 cup water, chicken broth and pineapple. Bring to a boil over high heat. Add shrimp, stirring well to coat with sauce. Serve immediately. Makes 4 servings.

Abalone with Oyster Sauce

Cantonese

Use canned abalone if fresh is not available.

12 oz. fresh or canned abalone
1/4 teaspoon baking soda
3 cups boiling water
1 (1-lb.) head lettuce
1/2 cup chicken broth
1 cup water
1/2 teaspoon salt
3 tablespoons vegetable oil

Seasoning sauce:
  3 tablespoons oyster sauce
  1-1/2 teaspoons soy sauce
  1 tablespoon rice wine or dry sherry
  1/2 teaspoon sugar
  1 tablespoon cornstarch

1 tablespoon vegetable oil
1 tablespoon sesame oil

Use a cleaver to slice abalone 1/8-inch thick. Place in a medium bowl. Sprinkle with baking soda and let stand 15 minutes. Put abalone and 3 cups boiling water in a medium saucepan. Cook 3 to 5 minutes over medium heat. Remove abalone with a slotted spoon, draining well over saucepan; set aside. Cut lettuce head into quarters. Combine chicken broth, 1 cup water, salt and 3 tablespoons oil in a medium saucepan. Bring to a boil. Add lettuce quarters. Cook about 10 seconds. Remove lettuce and drain well, reserving liquid in saucepan. Arrange lettuce on a small platter. Reheat liquid and bring to a boil. Mix ingredients for seasoning sauce in a small bowl. Add to boiling liquid and bring to a second boil. Add cooked abalone. When sauce thickens slightly, add 1 tablespoon vegetable oil and sesame oil. Mix well and spoon sauce and abalone over lettuce quarters. Serve immediately. Makes 4 servings.

How to Shell and Devein Shrimp

1/Gently but firmly press shrimp to crack shell. Remove loosened shell.

2/Slit skin on outside curve of shrimp to expose black vein. Use the point of the knife to remove vein.

Fried Oyster Rolls

Cantonese

Marinated oysters are rolled in breadcrumbs before they are deep-fried.

1-1/3 lbs. fresh oysters, shelled
3 cups boiling water

Marinade:
  2 tablespoons rice wine or dry sherry
  1/2 cup chopped green onions
  1-1/2 teaspoons minced fresh
    ginger root
  1/4 teaspoon pepper
  2 teaspoons sesame oil

3/4 teaspoon salt
1/4 teaspoon pepper
1 tablespoon all-purpose flour
5 tablespoons cornstarch
1 egg, slightly beaten
1/2 cup fine breadcrumbs
6 cups oil for deep-frying
Sweet & Sour Sauce, page 64, or
  Peppersalt, page 88

Rinse oysters with cold water. Cook in 3 cups boiling water 10 seconds. Drain well and pat dry with a paper towel. Mix marinade ingredients in a medium bowl. Add oysters; mix well. Let stand 20 minutes. Pat marinated oysters dry with a paper towel. Mix oysters, salt and pepper in a small bowl. Combine flour and cornstarch. Have 12 wooden picks ready. Spear 5 or 6 oysters on a bamboo skewer, dust with cornstarch mixture, dip in beaten egg and roll in breadcrumbs. Repeat with remaining oysters. Heat 6 cups oil in a wok over high heat to 350°F (175°C). Reduce heat to medium. Carefully lower oysters into hot oil with a slotted metal spoon. Deep-fry several oysters at a time about 1 minute until golden. Remove with slotted spoon. Drain on paper towels. Serve hot with Sweet & Sour Sauce or Peppersalt. Makes 12 large appetizers.

Fish with Black Bean Sauce

Cantonese

Salty fermented black beans are often used to season seafood.

1 lb. fresh white fish, boned, filleted
Marinade:
   1 tablespoon rice wine or dry sherry
   1/2 teaspoon salt

1 tablespoon sesame oil
1 tablespoon vegetable oil
1 teaspoon sugar
2 tablespoons soy sauce
1 tablespoon cornstarch
2 tablespoons salty black beans,
   rinsed, minced
2 tablespoons minced garlic
About 8 cups boiling water
1 tablespoon chopped dried
   hot red pepper or
   shredded green onion, page 11

Cut fish into 1-1/2" x 2" pieces. Mix marinade ingredients in a medium bowl. Add fish; mix well. Let stand 15 minutes. Pat dry with paper towels. Add sesame oil, vegetable oil, sugar, soy sauce, cornstarch, black beans and garlic to fish marinade; mix well. Pour 4 cups boiling water into a wok or large pot. Place fish pieces in a shallow baking dish in a steamer or on a steamer rack over boiling water. Cover steamer or baking dish. Steam over high heat 20 minutes, adding more boiling water as needed. Remove wok from heat and let cool about 1 minute. Remove fish pieces and place on a small platter. Sprinkle with chopped red pepper or shredded green onion. Makes 4 servings.

Cantonese Fried Oysters

Cantonese

Sweet & Sour Sauce, page 64, or Hot Mustard Sauce, page 23, go well with batter-fried oysters.

2-1/2 teaspoons salt
1 lb. fresh oysters, shucked
8 cups water
Batter:
   1 egg yolk
   1/4 cup all-purpose flour
   1/4 cup cornstarch
   1 tablespoon shortening or
     2 tablespoons vegetable oil
   1/8 teaspoon pepper
   1 teaspoon salt
   1 teaspoon baking powder
   6 tablespoons ice water

6 cups vegetable oil
2 teaspoons Peppersalt, page 88

Rub salt into oysters with your fingers. Rinse with cold water until water is clear; drain. Bring 8 cups water to a boil in a large saucepan. Add oysters. Remove from heat. Let stand about 5 seconds, then drain immediately. Pat dry with paper towels. Combine batter ingredients in a medium bowl; mix well. Heat 6 cups oil in a wok over high heat to 350°F (175°C). Reduce heat to medium. Dip each oyster into batter. Carefully lower into hot oil with a slotted metal spoon. Deep-fry several oysters at a time about 2 minutes until golden brown. Remove from oil with slotted spoon. Drain on paper towels, then arrange on a small platter. Sprinkle with Peppersalt. Makes 4 to 6 servings.

Shrimp with Cashews

Cantonese

Raw cashews are roasted ahead of time and stored in a tightly covered container.

1/2 lb. fresh shrimp
Marinade:
    1/2 teaspoon rice wine or dry sherry
    1/4 teaspoon salt
    1 teaspoon cornstarch
    1 egg white
Seasoning sauce:
    1 teaspoon rice wine or dry sherry
    1 teaspoon Worcestershire sauce
    1/4 teaspoon salt
    1/4 teaspoon pepper
    1/4 teaspoon sesame oil
    1-1/2 teaspoons soy sauce
    1/2 teaspoon cornstarch
    1/4 cup water
    2 tablespoons chicken broth

7 tablespoons oil
10 green onions,
  chopped in 1-inch lengths
6 slices fresh ginger root, page 16
1/4 cup sliced bamboo shoots
1/4 cup sliced cooked carrot
1/3 cup Crisp Cashews, page 80

Shell and devein shrimp, page 59. Rinse and pat dry with a paper towel. Combine marinade ingredients in a medium bowl. Add shrimp; mix well. Let stand 20 minutes. Combine ingredients for seasoning sauce in a small bowl; mix well and set aside. Heat 4 tablespoons oil in a wok over high heat 1 minute. Pat shrimp dry with a paper towel. Stir-fry 1 minute or until pink. Remove shrimp with a slotted spoon, draining well over wok; set aside. Add remaining 3 tablespoons oil to wok. Heat 1 minute. Stir-fry green onions and ginger root in wok until fragrant, about 1 minute. Add bamboo shoots and carrot to green onions. Stir-fry 1 minute. Add seasoning sauce and stir-fry until sauce thickens slightly. Add shrimp. Stir-fry to coat with sauce. Remove from heat. Add roasted cashews and mix well. Serve immediately. Makes 4 servings.

中國菜

If you are using frozen fish in a recipe, the mixture may be soupy. Turn heat to high and boil until the sauce is reduced slightly.

Stir-Fried Turbot with Hot Sauce

Szechuan

This spicy dish takes only minutes to cook.

1-1/2 lbs. turbot fillet

Seasoning sauce:
 3 tablespoons soy sauce
 1/2 teaspoon salt
 1 teaspoon sugar
 1/2 cup water
 1 teaspoon cornstarch
 3 tablespoons chicken broth
 1/4 teaspoon pepper

5 tablespoons lard or vegetable oil
1 tablespoon hot bean sauce
**4-1/2 teaspoons minced fresh
 ginger root**
1 tablespoon rice wine or dry sherry
4-1/2 teaspoons minced garlic
1/4 cup chopped green onions
1 tablespoon sesame oil

Cut turbot into 1-1/2-inch squares with a sharp knife. Rinse with cold water and pat dry with paper towels. Combine ingredients for seasoning sauce in a small bowl; mix well and set aside. Heat lard or oil in a wok over high heat 1 minute. Add turbot squares. Stir-fry about 30 seconds until fish becomes white. Add hot bean sauce, ginger root, wine and garlic. Stir-fry 30 seconds. Add seasoning sauce and green onions. Stir-fry 1 minute. Sprinkle with sesame oil. Serve hot. Makes 4 servings.

Stir-Fried Squid with Red Peppers

Szechuan

Farmers in Szechuan like hot spicy food, so this is sometimes called country-style *squid.*

1 lb. fresh or thawed frozen squid
1 cup vegetable oil
**3 dried hot red peppers,
 chopped in small pieces**
**1-1/2 teaspoons rice wine or
 dry sherry**
1/2 teaspoon minced garlic
1 fresh carrot, chopped in thin slices
1/2 teaspoon baking soda

Seasoning sauce:
 1/2 teaspoon salt
 3 tablespoons soy sauce
 1-1/2 teaspoons sugar
 1 teaspoon sesame oil
 1 teaspoon Worcestershire sauce
 1/2 teaspoon cornstarch
 **1 teaspoon rice wine or
 dry sherry**
 1/4 cup water

Remove squid head and tail; rinse off any ink. Remove skin; rinse again and pat dry with a paper towel. Cut squid into 3 strips. Lightly score inside surface with a cleaver in crisscross diagonal cuts without cutting through meat. Cut the squid into 2'' x 1-1/2'' pieces. Sprinkle with baking soda; mix well. Let stand 20 minutes. Heat oil in a wok over medium heat to 350°F (175°C). Carefully lower squid pieces into hot oil with a slotted metal spoon. Stir-fry 20 seconds. Remove with slotted spoon. Remove oil from wok except 3 tablespoons. Reheat oil remaining in wok over medium heat 1 minute. Stir-fry dried red peppers, wine and garlic about 1 minute until fragrant. Add carrot. Stir-fry 1 minute. Combine ingredients for seasoning sauce in a small bowl; mix well. Add seasoning sauce to wok. Stir-fry until sauce thickens slightly. Add squid. Toss lightly to coat squid with sauce before serving. Makes 4 servings.

Princess Shrimp

Szechuan

Removing peppercorns is easy if you use a small strainer to lift them from the hot oil.

1 lb. fresh shrimp
Marinade:
  2 teaspoons rice wine or dry sherry
  1 teaspoon minced fresh ginger root
  1/2 teaspoon salt

Seasoning sauce:
  1/3 cup water
  1/2 teaspoon salt
  1 tablespoon soy sauce
  1 teaspoon cornstarch
  1 tablespoon rice wine or dry sherry
  1/2 teaspoon sugar
  1 teaspoon sesame oil

6 tablespoons vegetable oil
1 teaspoon sliced garlic
1 teaspoon Szechuan peppercorns
4 dried hot red peppers,
  chopped in small pieces
1/4 cup sliced water chestnuts
1/4 cup sliced bamboo shoots

Shell and devein shrimp, page 59. Rinse and pat dry with a paper towel. Combine marinade ingredients in a medium bowl. Add shrimp; mix well. Let stand 15 minutes. Combine ingredients for seasoning sauce in a small bowl; mix well. Heat oil in a wok over medium heat 1 minute. Stir-fry garlic, peppercorns and red peppers until peppers darken. Remove peppercorns. Add shrimp to mixture in wok and stir-fry about 3 minutes until shrimp are pink. Remove shrimp from wok with a slotted spoon and drain on paper towels. Add water chestnuts and bamboo shoots to mixture in wok. Stir-fry 2 minutes. Add seasoning sauce. Stir-fry until sauce thickens slightly. Add cooked shrimp. Stir-fry to mix well and heat through. Makes 4 servings.

Shrimp with Hot Sauce

Szechuan

Dried red peppers are the key to this spicy sauce.

1 lb. fresh shrimp
7 tablespoons vegetable oil
8 dried red peppers,
  chopped in small pieces
1/2 teaspoon minced garlic
1 fresh carrot, chopped in thin slices
Seasoning Sauce:
  1 teaspoon salt
  3 tablespoons soy sauce
  1-1/2 teaspoons sugar
  1 teaspoon sesame oil
  1 teaspoon Worcestershire sauce
  1 teaspoon cornstarch
  2 tablespoons water
1/2 tablespoon rice wine or dry sherry

Shell and devein shrimp, page 59. Rinse and pat dry with a paper towel. Heat oil in a wok over high heat 30 seconds. Stir-fry shrimp 1 minute or until pink. Remove from wok with a slotted spoon, draining well over wok; set aside. Remove oil from wok except 1/4 cup. Stir-fry red peppers and garlic about 1 minute until fragrant. Add carrot. Stir-fry 1 minute longer. Combine ingredients for seasoning sauce in a small bowl; mix well. Add wine, shrimp and seasoning sauce to carrot mixture in wok. Stir-fry until sauce thickens slightly. Toss lightly to coat shrimp with sauce. Serve hot. Makes 4 servings.

Sizzling Rice Shrimp

Szechuan

If the rice is too oily after frying, it will fly off the platter when you add the shrimp mixture.

2/3 lb. fresh shrimp
Marinade:
   1/4 teaspoon salt
   1 teaspoon rice wine or dry sherry
   2 teaspoons cornstarch
   1 egg white
6 tablespoons vegetable oil
1 medium tomato
1 (4-oz.) can sliced water chestnuts,
   drained
1 tablespoon frozen peas
1/4 cup diced pineapple
1/4 teaspoon salt
2/3 cup Sweet & Sour Sauce,
   see below
1/3 cup water
2 tablespoons chicken broth
1 teaspoon sesame oil
3 cups oil for deep-frying
16 (2-inch) squares Crisp Rice,
   page 151

Shell and devein shrimp, page 59. Rinse and pat dry with a paper towel. Combine marinade ingredients in a medium bowl. Add shrimp; mix well. Let stand about 30 minutes. Heat 6 tablespoons oil in a wok over high heat 30 seconds. Stir-fry shrimp 1 minute until pink. Remove shrimp from wok with slotted spoon, draining well over wok; set aside. Remove oil from wok except 2 tablespoons. Dice tomato into 1-inch cubes. Heat oil remaining in wok over medium heat 1 minute. Add water chestnuts and peas. Stir-fry 1 minute. Add tomato cubes and salt. Stir-fry 1 minute longer. Add sweet and sour sauce, water and chicken broth. Bring to a boil. Add pineapple, cooked shrimp and sesame oil. Stir-fry to mix and pour into a large bowl; cover and keep warm. Heat 3 cups oil in a heavy pot or another wok to 400°F (205°C). Test oil for deep-frying rice by dropping in a piece of crisp rice. The oil is hot enough if the rice puffs in 3 seconds. Carefully lower rice squares into hot oil with a slotted metal spoon. Deep-fry over high heat until rice puffs out and turns golden. Quickly remove rice with slotted spoon, draining well over wok. Place drained rice on a platter and carefully pour shrimp mixture over rice. The rice will pop and sizzle. Makes 4 servings.

Sweet & Sour Sauce

If the sauce is not sweet or sour enough, add more sugar or a little vinegar.

1 (18-oz.) bottle ketchup (1-1/2 cups)
2/3 cup packed brown sugar
2/3 cup granulated sugar
1/2 teaspoon ground cinnamon
2 slices fresh ginger root, page 16
1 lemon

Mix ketchup, brown sugar, granulated sugar, cinnamon and ginger root in a small saucepan. Cut lemon in half and squeeze juice into saucepan; mix well. Bring to a boil over low heat. Cook 45 minutes over low heat, stirring occasionally. Set sauce aside to cool. Remove and discard ginger root. Sauce may be refrigerated in a covered container about 6 months. Makes 3 cups.

Stir-Fried Shrimp with Chicken

Shanghai

If shrimp are large, cut them in half before stir-frying.

6 large fresh shrimp (about 4 oz.)
1/2 lb. skinned, boned chicken breast
1/2 lb. skinned, cleaned squid,
  if desired

Marinade:
  1 teaspoon rice wine or dry sherry
  1/2 teaspoon salt
  1/2 teaspoon cornstarch
  1 egg white

Seasoning sauce:
  1 tablespoon rice wine or dry sherry
  1/2 teaspoon salt
  1/2 teaspoon sugar
  1/4 teaspoon pepper
  1 teaspoon rice vinegar or
    white vinegar
  1 teaspoon sesame oil
  3 tablespoons chicken broth or water
  1 teaspoon cornstarch

2 fresh carrots
2 cups boiling water
1/4 lb. fresh snow peas
2 cups boiling water
1 cup vegetable oil
6 slices fresh ginger root, page 16
1/3 cup sliced bamboo shoots
1 teaspoon sesame oil

Shell and devein shrimp, page 59. Rinse and pat dry. Cut each shrimp in half. Cut chicken into thin slices. Chop slices into bite-size pieces. If using squid, cut into bite-size pieces. Mix marinade ingredients in a medium bowl. Add shrimp halves, chicken pieces and squid pieces; mix well. Let stand 20 minutes. Mix ingredients for seasoning sauce in a small bowl; set aside. Cook whole carrots in 2 cups boiling water in a small saucepan 10 minutes. Remove with a slotted spoon, drain well and slice into thin pieces. Remove strings from snow peas. Blanch snow peas by submerging in 2 cups boiling water 15 seconds; then plunge into cold water, drain and set aside. Heat oil in a wok over medium heat 2 minutes. Add marinated shrimp, chicken and squid, if desired. Stir-fry about 2 minutes. Remove with a slotted spoon, draining well over wok; set aside. Drain oil from wok except 1/4 cup. Heat oil remaining in wok over medium heat 30 seconds. Stir-fry ginger root until fragrant, about 30 seconds. Remove and discard ginger root. Add bamboo shoots, sliced cooked carrots and blanched snow peas to oil. Stir-fry 1 minute. Add cooked shrimp, chicken and squid, if desired. Stir in seasoning sauce. Stir-fry until sauce thickens slightly. Add sesame oil. Mix well and serve hot. Makes 4 servings.

Deep-Fried Fish with Tomato Sauce

Shanghai

Deep-frying twice makes the meat tender and the coating extra-crisp.

1 (2-1/2- to 3-lb.) red snapper, scaled, boned and filleted, leaving skin on (2 fillets)

Marinade:
  2 teaspoons rice wine or dry sherry
  1/2 teaspoon salt

Batter:
  1 egg yolk
  1 teaspoon shortening
  1/4 cup all-purpose flour
  1/4 cup cornstarch
  6 tablespoons ice water
  1/4 teaspoon salt

Seasoning sauce:
  1 tablespoon rice wine or dry sherry
  1-1/2 teaspoons soy sauce
  1/4 cup sugar
  1/4 cup rice vinegar or white vinegar
  1/4 cup ketchup
  1 tablespoon cornstarch
  1/2 teaspoon salt
  2 tablespoons chicken broth
  6 tablespoons water

6 cups oil for deep-frying
1/4 cup diced onion
1 small tomato, peeled, diced
1/4 cup diced fresh or
  drained canned mushrooms
1/4 cup diced fresh carrot
1/4 cup thawed frozen peas

Score the inside of each fillet 3 times lengthwise and 5 times across, making deep cuts but not going through the skin. Combine marinade ingredients in a shallow bowl. Add scored fish, turning to coat with marinade. Let stand 15 minutes. Combine batter ingredients in a medium bowl to make a smooth mixture; set aside. Combine ingredients for seasoning sauce in a small bowl; set aside. Heat 6 cups oil in a wok over high heat to 350°F (175°C). Reduce heat to medium. Holding 1 fillet by tail with tongs, dip in batter to coat well. Carefully dip fillet in and out of hot oil several times to separate scored surfaces. Then lower skin-side down into oil and deep-fry about 2 minutes. Remove with tongs. Let cool on a plate 2 minutes and then return to hot oil. Cook 2 minutes longer until crust is golden brown. Remove with tongs, draining well over wok. Place on a paper towel on a platter. Repeat with remaining fillet. Remove oil from wok except 3 tablespoons. Stir-fry onion over medium heat 1 minute. Add tomato, mushrooms, carrot and peas. Stir-fry 2 minutes. Add seasoning sauce to vegetables. Stir-fry until sauce thickens slightly. Spoon sauce and vegetables over fish. Serve hot. Makes 4 servings.

Variation

Shrimp with Tomato Sauce: Substitute 1 pound shrimp, shelled and deveined, page 59, for the scored fish.

中國菜

To make a smooth batter for deep-frying, combine the batter ingredients with a whisk.

How to Make Deep-Fried Fish with Tomato Sauce

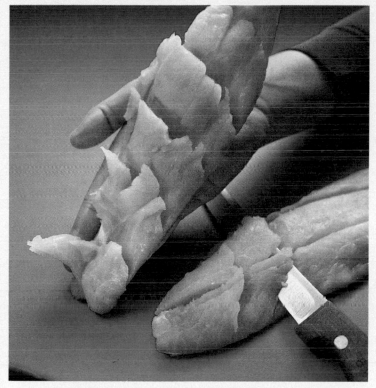

1/Diagonally score fish both down and across to provide more surface area for cooking.

2/After dipping fish in hot oil several times, deep-fry 2
minutes, drain, and deep-fry again 2 minutes.

Sautéed Shrimp

Shanghai

A simple marinade brings out the natural flavor of fresh shrimp.

3/4 lb. fresh shrimp

Marinade:
  2 teaspoons rice wine or dry sherry
  1/2 teaspoon salt
  1 tablespoon cornstarch

Seasoning sauce:
  2 teaspoons rice wine or dry sherry
  1 teaspoon cornstarch
  1 tablespoon chicken broth
  3 tablespoons water
  1/2 teaspoon salt

1/2 cup vegetable oil
1 garlic clove, sliced
1 cup sliced fresh or drained
  canned mushrooms (about 4 oz.)
1/2 (4-oz.) can sliced water chestnuts,
  drained
2 tablespoons frozen peas
1 tablespoon sesame oil

Shell and devein shrimp, page 59. Rinse and pat dry with a paper towel. Combine marinade ingredients in a medium bowl; mix well. Add shrimp. Let stand 1 hour. Pat marinated shrimp dry with a paper towel. Combine ingredients for seasoning sauce in a small bowl; mix well and set aside. Heat vegetable oil in a wok over medium heat 1 minute. Stir-fry marinated shrimp about 1 minute or until pink. Remove with a slotted spoon, draining well over wok; set aside. Remove oil from wok except 1/4 cup. Add garlic, mushrooms, water chestnuts and peas to oil remaining in wok. Stir-fry 1 minute. Turn heat to high and add seasoning sauce. Stir-fry until sauce thickens slightly. Add cooked shrimp. Stir-fry to coat with sauce and heat through. Stir in sesame oil. Serve hot. Makes 4 servings.

Braised Fish with Tomato Sauce

Shanghai

For a lovely garnish, shred both ends of a green onion and chill it in ice water until it curls.

1 (1-1/2-lb.) whole fresh fish such as
  trout, carp, whitefish or perch
1/2 teaspoon salt
3 tablespoons cornstarch
1/3 cup lard or vegetable oil

Tomato Sauce:
  2 tablespoons vegetable oil
  1/4 cup diced onion
  1 small tomato, peeled, diced
  1/4 cup diced fresh or
    drained canned mushrooms
  1/4 cup diced fresh carrot
  1/4 cup thawed frozen peas

Seasoning sauce:
  1 tablespoon rice wine or dry sherry
  1-1/2 teaspoons soy sauce
  1/4 cup sugar
  1/4 cup rice vinegar or white vinegar
  1/4 cup ketchup
  1 tablespoon cornstarch
  1/4 teaspoon salt
  2 tablespoons chicken broth
  6 tablespoons water

Clean fish and pat dry with a paper towel. Score fish several times on each side in a crisscross pattern for faster cooking and easier serving. Sprinkle fish with salt and let stand 10 minutes. Pat dry with a paper towel. Pat cornstarch on both sides of fish. Heat lard or vegetable oil in a large skillet over medium heat 1 minute. Carefully place whole fish in skillet. If fish is too long, carefully cut in 2 pieces. Cover and cook until bottom of fish is golden brown. Turn fish carefully and cook until other side is golden brown. Remove from skillet and keep warm on a platter. Combine ingredients for seasoning sauce in a small bowl; set aside. To make Tomato Sauce, add 2 tablespoons oil to skillet. Stir-fry onion over medium heat 1 minute. Add tomato, mushrooms, carrot and peas. Stir-fry 2 minutes. Add seasoning sauce to vegetables. Stir-fry until sauce thickens slightly. Spoon sauce and vegetables over fish. Serve hot. Makes 4 servings.

Smoked Fish

Shanghai

The smoked flavor comes from the blend of ingredients in the seasoning sauce.

2 lbs. fresh trout or carp fillets
3 tablespoons rice wine or dry sherry
6 cups oil for deep frying

Seasoning sauce:
  3 slices fresh ginger root, page 16
  3 tablespoons soy sauce
  1/2 teaspoon five-spice powder
  1/4 cup water
  1/4 teaspoon cinnamon

1 tablespoon sesame oil
4 lettuce leaves

Pat fish dry with a paper towel and slice into pieces 1/3 inch thick. Place in a medium bowl and sprinkle with wine. Let stand 15 minutes. Heat 6 cups oil in a wok over high heat to 350°F (175°C). Reduce heat to medium. Carefully lower fish slices into hot oil with a slotted metal spoon. Deep-fry about 10 minutes until fish slices are very dry. Remove from wok with slotted spoon. Drain on paper towels. Remove oil from wok. Combine ingredients for seasoning sauce in a small bowl; mix well. Heat sesame oil in wok over medium heat 30 seconds. Add seasoning sauce to hot sesame oil. Bring to a boil. Add cooked fish slices. Stir-fry until fish has absorbed all the sauce. Remove and discard ginger root. Serve warm or cold on a plate garnished with lettuce leaves. Makes 4 servings.

CHICKEN & FOWL

The Chinese have so many recipes for chicken that you could serve it night and day for weeks before eating the same dish twice. Chicken is popular in all regional cuisines and is served in the homes of both rich and poor. Cooked chicken can be purchased in grocery stores. Because of the Chinese emphasis on fresh foods, live chickens are often transported to markets and butchered at the last moment.

Steaming produces a very tender and juicy chicken. For Steamed Chicken with Green Onions, a whole chicken is marinated for several hours and then steamed for 45 minutes. After the chicken is chopped into small pieces, a seasoning sauce is poured over it.

Shanghai ingenuity is evident in their specialty, Drunk Chicken. The only seasonings used are salt and rice wine. After a whole chicken has been steamed for half an hour, it is cut into quarters and refrigerated in a marinade for two days. When the chicken is ready to be served, it is chopped into small pieces and eaten cold. Drunk Chicken is easy to prepare for a picnic. Serve it with a bowl of cold vegetables such as Garlic Cucumber Salad, page 135, or cold noodles such as Tossed Noodles, page 162.

Ducks are eaten frequently in China. They are salted, roasted, braised, deep-fried and simmered in soup. It's traditional to serve duck during the Moon Festival.

Peking Duck is a Mandarin specialty not available in homes because an oven is required for roasting the duck. Most restaurants require 24 hours notice to prepare Peking Duck. You can prepare our simplified version in your kitchen. It requires six to eight hours of waiting time before cooking. Before serving, the skin is sliced into small pieces and the meat is cut into strips. A piece of burnished skin, another of tender meat, a few green onion shreds and a dab of Duck Sauce are placed in the middle of a Mandarin Pancake. The pancake is rolled up so the delicacy can be picked up easily in your fingers.

Peking Duck   Photo on pages 72 and 73.

Mandarin

Duck is basted with honey and then roasted, so the skin is crisp and delicious.

1 (5-lb.) Long Island duckling
2 tablespoons rice wine or dry sherry
1 tablespoon lard
3 tablespoons honey
1 tablespoon rice vinegar or
    white vinegar
12 Mandarin Pancakes, page 153
Duck Sauce, see below
6 green onion brushes, page 21

Clean duck as you would a chicken and remove excess fat at openings at each end. Pat dry with a paper towel. Place duck in a large bowl and baste thoroughly with wine. Tie a string around neck or wing of duck and hang it in a cool place. Let dry 2 hours. Rub lard all over the duck. Hang duck again and let dry 2 hours longer. Mix honey and vinegar in a small bowl. Brush honey mixture all over the duck and let dry another 2 hours. Brush duck with honey mixture again just before roasting. Preheat oven to 350°F (175°C). Pour about 2 cups water into a baking pan and place on bottom shelf of oven. This will prevent glaze on duck from burning and smoking. Roast duck on a rack in a roasting pan 30 minutes. Turn duck over and roast 20 minutes longer. Increase oven temperature to 475°F (245°C). Roast duck 3 to 5 minutes on each side. Skin will be crisp and golden brown when done. While duck is cooking prepare Mandarin Pancakes and Duck Sauce. Remove duck from oven. Slice off skin and cut skin into 1-1/2" x 2" pieces. Slice meat into thin bite-size pieces. Serve skin and duck meat with shredded green onions, Duck Sauce and Mandarin Pancakes. To eat: Place 1/2 teaspoon Duck Sauce and several green onion shreds in the center of a pancake. Add a few pieces of duck. Roll up pancake and fold one end over. This makes a neat little package that can be picked up with your fingers. Makes 6 servings.

Duck Sauce   Photo on pages 72 and 73.

Mandarin

This delicious sauce is served with Peking Duck, see above, and Mu Shu Pork, pages 96 and 97.

3 tablespoons sweet bean sauce
3 tablespoons hoisin sauce
1 teaspoon sugar
1 tablespoon sesame oil

Mix bean sauce, hoisin sauce, sugar and sesame oil in a small bowl until smooth. Serve at room temperature. Makes about 1/2 cup.

Peking New Year's Supper is shown on the following pages. Top row: Duck Sauce, page 71; Peking Duck, page 71; Mandarin Pancakes, page 153. Bottom row: Three-Color Balls with Scallops, page 136; Hot Mustard Sauce, page 23; Peking Spareribs, page 93; Chicken-Cucumber Salad, page 75.

Stuffed Chicken Breasts

Mandarin

Peppersalt is the traditional garnish and seasoning for deep-fried chicken.

2 dried black mushrooms
1 cup hot water
2 (3/4-lb.) skinned,
 boned chicken breasts
Marinade:
 1 tablespoon rice wine or dry sherry
 1 teaspoon minced fresh ginger root
 1 teaspoon salt
 1/4 teaspoon pepper
 1 teaspoon sesame oil
 1 egg white
 2 tablespoons cornstarch
6 oz. fresh shrimp
1/4 cup shredded water chestnuts,
 page 11
1/4 cup shredded fresh carrot,
 page 11
1/4 cup shredded green onion,
 page 11
2 tablespoons cornstarch
6 cups oil for deep-frying
Peppersalt, page 88

Soak black mushrooms in 1 cup hot water until soft, 15 to 20 minutes. Drain; remove any hard stems and chop very fine with a cleaver. Slice each chicken breast in half lengthwise. Lightly pound each piece with the blunt edge of cleaver to make 4 thin slices. Combine marinade ingredients in a medium bowl. Pour two-thirds of the marinade into a shallow bowl. Add chicken; mix well. Let stand 20 minutes. Shell and devein shrimp, page 59. Rinse and pat dry with a paper towel. Chop shrimp into a fine paste. Add shrimp paste, water chestnuts, carrot, black mushrooms and green onion to remaining third of the marinade; mix well. Lay each chicken rectangle skin-side down. Sprinkle cornstarch lightly on top of each chicken rectangle. Sprinkle a fourth of the shrimp mixture over cornstarch. Use a spoon dipped in water to press and smooth filling. Heat 6 cups oil in a wok over high heat to 350°F (175°C). Carefully lower stuffed chicken breasts into hot oil with a slotted metal spoon. Deep-fry until golden, about 4 minutes. Carefully remove from oil with slotted spoon. Drain on paper towels. Chop each piece into 2" x 1" rectangles. Serve hot with Peppersalt. Makes 4 servings.

Deep-Fried Five-Spice Chicken Wings

Mandarin

Five-spice powder is a mixture of ground cloves, star anise, cinnamon, fennel and Szechuan peppercorns.

Marinade:
 4-1/2 teaspoons rice wine or
 dry sherry
 3 slices fresh ginger root, page 16
 3 green onions, chopped
 5 tablespoons soy sauce
2 lbs. chicken wings
Coating:
 1/3 cup all-purpose flour
 1/3 cup cornstarch
 1/2 teaspoon salt
 1/2 teaspoon five-spice powder
8 cups oil for deep-frying

Combine marinade ingredients in a large bowl. Add chicken pieces; mix well. Let stand 2 hours. Mix coating ingredients in a large bowl and place in clean plastic bag. Pat chicken pieces dry with a paper towel and place in bag. Twist top of bag to close and shake well to coat chicken with flour mixture. Heat 8 cups oil in a wok over high heat to 350°F (175°C). Reduce heat to medium. Carefully lower chicken pieces into hot oil with a slotted metal spoon. Deep-fry 2 to 3 minutes. Turn and deep-fry 2 to 3 minutes longer. Carefully remove from oil with slotted spoon and set aside. Remove with slotted spoon and drain on paper towels. Serve hot. Makes 4 servings.

Chicken-Cucumber Salad   Photo on pages 72 and 73.

Mandarin

Mustard sauce and sesame paste add zest to this chicken salad. Agar agar, a seaweed, adds crunch.

1/2 oz. agar agar strips
2 cups warm water
1 cup sliced or shredded
   peeled cucumber, page 11
1 whole chicken breast, cooked, boned,
   shredded, page 11
2 tablespoons minced ham
1 tablespoon dry mustard
2 tablespoons water
1 tablespoons sesame seed paste or
   2 teaspoons peanut butter
2 tablespoons soy sauce
8 teaspoons rice vinegar or
   white vinegar
1/2 teaspoon salt
1-1/2 teaspoons sugar
4-1/2 teaspoons sesame oil

Soak agar agar in 2 cups warm water 15 minutes to soften. Drain and squeeze dry. Chop softened agar agar into 2-inch pieces with a cleaver. Arrange on a large plate. Arrange cucumber on top of agar agar. Arrange chicken on top of cucumber. Sprinkle ham on chicken for garnish. Place in refrigerator. Mix dry mustard with 1 tablespoon water in a small cup. Cover and let stand 1 minute. Add another tablespoon water and mix well; set aside. Mix sesame seed paste or peanut butter and soy sauce in a medium bowl. Add vinegar, salt, sugar and sesame oil; mix well. Pour sesame mixture and mustard mixture over salad. Serve cold. Makes 4 to 6 servings.

Stewed Chicken with Chestnuts

Mandarin

Fresh chestnuts can be peeled easily if they are boiled first.

10 oz. fresh chestnuts or
   5 oz. dried chestnuts
1 (2-lb.) chicken
5 cups oil for deep-frying
1 tablespoon rice wine or dry sherry
5 tablespoons soy sauce
1 tablespoon sugar
2 slices fresh ginger root, page 16
4 green onions,
   chopped in 2-inch lengths
2-1/2 cups water
2 teaspoons cornstarch
4 teaspoons water
1 tablespoon vegetable oil
4 lettuce leaves

If using dried chestnuts, soak in warm water 8 hours. To remove shell and skin from fresh chestnuts, use a sharp paring knife to score an X on each side of the chestnut shell. Drop scored chestnuts in a small saucepan of boiling water and boil 2 minutes to soften shell. Drain and cool slightly. While chestnuts are still warm, peel off hard shell and furry inner skin. Use a cleaver to chop chicken into 2-inch square pieces. Pat chicken dry with a paper towel. Heat 5 cups oil in a wok over high heat to 350°F (175°C). Reduce heat to medium. Carefully lower chicken pieces into hot oil with a slotted metal spoon. Deep-fry half the chicken pieces 2 minutes or until golden. Remove chicken with slotted spoon, draining well over wok; set aside. Repeat with remaining chicken pieces. Remove oil from wok. Place fried chicken and chestnuts in a medium saucepan. Add wine, soy sauce, sugar, ginger root, green onions and water; stir to mix. Bring to a boil over high heat. Reduce heat to low and cook 30 to 40 minutes until only 1/3 cup of liquid remains. Remove green onions and ginger root. Dissolve cornstarch in water to make a paste. Add to saucepan and stir until sauce thickens slightly. Stir in 1 tablespoon oil. Serve chicken and sauce on a small platter garnished with lettuce. Makes 4 servings.

Eight-Treasure Duckling

Mandarin

Indescribably delicious because it's stuffed with eight sweet and savory ingredients.

1 (4-1/2-lb.) duck

Marinade:
2 tablespoons rice wine or dry sherry
1 teaspoon salt
3 star anise
1 teaspoon Szechuan peppercorns

1 cup sweet rice
3 cups water
5 dried black mushrooms
3 cups hot water
2 tablespoons dried shrimp
3 tablespoons vegetable oil
1 garlic clove, crushed
1/2 cup diced fresh carrot
1/2 cup thawed frozen peas
1/2 cup diced bamboo shoots or
water chestnuts
2 Chinese sausages,
removed from casing, diced
1/4 cup water

Seasoning sauce:
3 tablespoons soy sauce
1 teaspoon cornstarch
1/8 teaspoon pepper
1 teaspoon sugar
1/2 cup water
2 slices fresh ginger root, page 16

Use the back of a knife blade or cleaver blade to hit the joints of the wings and legs and crack them. Use kitchen scissors or a sharp knife to cut through skin and flesh around breast cavity. Cut tough tendons around wing joints. Working slowly and carefully, pull flesh and membranes away from bones in one piece. Cut tendons around leg joints and pull out carcass. Use your hands to mold and pat duck to its original shape. Combine marinade ingredients in a large bowl; mix well. Add duck, mixing thoroughly. Let stand 6 to 8 hours. Soak sweet rice in 3 cups water 2 hours. Soak black mushrooms in 1 cup hot water and dried shrimp in 2 cups hot water until soft, 15 to 20 minutes. Drain rice, mushrooms and shrimp well; discard water. Remove hard stems from mushrooms. Dice softened mushrooms with a cleaver. Heat oil in a wok over medium heat 30 seconds. Stir-fry garlic until golden, 30 seconds; remove and discard. Add shrimp and diced black mushrooms. Stir-fry 1 minute. Add carrot, peas, bamboo shoots or water chestnuts, Chinese sausages, softened sweet rice and 1/4 cup water. Stir-fry until rice is almost tender, about 10 minutes. Remove from heat and let cool 10 minutes. Preheat oven to 375°F (190°C). Remove duck from marinade and place on a flat surface. Use your hands to fill breast cavity with cooled rice mixture. Overlap skin and secure with long wooden picks or skewers. Place duck breast-side up on a roasting rack above a shallow pan of water. Bake about 45 minutes until skin is golden brown. Remove and turn duck over. Bake 15 to 20 minutes longer until skin is golden brown. Combine seasoning sauce ingredients in a small saucepan; mix well. Bring to a boil over medium heat. Remove ginger root from seasoning sauce. Remove duck from oven. Remove wooden picks. Slice duck into 4 to 6 pieces. Spoon seasoning sauce over duck and serve hot. Makes 4 to 6 servings.

How to Make Eight-Treasure Duckling

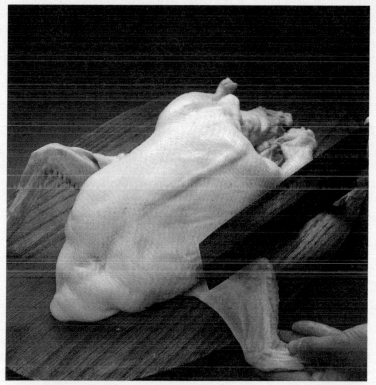

1/Crack wings and legs by hitting joints closest to the body of the duck with the back of the cleaver blade.

2/Cut through the skin and flesh to separate them from the breast bones.

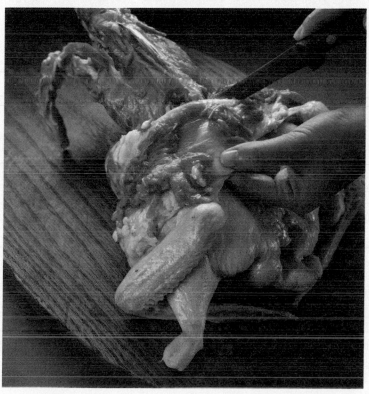

3/Pull flesh and membranes away from bones in one piece, cutting through any tendons with a sharp knife.

4/After duck is marinated, stuff it with sweet rice filling. Close opening with wooden skewers.

Mu Shu Chicken

Mandarin

Dried wood ears are softened in water, then shredded. They add a crunchy texture.

1/2 lb. skinned, boned chicken breast

Marinade:
  1 teaspoon rice wine or dry sherry
  1/4 teaspoon salt
  1 egg white
  1/2 teaspoon soy sauce

5 wood ears
2 cups hot water
14 to 16 Mandarin Pancakes,
  page 153
2 tablespoons Duck Sauce, page 71
3 eggs
7 tablespoons vegetable oil
1 garlic clove, chopped
4-1/2 teaspoons hoisin sauce
1/2 cup shredded bamboo shoots,
  page 11
1 cup shredded cabbage, page 11
1 medium, fresh carrot, shredded,
  page 11
1 teaspoon salt
4 to 5 tablespoons chicken broth
3 tablespoons shredded green onions,
  page 11

Cut chicken horizontally into thin slices with a cleaver. Chop slices into 1-1/2" x 1/4" shreds, page 11. Combine marinade ingredients in a medium bowl. Add shredded chicken; mix well. Let stand 15 minutes. Soak wood ears in 2 cups hot water until soft, 15 to 20 minutes. Wood ears will expand to several times their original size. Break off hard stems and shred wood ears with cleaver, page 11. Prepare Mandarin Pancakes and Duck Sauce; set aside. Beat eggs slightly in a small bowl. Heat 1 tablespoon oil in a wok over medium heat 1 minute. Rotate wok so all sides are coated with oil. Pour in beaten eggs. Rotate wok so bottom and sides are coated with egg. Push cooked egg to center of wok and rotate to swirl liquid eggs on sides to make a large thin omelette. Remove cooked eggs from wok as soon as they are dry but before they turn brown. Shred eggs with cleaver, page 11; set aside. Heat 4 tablespoons oil in wok over high heat 1 minute. Stir-fry garlic until golden, 30 seconds. Add chicken shreds. Stir-fry until very lightly browned, about 1 minute. Remove chicken shreds with a slotted spoon, draining well over wok; set aside. Add hoisin sauce and 2 tablespoons oil to wok. Stir-fry 2 minutes. Add bamboo shoots, cabbage, carrot and shredded wood ears. Reduce heat to medium and stir-fry 5 minutes. Add salt, chicken broth, cooked chicken and shredded egg. Mix well over high heat 1 minute. Serve hot with shredded green onions, Duck Sauce and Mandarin Pancakes. To eat: Spread a pancake flat on a plate. Place 1/2 teaspoon Duck Sauce and several green onion shreds in the center. Add 2 or 3 tablespoons chicken and vegetable mixture. Roll up pancake and fold ends over to make a neat little package that can be picked up with fingers. Makes 4 servings.

Variation

Substitute 1/2 pound fresh mushrooms for softened wood ears.

Stir-Frying Chicken & Pork

Many stir-fry dishes contain chicken or pork and the only cooking required is stir-frying. The pieces of chicken and pork are sliced thin so they will cook quickly and all the way through. The meat will change color as it cooks, losing its raw look and becoming a very light brown. Pork will turn from red to pale golden and chicken will become light beige.

Chicken with Lemon Sauce

Cantonese

Tangy lemon sauce brings out the flavor of deep-fried chicken and gives the dish a glossy appearance.

3/4 lb. skinned, boned chicken breasts
Marinade:
  1/2 teaspoon salt
  2 teaspoons rice wine or dry sherry
  1 teaspoon soy sauce
  1 egg yolk
  1/8 teaspoon pepper
Lemon Sauce:
  1/4 cup sugar
  1/4 cup chicken broth
  2 tablespoons water
  1/2 teaspoon salt
  2 teaspoons cornstarch
  1 teaspoon sesame oil
  Juice of 1 lemon (about 1/4 cup)

6 tablespoons cornstarch
2 tablespoons all-purpose flour
8 cups oil for deep-frying
1 tablespoon vegetable oil
1 sliced lemon, if desired

Cut chicken breasts into very thin 2" x 1-1/2" slices. Combine marinade ingredients in a medium bowl. Add chicken; mix well. Let stand 15 minutes. Combine ingredients for Lemon Sauce in a small bowl; mix well and set aside. Mix flour and cornstarch in a medium bowl. Dip chicken in flour mixture to coat. Heat 8 cups oil in a wok over medium heat to 350°F (175°C). Reduce heat to low. Carefully lower flour-coated chicken into hot oil with a slotted metal spoon. Deep-fry about 30 seconds until light golden. Remove chicken with slotted spoon, drain well over wok. Arrange on a platter. Remove oil from wok except 1 teaspoon. Heat oil remaining in wok over medium heat. Stir Lemon Sauce into hot oil. Bring to a boil. When sauce thickens slightly, add 1 tablespoon oil to make sauce glossy. Stir sauce and pour over chicken slices. If desired, garnish with lemon slices. Serve immediately. Makes 4 servings.

Chicken with Black Bean Sauce

Cantonese

Salty black beans are sold in cans and, once opened, can be stored tightly covered at room temperature.

1-1/2 lbs. chicken thighs
1/4 cup vegetable oil
1 tablespoon rice wine or dry sherry
4-1/2 teaspoons chopped garlic
4-1/2 teaspoons salty black beans,
  rinsed, chopped
1/4 cup soy sauce
1 teaspoon sugar
3 tablespoons chopped green onion
1 cup boiling water

Use a cleaver to chop each chicken thigh into 2 or 3 pieces. Heat oil in a wok over medium-high heat. Stir-fry chicken pieces 5 minutes or until golden brown. Add wine, garlic and black beans. Stir-fry 10 seconds. Add soy sauce, sugar, green onion and 1 cup boiling water. Reduce heat to medium. Cover and cook 10 minutes or until only 3 tablespoons sauce remain; mix well. Serve hot. Makes 4 to 6 servings.

Almond Chicken

Cantonese

This Chinese restaurant favorite is easy to make at home.

1 lb. skinned, boned chicken
Marinade:
    1/4 teaspoon salt
    1/8 teaspoon pepper
    1 teaspoon cornstarch
    1 tablespoon soy sauce
    1 egg white

1 cup vegetable oil
5 slices fresh ginger root, page 16
3 green onions,
    chopped in 1-inch lengths
1 green pepper,
    chopped in 1-inch pieces
1/2 cup diced whole bamboo shoots

Seasoning sauce:
    1 tablespoon rice vinegar or
      white vinegar
    2 tablespoons soy sauce
    1 tablespoon rice wine or dry sherry
    1/2 teaspoon salt
    1 teaspoon sugar
    1/2 teaspoon cornstarch
1/3 cup Crisp Almonds, see below

Dice chicken into 1-inch cubes. Combine marinade ingredients in a medium bowl. Add diced chicken; mix well. Let stand 30 minutes. Heat oil in a wok over high heat 30 seconds. Add chicken to oil. Stir-fry 30 seconds until very lightly browned. Remove chicken with a slotted spoon; drain well and set aside. Remove oil from wok except 2 tablespoons. Reheat oil over medium heat 30 seconds. Stir-fry ginger slices 30 seconds, remove and discard. Add green onion, green pepper and bamboo shoots to oil. Stir-fry 1 or 2 minutes until vegetables are crisp-tender. Combine ingredients for seasoning sauce in a small bowl; mix well and add to wok. Bring to a boil. Add chicken to boiling sauce. Stir-fry until chicken is coated with sauce. Add almonds; mix well and serve hot. Makes 4 servings.

Variations

Cashew Chicken: Substitute Crisp Cashews, see below, for Crisp Almonds.

Crisp Almonds

Shrimp with Cashews, page 61, and Almond Chicken, see above, are enhanced by these deep-fried nuts.

4 cups oil for deep-frying
1 cup blanched almond halves

Heat 4 cups oil in a wok over medium heat to 350°F (175°C). Add nuts and stir 2 to 3 minutes until golden brown. Remove from hot oil and drain well on paper towels. Let stand 5 minutes before using. Makes about 1 cup.

Variation

Crisp Cashews: Substitute 1 cup blanched cashew halves for the almond halves.

Chicken in a Bird's Nest

Cantonese

Chicken and vegetables are served in a nest made from deep-fried potato shreds.

1 lb. skinned, boned chicken

Marinade:
    1 tablespoon soy sauce
    1 tablespoon cornstarch
    1 egg white

Seasoning sauce:
    1 tablespoon rice wine or dry sherry
    2 tablespoons soy sauce
    1/2 teaspoon salt
    1/2 teaspoon sugar
    1/4 teaspoon pepper
    1 teaspoon sesame oil
    1 teaspoon cornstarch

2/3 lb. potatoes, peeled
1/2 cup cornstarch
1/4 teaspoon salt
8 cups oil for deep-frying
1 teaspoon minced fresh ginger root
1 teaspoon minced garlic
1/2 lb. fresh mushrooms, diced
1/3 cup diced water chestnuts
1/3 cup diced cooked carrots
1/2 cup diced green pepper
Shredded lettuce

Dice chicken into 1/2-inch cubes. Combine marinade ingredients in a medium bowl. Add chicken cubes; mix well. Let stand 30 minutes. Combine ingredients for seasoning sauce in a small bowl; mix well and set aside. Shred potatoes, page 11. Rinse well with cold water. Drain quickly then toss with cornstarch and salt; be sure each potato shred is coated with the cornstarch mixture. Place potato mixture in a large strainer with a long handle; place another strainer of the same size on top. Press potato mixture between the 2 strainers. Heat 8 cups oil in a wok over high heat to 350°F (175°C). Submerge strainers in hot oil and deep-fry potato nest 5 minutes until shreds are crisp and golden brown. Drain nest well over wok, then let cool between strainers on a paper towel about 2 minutes. Remove nest from strainers and place upright on a small platter. Remove oil from wok except 5 tablespoons. Heat oil remaining in wok over medium heat 30 seconds. Add chicken cubes. Stir-fry about 1 minute until very lightly browned. Remove with a slotted spoon, draining well over wok; set aside. Reheat oil. Stir-fry ginger, garlic, mushrooms, water chestnuts, carrots and green pepper about 2 minutes. Stir seasoning sauce to dissolve any lumps. Turn heat to high, add cooked chicken and seasoning sauce to vegetable mixture. Stir-fry 5 minutes. Spoon chicken mixture into nest. Garnish with shredded lettuce. Makes 4 servings.

Variation

Substitute 1 (12-ounce) can whole mushrooms or straw mushrooms, drained, for the fresh mushrooms.

How to Make Chicken in a Bird's Nest

1/After coating potato shreds in cornstarch, press shreds between 2 strainers and deep-fry.

2/Serve chicken and vegetable mixture in nest on a platter garnished with shredded lettuce.

Princess Chicken

Szechuan

Crunchy peanuts and tender chicken in a hot but delicious sauce.

**2 lbs. chicken thighs or
  1 lb. chicken breasts
2 tablespoons cornstarch
1 tablespoon soy sauce
10 (1-inch) dried hot red peppers**

Seasoning sauce:
  **1 tablespoon rice wine or dry sherry
  2 tablespoons soy sauce
  1 tablespoon sugar
  1 teaspoon salt
  1 teaspoon cornstarch
  1 teaspoon sesame oil**

**1 cup vegetable oil
1 teaspoon Szechuan peppercorns
1 teaspoon minced fresh ginger root
1/2 cup chopped roasted peanuts**

Use a knife to remove bones from chicken. Lightly pound meat with the broad side of a cleaver. Chop into 1-inch pieces. Combine cornstarch and soy sauce in a medium bowl. Add chicken; mix well. Let stand 30 minutes. Cut stems from dried peppers. Combine ingredients for seasoning sauce in a small bowl; mix well and set aside. Heat oil in a wok over high heat 1 minute. Stir-fry chicken pieces about 2 minutes until very lightly browned. Remove chicken with a slotted spoon, draining well over wok; set aside. Remove oil from wok except 2 tablespoons. Heat oil remaining in wok over medium heat. Stir-fry red peppers and peppercorns until red peppers turn dark brown. Add ginger root and cooked chicken. Stir-fry 1 minute. Add seasoning sauce. Stir well and cook until sauce thickens slightly. Remove wok from heat. Stir in chopped peanuts. Serve hot. Makes 6 to 8 servings.

Bon Bon Chicken

Szechuan

Cold shredded chicken is tossed with a sesame seed sauce before serving.

4 cups water
1-1/4-lbs. skinned, boned chicken
1 cucumber, peeled, thinly sliced
1/2 teaspoon salt
4 bean sheets or 2 oz. bean noodles
3 cups hot water
1/2 teaspoon Peppersalt, page 88
1/2 teaspoon minced garlic
2 teaspoons minced fresh ginger root

Seasoning sauce:
   2 teaspoons sugar
   1 tablespoon Worcestershire sauce
   3 tablespoons soy sauce
   1 tablespoon Chili Oil, page 85
   4-1/2 teaspoons sesame oil
   4-1/2 teaspoons sesame paste or
      peanut butter

Bring 4 cups water to a boil in a large saucepan; reduce heat to medium. Add chicken. Cover and simmer 20 minutes. Remove chicken and let cool, reserving broth in saucepan. Sprinkle cucumber slices with salt and let stand about 15 minutes. Squeeze slices to remove water. Arrange on a platter. Soak bean sheets or bean noodles in 3 cups hot water 5 minutes to soften. Bring chicken broth to a boil. Cut bean sheets into 1/2-inch widths or bean noodles into 4-inch lengths; place in a large strainer. Dip cut bean sheets or noodles in boiling broth 3 to 5 seconds; drain well and arrange on top of cucumbers. Remove bones from chicken. Chop chicken into 2" x 1/3" shreds with a cleaver, page 11. Place chicken shreds on top of bean sheets or noodles. Sprinkle with Peppersalt, garlic and ginger root. Combine ingredients for seasoning sauce in a small bowl; mix well. Pour sauce over chicken. Serve at room temperature. Toss at the table just before serving. Makes 4 servings.

Garlic Chicken

Szechuan

Remove the bone from the chicken breasts if you prefer.

1 lb. skinned chicken breasts
Marinade:
   1 teaspoon rice wine or dry sherry
   1/4 teaspoon salt
   1 tablespoon sesame oil
   1 egg white

1 cup vegetable oil
1/4 teaspoon cornstarch
3 tablespoons chicken broth
1/4 cup chopped garlic
1/3 cup sliced water chestnuts
1/3 cup sliced bamboo shoots or
   cooked carrots
1/2 teaspoon salt
1/2 teaspoon sugar
3 tablespoons soy sauce
1/2 cup water
1 teaspoon sesame oil

Chop chicken breasts into 2-inch square pieces. Mix marinade ingredients in a medium bowl. Add chicken pieces; mix well. Let stand 20 minutes. Heat 1 cup oil in a wok over medium heat 1 minute. Add chicken pieces. Stir-fry until chicken is almost cooked, 3 to 4 minutes. Remove chicken, draining well over wok; set aside. Remove oil from wok except 4 tablespoons. Dissolve cornstarch in chicken broth to make a paste; set aside. Heat oil in wok over medium heat 1 minute. Add cooked chicken, garlic, water chestnuts and bamboo shoots or carrots. Stir-fry about 2 minutes. Add salt, sugar, soy sauce and water. Cover and cook over low heat 10 minutes. Add cornstarch paste. Stir-fry until sauce thickens slightly, about 30 seconds. Stir in 1 teaspoon sesame oil. Serve hot. Makes 4 servings.

Chengtu Chicken

Szechuan

Sesame oil is splashed on just before serving to add flavor and shine to the sauce.

2/3 lb. skinned, boned chicken breasts
Marinade:
  1 teaspoon rice wine or dry sherry
  1 tablespoon soy sauce
  1 egg white
Seasoning sauce:
  1 teaspoon rice wine or dry sherry
  1 tablespoon soy sauce
  1-1/2 teaspoons sugar
  1 teaspoon rice vinegar or
    white vinegar
  2 tablespoons chicken broth
  2 teaspoons oyster sauce
  1 teaspoon cornstarch
  2 tablespoons water
  1/4 teaspoon Peppersalt, page 88

1 cup vegetable oil
2/3 lb. fresh spinach
1/4 teaspoon salt
3 tablespoons vegetable oil
1 teaspoon chopped fresh ginger root
1 tablespoon chopped garlic
1 tablespoon chopped green onion
1 tablespoon hot bean sauce
1 teaspoon sesame oil

Dice chicken into 1-inch cubes. Mix marinade ingredients in a medium bowl. Add chicken cubes; mix well. Let stand 20 minutes. Mix ingredients for seasoning sauce in a small cup; set aside. Heat 1 cup oil in a wok over medium heat 1 minute. Stir-fry marinated chicken cubes until very lightly browned, about 1 minute. Remove chicken cubes with a slotted spoon, draining well over wok; set aside. Remove oil from wok except 2 tablespoons. Heat oil remaining in wok over medium heat 30 seconds. Add spinach and salt. Stir-fry until spinach is tender, about 1 minute. Remove from wok with a slotted spoon, draining well over wok. Arrange on outside of a platter. Add 3 tablespoons oil to wok. Heat over medium heat 1 minute. Add ginger root, garlic, green onion and hot bean sauce to oil in wok. Stir-fry until fragrant, 1 to 2 minutes. Add cooked chicken cubes and seasoning sauce. Stir-fry until sauce thickens slightly. Add 1 teaspoon sesame oil to wok and stir to mix. Place chicken mixture in the middle of spinach on platter. Makes 4 servings.

Chili Oil

Chili oil bought in Chinese grocery stores is usually very mild. Make your own for better flavor.

1 cup peanut oil or corn oil
1/2 cup sesame oil
1 cup chopped dried hot red peppers
5 teaspoons red (cayenne) pepper

Heat oil in a small saucepan over medium low heat 1 minute until a piece of chopped pepper sizzles when dropped into oil. Remove saucepan from heat. Add chopped peppers with seeds to hot oil. Cover and let stand 10 minutes. Stir in cayenne pepper to mix well. Cover and let stand at room temperature 8 hours. Strain into a jar. Cover and refrigerate. Makes 1-1/2 cups.

Hunan Chicken

Szechuan

Substitute creamy peanut butter if you don't have sesame seed paste.

1 (2-lb.) chicken
10 cups boiling water
1/2 cup sliced water chestnuts

Seasoning sauce:
  2 tablespoons sesame paste
  1 tablespoon rice vinegar or
    white vinegar
  1 tablespoon sesame oil
  1 teaspoon Chili Oil, page 85
  1 tablespoon soy sauce
  1-1/2 teaspoons crushed Szechuan
    peppercorns
  1-1/2 teaspoons minced fresh
    ginger root
  3 tablespoons shredded green onion,
    page 11
  1 tablespoon chopped garlic
  3 tablespoons chopped
    Chinese parsley
  1-1/2 teaspoons chili powder

1 sliced cucumber
Tossed Noodles, page 162

Cook chicken in a large saucepan of boiling water 30 to 40 minutes. Remove, let cool. Remove bones. Shred chicken with a cleaver, page 11. Combine with water chestnuts. Mix ingredients for seasoning sauce in a small bowl. Pour over chicken and mix well. Refrigerate until ready to serve. To serve, peel and halve cucumber; scoop out seeds. Cut cucumber halves in diagonal slices. Arrange on a platter with chicken mixture. Serve with Tossed Noodles. Makes 4 servings.

Crisp Chicken

Szechuan

Sprinkle with Peppersalt and serve with Steamed Flower Buns, pages 154 and 155.

3 tablespoons Peppersalt, page 88
1 tablespoon rice wine or dry sherry
4 green onions
1 (2-1/2-lb.) chicken
About 8 cups boiling water
2 tablespoons soy sauce
2 tablespoons all-purpose flour
1 tablespoon cornstarch
8 cups oil for deep-frying

Put Peppersalt and wine in a large bowl. Pound green onions with the broad side of a cleaver, then chop into 1-inch lengths and add to Peppersalt mixture. Rinse chicken with cold water; pat dry with a paper towel. Rub both inside and outside of chicken with Peppersalt mixture. Refrigerate chicken 8 hours. Pour 4 cups boiling water into a wok or large pot. Place chicken in a baking dish in steamer or on steamer rack over boiling water. Cover wok and steam chicken over medium heat about 2 hours until meat is very tender, adding more boiling water as needed. Remove wok from heat. Let cool slightly before removing chicken. Pat chicken dry and let cool. Brush soy sauce all over chicken. Combine flour and cornstarch. Dust chicken with flour mixture. Heat 8 cups oil in a wok over high heat to 350°F (175°C). Carefully lower chicken into hot oil with large tongs. Deep-fry 2 minutes. Remove chicken from oil with tongs; set aside. Reheat oil to 350°F (175° C). Carefully submerge chicken in hot oil again. Deep-fry about 1 minute until chicken is browned and crisp. Remove and let cool a few minutes. Use a sharp cleaver to chop cooked chicken into small pieces. Makes 4 servings.

Hunan Chicken with Tossed Noodles

Sizzling Rice Chicken

Szechuan

Pour the sauce over the rice at the table. Then listen to it pop and sizzle!

**1 (1/2-lb.) chicken breast,
skinned, boned**

Marinade:
  1 teaspoon rice wine or dry sherry
  1 tablespoon soy sauce
  1 tablespoon water
  1 teaspoon cornstarch

1 cup vegetable oil

Seasoning sauce:
  1-1/2 cups water
  2-1/2 teaspoons cornstarch
  1/3 cup chicken broth
  1 teaspoon salt

1/3 cup mixed frozen peas and carrots
**1/2 (4-oz.) can sliced mushrooms,
drained, or 4 oz. fresh mushrooms,
sliced**
1/4 teaspoon pepper
1 teaspoon sesame oil
5 cups oil for deep-frying
**9 (2-inch) squares Crisp Rice,
page 151**

Using blunt edge of a cleaver, lightly pound chicken. Chop into 1-inch pieces with cleaver. Mix marinade ingredients in a medium bowl. Add chicken pieces; mix well. Let stand 20 minutes. Heat 1 cup oil in a wok over high heat to 350°F (175°C). Stir-fry marinated chicken until very lightly browned, 1 to 2 minutes. Remove chicken with a slotted spoon, draining well over wok; set aside. Remove oil from wok. Mix ingredients for seasoning sauce in a medium saucepan. Bring to a boil over high heat. Add peas and carrots and mushrooms. Reduce heat to medium. Cook until sauce thickens slightly, stirring constantly. Add cooked chicken, pepper and sesame oil. Cook about 1 minute. Put in a large bowl and cover to keep hot. Heat 5 cups oil in wok over high heat to 400°F (205°C). Test oil temperature by dropping in a piece of crisp rice. Oil is hot enough if rice puffs out in 3 seconds. Add crisp rice squares to wok and deep-fry until rice puffs out and turns golden. Quickly remove rice squares with slotted spoon. Place in a shallow serving dish. Pour chicken mixture over rice. Rice will pop and sizzle. Makes 4 servings.

Peppersalt

Sprinkle it over fried foods—it's especially good on crisp-fried seafood.

2 tablespoons Szechuan peppercorns
2 tablespoons salt

Heat a medium saucepan over medium-low heat 1 minute. Add peppercorns and stir-fry 5 minutes. Remove saucepan from heat and let cool. Grind peppercorns into a fine powder with a mortar and pestle or pepper grinder. Add salt; mix well. Store in a tightly covered container. Makes about 1/4 cup.

Steamed Chicken with Green Onions

Szechuan

If you like hot foods, add a little Chili Oil, page 85, or Hot Chili Sauce, page 143, to the seasoning sauce.

2 lbs. skinned, boned chicken

Marinade:
  1 tablespoon rice wine or dry sherry
  3 slices fresh ginger root, page 16
  4 green onions,
    chopped in 2-inch pieces
  1/2 teaspoon salt

About 8 cups boiling water

Seasoning sauce:
  1 cup juice from steamed chicken
  1 tablespoon rice wine or dry sherry
  4-1/2 teaspoons minced fresh
    ginger root
  4 teaspoons minced garlic
  1/2 cup chopped green onions
  3 tablespoons soy sauce
  1/2 teaspoon sugar
  2 teaspoons sesame oil

Rinse chicken with cold water and drain well. Combine marinade ingredients in a large bowl. Add chicken; mix well. Let stand 20 minutes. Pour 4 cups boiling water into a wok or large pot. Place chicken in a baking dish in steamer or on steamer rack over boiling water. Cover wok and steam over high heat 45 minutes to 1 hour until meat is very tender, adding more boiling water as needed. Remove wok from heat. Let cool slightly before removing chicken; reserve juice in baking dish for seasoning sauce. Use a sharp cleaver or boning knife to chop chicken into 2-inch square pieces. Place on a platter. Combine ingredients for seasoning sauce in a small bowl and pour over chicken. Serve hot. Makes 6 servings.

Deep-Fried Chicken with Walnuts

Shanghai

Chicken coated with crushed walnuts before it's deep-fried is a crunchy treat.

1 cup walnuts
3/4 lb. skinned, boned chicken
  breasts

Marinade:
  1 teaspoon rice wine or dry sherry
  1 teaspoon sesame oil
  1 teaspoon salt

6 cups oil for deep-frying
1/4 cup cornstarch
1 egg, well beaten
1 teaspoon Peppersalt, page 88,
  if desired
Orange or pineapple slices

Crush walnuts into rice-size pieces with the flat side of a cleaver. Slice chicken breasts into 2-inch square pieces. Combine marinade ingredients in a medium bowl. Add chicken; mix well. Let stand 15 minutes. Heat 6 cups oil in a wok over high heat to 350°F (175°C). Dust each piece of chicken with cornstarch, dip in beaten egg and coat with crushed walnuts. Reduce heat to medium-low. Carefully lower chicken pieces into hot oil with a slotted metal spoon. Deep-fry about 2 minutes until golden. Remove with slotted spoon, draining well over wok. Place on a small platter and serve warm. Sprinkle with Peppersalt, if desired. Garnish with orange or pineapple slices. Makes 4 servings.

Chicken with Papaya

Shanghai

It's best if you use a very firm papaya that is not yet ripe.

1/2 lb. skinned, boned
chicken breast

Marinade:
1 teaspoon rice wine or dry sherry
1/2 teaspoon salt
1/2 teaspoon minced fresh
ginger root
1-1/2 teaspoons soy sauce
1 egg white

Seasoning sauce:
3 tablespoons chicken broth
1/4 cup water
1 teaspoon cornstarch
1/4 teaspoon pepper
1 teaspoon sesame oil

1 cup vegetable oil
8 green onions,
chopped in 1-inch lengths
1-1/2 cups shredded fresh papaya,
page 11
2 tablespoons shredded fresh carrot,
page 11
1/2 teaspoon salt

Cut chicken into thin slices. Chop slices into thin 1" x 1/4" shreds with a cleaver, page 11. Mix marinade ingredients in a medium bowl. Add chicken shreds; mix well. Let stand 20 minutes. Combine ingredients for seasoning sauce in a small bowl. Mix well and set aside. Heat oil in a wok over medium heat 1 minute. Stir-fry chicken shreds 2 to 3 minutes until very lightly browned. Remove chicken with a slotted spoon, draining well over wok; set aside. Remove oil from wok except 4 tablespoons. Heat oil remaining in wok 30 seconds over medium heat. Add green onions; stir-fry 10 seconds. Turn heat up to high. Add papaya, carrot and salt. Stir-fry 2 minutes or until papaya is tender. Add seasoning sauce and cooked chicken to wok. Stir-fry until sauce thickens slightly. Mix well and serve hot. Makes 4 servings.

Variation

Pork with Papaya: Substitute 1/2 pound pork butt or shoulder for the chicken. Omit egg white.

Drunk Chicken

Shanghai

Steamed chicken is soaked in wine for 24 hours and then served cold.

1 (2- to 2-1/2-lb.) chicken
4-1/2 teaspoons salt
About 8 cups boiling water
1 cup chicken broth
1-1/4 cups rice wine or dry sherry

Pat chicken dry with paper towels. Rub inside and outside of chicken with salt. Refrigerate at least 6 hours. Pour 4 cups boiling water into a wok or large pot. Place chicken in a large baking dish in steamer or on steamer rack over boiling water. Cover wok and steam over high heat 25 to 30 minutes, adding more boiling water as necessary. Remove wok from heat. Let cool before removing chicken. Reserve juice from chicken. Cut chicken into quarters and place in a deep bowl. Strain chicken juice and pour over chicken. Add chicken broth and wine. Shake bowl to mix well. Cover and refrigerate 48 hours, turning chicken once after 6 to 8 hours. Aspic-like jelly will form around chicken. Serve with chicken or remove from chicken. Chop chicken into 2-inch pieces and serve cold. Makes 4 to 6 servings.

Fifteen-Minute Chicken

Shanghai

Chicken thighs are stir-fried for five minutes then simmered for 10 to 15 minutes.

1-1/2 lbs. chicken thighs
2 tablespoons vegetable oil
1 tablespoon rice wine or dry sherry
1 tablespoon chopped garlic
1 teaspoon minced fresh ginger root
1/3 cup soy sauce
1 tablespoon sugar
3 tablespoons chopped green onion
1 cup boiling water

Use a cleaver to chop each chicken thigh into 2 or 3 pieces. Heat oil in a wok over medium-high heat 30 seconds. Stir-fry chicken pieces 5 minutes or until golden brown. Add wine, garlic and ginger root. Stir-fry 10 seconds. Add soy sauce, sugar, green onion and 1 cup boiling water. Reduce heat to medium. Cover and cook 10 to 15 minutes or until about 1/4 cup of sauce remains. Serve hot. Makes 4 servings.

Shanghai Chicken

Shanghai

Let the chicken stand on a roasting rack or hang it until the soy sauce dries.

1 (2-1/2-lb.) chicken
3 tablespoons soy sauce
4 wood ears
12 dried tiger lily buds
4 dried black mushrooms
3 cups hot water

Seasoning sauce:
  1 tablespoon soy sauce
  1 teaspoon salt
  1 teaspoon sugar
  2 teaspoons rice wine or dry sherry
  1/4 teaspoon pepper
  2 cups water
  2 tablespoons chicken broth

6 cups oil for deep-frying
3 green onions,
  chopped in 1-inch lengths
6 slices fresh ginger root, page 16
1 teaspoon cornstarch
3 tablespoons water
1 teaspoon sesame oil
6 parsley sprigs

Cut chicken into 4 pieces. Place in a large bowl. Pour soy sauce over chicken. Place chicken pieces on a roasting rack at room temperature 20 minutes until dry. Soak wood ears, tiger lily buds and black mushrooms in 3 cups hot water until all are soft, 15 to 20 minutes. Drain. Remove hard stems from wood ears and black mushrooms. Chop softened wood ears and mushrooms into 1-inch pieces. Mix ingredients for seasoning sauce in a small bowl; set aside. Heat 6 cups oil in a wok over high heat to 350°F (175°C). Carefully submerge chicken pieces in hot oil with tongs. Deep-fry until golden brown, 3 to 5 minutes. Carefully remove chicken with tongs, draining well over wok; set aside. Remove oil from wok except 1 tablespoon. Heat oil remaining in wok over medium heat 1 minute. Add green onions and ginger root. Stir-fry until fragrant, 1 to 2 minutes. Stir in wood ear pieces, lily buds, black mushroom pieces and seasoning sauce. Place chicken in wok and bring liquid to a boil. Cover, reduce heat to low and simmer 25 minutes. Remove chicken with tongs, draining well over wok; set aside. Remove vegetables with a spatula and arrange in the center of a large platter. Chop chicken into pieces. Arrange chicken on vegetables. Bring seasoning sauce left in wok to a boil over medium heat. Dissolve cornstarch in water to make a paste. Add cornstarch paste to sauce. Stir-fry until sauce thickens slightly. Stir in sesame oil. Pour sauce over chicken. Garnish with parsley and serve. Makes 4 to 6 servings.

PORK

豬肉

Pork has traditionally been the most popular meat in China. It's more abundant than beef because less land is needed to raise pigs and they are easier to feed.

Stir-fried pork is more tender and succulent than beef or lamb. Chinese cooks also deep-fry and steam pork, then use the bones to make broth. To be sure stir-fried pork is thoroughly cooked, it must be sliced to a size that will cook quickly. First slice it against the grain and then into thin strips or shreds. It's absolutely necessary to cook pork thoroughly because uncooked pork may contain microscopic parasites. It's a good idea to scrub your butcher block with a wire brush and a household bleach solution after chopping uncooked pork.

Ground pork is not sold in Chinese butcher shops. Chinese cooks mince their own with a sharp cleaver. Pork chops or another cut of pork with a little fat on it are best for making ground pork. Use a sharp cleaver to slice the pork across the grain into thin strips, then chop the strips into shreds. Mince these shreds with the cleaver until the pork is ground.

Chinese ham, which resembles Smithfield ham, is usually used as a garnish rather than as a main dish. It is shredded or minced and sprinkled on top of soups such as Velvet Corn Soup, page 42, or on appetizers such as Shrimp Toast, page 27. Pressed Shanghai Ham is very tender with a smooth texture and pungent flavor.

Sweet & Sour Pork, a well-known Cantonese favorite, uses pork tenderloin that is tenderized by light pounding. The pork is marinated, then coated with cornstarch and deep-fried. The tangy sweet and sour sauce provides a perfect flavor and texture contrast to the tender meat.

Mu Shu Pork is seasoned with hoisin sauce which is especially popular in Mandarin cooking. Stir-fried pork and vegetables, topped with crisp green onions and pungent Duck Sauce, are rolled up in Mandarin Pancakes and picked up in your fingers to eat.

Peking Spareribs   Photo on pages 72 and 73.

Mandarin

Deep-fried pork spareribs are mixed with a spiced seasoning sauce.

1 lb. pork spareribs

Marinade:
  1 teaspoon rice wine or dry sherry
  1 teaspoon minced fresh ginger root
  1 tablespoon soy sauce
  1/2 teaspoon baking soda or
    meat tenderizer
  1 tablespoon cornstarch
  1 tablespoon all-purpose flour
  1 tablespoon ice water

5 cups oil for deep-frying

Seasoning sauce:
  1 tablespoon Worcestershire sauce
  1 tablespoon ketchup
  1 tablespoon sugar
  1 teaspoon ground cinnamon
  2 tablespoons water
  1/2 teaspoon cornstarch

Chinese parsley, if desired
Peeled pineapple slices or lettuce,
  if desired

Cut spareribs in half lengthwise and cut between bones to make 2-inch pieces. Combine marinade ingredients and spareribs in a bowl; mix well and let stand 3 to 4 hours. Heat 5 cups oil in a wok over high heat to 350°F (175°C). Carefully lower spareribs into hot oil with a slotted metal spoon. Deep-fry over high heat about 3 minutes until spareribs are crisp and lightly browned. Remove with slotted spoon, draining well over wok; set aside. Remove oil from wok except 2 tablespoons. Combine ingredients for seasoning sauce in a small bowl; mix well. Heat oil remaining in wok over medium heat 30 seconds. Add seasoning sauce. Bring to a boil, stirring occasionally. Remove from heat. Add fried spareribs, mixing well to coat with sauce. Arrange spareribs and sauce on a platter. Garnish with Chinese parsley and pineapple slices or lettuce, if desired. Serve immediately. Makes 4 servings.

Pork with Green Onions

Mandarin

A little dried hot red pepper added to the oil before adding the pork changes this to a Szechuan dish.

2/3 lb. pork butt

Marinade:
  1 teaspoon rice wine or dry sherry
  1/2 teaspoon salt
  1 teaspoon cornstarch
  1/2 teaspoon minced ginger root

1/2 cup water
2 teaspoons cornstarch
1/4 cup chicken broth
1/2 teaspoon salt
1 cup vegetable oil
2 cups green onion slices,
  about 1-1/2 inches long

Slice pork into thin strips with a cleaver. Cut strips into 1" x 1/2" shreds, page 11. Combine marinade ingredients in a small bowl. Add pork shreds; mix well. Let stand 30 minutes. Combine water, cornstarch, chicken broth and salt in a small bowl; mix well. Heat oil in a wok over medium heat about 1 minute. Add marinated pork. Stir-fry until very lightly browned. Remove pork from wok with a slotted spoon, draining well over wok; set aside. Remove oil from wok except 2 tablespoons. Add chopped green onions and chicken broth mixture to oil in wok. Stir-fry until sauce thickens slightly. Stir in pork. Serve immediately. Makes 4 servings.

Shredded Pork with Sweet Bean Sauce

Mandarin

Sweet bean sauce is sold in cans in Chinese food markets.

3/4 lb. boneless pork loin

Marinade:
  4-1/2 teaspoons soy sauce
  1 teaspoon rice wine or dry sherry
  2 tablespoons water
  2 teaspoons cornstarch

Sweet Bean Sauce:
  4-1/2 teaspoons sweet bean sauce
  1-1/2 teaspoons rice wine or
    dry sherry
  1 tablespoon soy sauce
  2 teaspoons sugar

2 cups shredded green onions,
  page 11
1-1/2 cups vegetable oil

Use a cleaver to slice pork into 3" x 1/4" shreds, page 11. Combine marinade ingredients in a small bowl. Add pork shreds; mix well. Let stand 30 minutes. Combine ingredients for Sweet Bean Sauce in another small bowl; set aside. Arrange green onion shreds in a layer on a platter. Heat oil in a wok over medium heat to 375°F (190° C). Carefully lower pork shreds into hot oil with a slotted metal spoon. Stir-fry about 2 minutes until pork shreds are no longer pink. Remove pork from oil with slotted spoon, draining well over wok; set aside. Remove oil from wok except 3 tablespoons. Add Sweet Bean Sauce to oil remaining in wok. Stir-fry until sauce thickens slightly. Add cooked pork shreds, mixing well. Place pork and Sweet Bean Sauce on top of green onions. Serve immediately. Makes 4 servings.

Stewed Pork Balls with Chinese Cabbage

Mandarin

Deep-frying is the secret for making crisp Chinese meatballs.

Marinade:
  1 tablespoon rice wine or dry sherry
  1-1/2 teaspoons minced fresh
    ginger root
  1 cup chopped green onions
  1 teaspoon salt
  3 tablespoons soy sauce
  1 tablespoon cornstarch
  1 egg
  1/4 teaspoon sugar
  1 teaspoon sesame oil

1 lb. ground pork
1-1/4 lb. Chinese cabbage
2 oz. bean noodles
3 cups hot water
6 cups oil for deep-frying
1 large star anise
1 garlic clove, crushed
3 tablespoons soy sauce
3 cups water
1 teaspoon salt

Combine marinade ingredients and ground pork in a small bowl. Stir mixture with a chopstick or a wooden spoon in one direction until pork and marinade are mixed well, 5 to 7 minutes. Remove pork mixture from bowl and gently toss back into bowl. Repeat tossing back into bowl about 3 minutes until pork mixture is very sticky. Cut Chinese cabbage into bite-size pieces. Soak bean noodles in 3 cups hot water 15 minutes. Drain well. Chop noodles into 4-inch lengths; set aside. Heat 6 cups oil in a wok over medium-high heat to 350°F (175°C). While oil is heating, use a teaspoon dipped in water and about 2 tablespoons pork mixture to make 1 pork ball. Repeat with remaining pork mixture. Carefully lower pork balls into hot oil with a slotted metal spoon. Deep-fry several at a time about 3 minutes until golden brown. Remove from oil with slotted spoon; drain on paper towels. Remove oil from wok except 7 tablespoons. Heat oil remaining in wok over medium heat 30 seconds. Stir-fry star anise and garlic about 1 minute until garlic turns golden. Add cabbage pieces. Stir-fry 2 minutes. Add soy sauce; stir-fry 1 minute longer. Add water, salt and pork balls. Cover and bring to a boil over high heat. Reduce heat to medium and cook 5 minutes. Add softened bean noodle pieces. Stir to mix with pork balls and cabbage. Cook 10 minutes. Serve hot. Makes 6 servings.

How to Make Shredded Pork with Sweet Bean Sauce

1/Use a cleaver or the point of a sharp paring knife to shred green onions.

2/Spread shredded green onions on a platter. Spoon pork and sauce mixture on top of green onions.

Deep-Fried Pork Chops

Mandarin

Oil for deep-frying can be oil you've used before; see page 14.

1 lb. pork chops, with or without bone

Marinade:
  2 teaspoons rice wine or dry sherry
  1-1/4 teaspoons salt
  1/2 teaspoon pepper
  1 teaspoon soy sauce
  1/4 teaspoon sugar

1/2 cup cornstarch
1 egg, beaten
1 cup fine breadcrumbs
6 cups oil for deep-frying

Trim fat off pork chops and pound each side with a meat hammer to tenderize. Combine marinade ingredients in a shallow bowl. Add pork chops; mix well. Let stand 30 minutes. Pat pork chops dry with a paper towel. Dust with cornstarch, dip into beaten egg and coat with breadcrumbs. Heat 6 cups oil in a wok over high heat to 350°F (175°C). Carefully lower pork chops into hot oil with a slotted metal spoon. Deep-fry several at a time about 2 minutes until golden brown. Turn and deep-fry other side about 1 minute until golden brown. Remove from oil with slotted spoon. Drain on paper towels. Serve hot. Makes 4 servings.

Mu Shu Pork

Mandarin

Traditionally served with shredded green onions, Duck Sauce and Mandarin Pancakes.

1/2 lb. boneless pork loin or pork shoulder

Marinade:
  1-1/2 teaspoons rice wine or dry sherry
  1 tablespoon sesame oil
  1 teaspoon soy sauce

5 wood ears
2 cups hot water
14 to 16 Mandarin Pancakes, page 153
2 tablespoons Duck Sauce, page 71
3 eggs
7 tablespoons vegetable oil
1 garlic clove, minced
4-1/2 teaspoons hoisin sauce
1 cup shredded bamboo shoots, page 11
2 cups shredded cabbage, page 11
1 medium carrot, shredded, page 11
1 teaspoon salt
4 to 5 tablespoons chicken broth
1/4 cup shredded green onions, page 11

Cut pork horizontally into thin slices with a cleaver. Chop slices into 1-1/2" x 1/4" shreds, page 11. Mix marinade ingredients in a small bowl. Add shredded pork; mix well. Let stand 15 minutes. Soak wood ears in 2 cups hot water 15 minutes to soften. Wood ears will expand to several times their original size. Break off hard stems and shred wood ears with a cleaver, page 11. Prepare Mandarin Pancakes and Duck Sauce; set aside. Beat eggs slightly in a small bowl. Heat 1 tablespoon oil in a wok over medium heat 1 minute. Rotate wok to coat sides with oil. Pour in beaten eggs. Slowly rotate wok several times to spread eggs thinly over surface. When eggs are lightly browned on bottom, turn with a spatula and cook other side. Remove from wok. Shred cooked eggs with a cleaver, page 11, and set aside. Heat 1/4 cup oil over high heat 1 minute. Add garlic. Stir-fry until golden, about 1 minute. Add marinated pork shreds. Stir-fry until very lightly browned, about 2 minutes. Remove pork shreds with a slotted spoon, draining well over wok; set aside. Add hoisin sauce and 2 tablespoons oil to wok. Stir-fry 2 minutes. Add bamboo shoots, cabbage, carrot and wood ears. Stir-fry over high heat 5 minutes. Add salt, chicken broth, cooked pork shreds and shredded egg. Mix well over high heat 1 minute. Serve with shredded green onions, Duck Sauce and Mandarin Pancakes. To eat: Place 1/2 teaspoon Duck Sauce and several green onion shreds in the center of a pancake. Add 2 or 3 tablespoons hot pork and vegetable mixture. Roll up one side of pancake and fold bottom over. Fold up other side of pancake to make a neat little package that can be picked up with your fingers. Makes 4 servings.

Variations

Mu Shu Shrimp: Substitute 3/4 pound shrimp, shelled and deveined, page 59, for the pork slices.

Substitute 1/2 pound fresh mushrooms for the wood ears.

How to Serve Mu Shu Pork

1/Spread Mandarin Pancakes with Duck Sauce. Add green onion shreds and pork mixture.

2/Fold one side of pancake over filling. Fold one end over, then fold up remaining side.

One, Two, Three, Four, Five

Mandarin

Stewed pork spareribs are as easy as counting from one to five!

1 lb. pork spareribs, cut in half
6 to 8 green onions, 4 to 5 inches long
1 tablespoon rice wine or dry sherry
2 tablespoons rice vinegar or
  white vinegar
3 tablespoons sugar
1/4 cup soy sauce
5 tablespoons water

Use a sharp knife to cut between spareribs. Put green onions in the bottom of a medium saucepan. Place spareribs on top of green onions. Add wine, vinegar, sugar, soy sauce and water. Cover and bring to a boil over high heat; reduce heat to low. Cook about 2 hours until almost all liquid is absorbed. Serve hot. Makes 4 servings.

Broiled Pork Roll with Sha Cha Sauce

Cantonese

Canned sha cha sauce can be purchased in an oriental food store.

1 (10-oz.) pork tenderloin

Marinade:
  1 teaspoon rice wine or dry sherry
  2 tablespoons soy sauce
  1/2 teaspoon salt
  1 tablespoon chicken broth
  1-1/2 teaspoons sugar
  1/4 teaspoon pepper
  1 teaspoon sesame oil
  3 tablespoons sha cha sauce

5 chicken livers
1 slice fresh ginger root, page 16
2 cups water
7 green onions,
  cut in 1-1/2-inch lengths

Use a cleaver to cut pork into 20 thin 2-inch square slices. Pound each slice with a meat hammer a few times. Combine marinade ingredients in a small bowl. Add pork; mix well. Let stand 20 minutes. Cut each chicken liver into 4 slices. Combine 2 cups water and ginger root in a small saucepan. Bring to a boil. Add chicken liver pieces and cook 1 minute over high heat. Remove chicken liver pieces with a slotted spoon, draining well over saucepan. Place 1 chicken liver piece and green onion in the center of each pork slice. Roll up, secure ends with a wooden pick and place on a baking sheet. Preheat oven to 475°F (245°C) 5 minutes. Place baking sheet in oven. Bake 7 to 10 minutes until pork rolls are golden brown. Remove and serve on a heated platter. Makes 4 servings.

Stewed Pork Rolls

Cantonese

Black mushrooms, green onions and bamboo shoots are wrapped in pork slices and cooked in a flavorful sauce.

5 large dried black mushrooms
2 cups hot water
5 green onions, chopped in
  1-1/2-inch lengths
14 bamboo shoot slices
1 lb. pork tenderloin

Marinade:
  1 tablespoon rice wine or
    dry sherry
  5 tablespoons soy sauce

5 cups oil for deep-frying
3 tablespoons Worcestershire sauce
2 tablespoons sugar
1-1/2 cups boiling water
2 teaspoons sesame oil

Soak dried black mushrooms in 2 cups hot water until soft, 15 to 30 minutes. Drain and remove hard stems. Slice softened mushrooms into 14 pieces. Chop green onions into 1-1/2-inch lengths, making 14 pieces. Cut pork into 14 slices about 2 inches square. Pound each slice with the broad side of a cleaver to flatten. Place a piece of mushroom, a piece of green onion and a bamboo shoot slice on each pork square. Roll up and secure with a wooden pick. Mix marinade ingredients in a shallow dish. Add pork rolls, coating with marinade. Let stand 20 minutes. Heat 5 cups oil in a wok over high heat to 350°F (175°C). Carefully lower 7 pork rolls into hot oil with a slotted metal spoon. Deep-fry until browned, about 1 minute. Remove with slotted spoon, draining well over wok; set aside. Repeat with 7 remaining pork rolls. Remove oil from wok except 1 tablespoon. Heat oil remaining in wok over medium heat 30 seconds. Add leftover marinade, Worcestershire sauce, sugar and boiling water; mix well. Add fried pork rolls. Cover and cook 30 minutes over medium heat. Add sesame oil, stirring to coat pork rolls with sauce. Remove wooden picks. Serve pork rolls hot. Makes about 4 servings.

Sweet & Sour Pork

Cantonese

Chicken coating mix simplifies the batter for this dish.

1 lb. pork tenderloin
Marinade:
  1/2 teaspoon salt
  1-1/2 teaspoons soy sauce
  1 tablespoon cornstarch
  1 tablespoon cold water
Batter:
  1/2 cup chicken coating mix
  1/2 cup ice water
  1 egg yolk
1/2 cup Sweet & Sour Sauce,
  page 64
1/4 cup chicken broth
1/4 cup water
1/2 teaspoon cornstarch
6 cups oil for deep-frying
1 green pepper,
  chopped in 1-inch pieces
1 medium carrot, sliced
1/2 cup sliced water chestnuts
4 slices canned or fresh pineapple,
  chopped in 1-inch pieces

Pound pork with the side of a cleaver to tenderize. Cut into 2/3-inch squares. Combine marinade ingredients in a small bowl. Add pork; mix well. Let stand 30 minutes. Combine batter ingredients in a medium bowl until just moistened; do not stir to blend. Combine Sweet & Sour Sauce, chicken broth, water and cornstarch in a small bowl; set aside. Heat 6 cups oil in a wok over high heat to 350°F (175°C). While oil is heating, coat each piece of pork with batter. Reduce heat to medium. Carefully lower coated pork into hot oil with a slotted metal spoon. Deep-fry pork 3 minutes or until browned. Remove from oil with slotted spoon. Turn heat up to high and heat oil to 400°F (205°C). Carefully place pork all at once in hot oil and deep-fry again until crisp, about 30 seconds. Remove pork with slotted spoon, draining well over wok; place cooked pork on a platter. Remove oil from wok except 2 tablespoons. Reduce heat to medium. Stir-fry green peppers, carrots and water chestnuts 1 minute. Add Sweet & Sour Sauce mixture. Stir in pineapple. Stir-fry until sauce has thickened. Remove from heat. Stir in pork and serve immediately. Makes 4 servings.

Pork with Broccoli

Cantonese

This dish is so easy and delicious you'll want to make it often.

1/3 lb. ground pork

Marinade:
  1 teaspoon rice wine or dry sherry
  1 tablespoon soy sauce
  1 teaspoon sesame oil
  1 teaspoon cornstarch
  1 teaspoon minced ginger root

1-1/2 lbs. fresh broccoli
3 tablespoons vegetable oil
1-1/2 teaspoons minced garlic
1 teaspoon salt
1/4 cup chicken broth
1/4 cup water

Combine marinade ingredients in a small bowl. Add pork; mix well. Let stand 15 minutes. Cut flowerets from broccoli stems and separate into small pieces. Slice stems into 2" x 1/4" pieces. Heat oil in wok over medium heat 1 or 2 minutes. Add 1 teaspoon minced garlic. Stir-fry until golden. Add pork. Stir-fry about 3 minutes until very lightly browned. Remove with a slotted spoon, leaving oil in wok. Add more oil to wok if necessary to measure 1/4 cup. Turn heat up to high. Add salt and broccoli stems. Stir-fry about 1 minute. Add flowerets. Stir-fry 1 minute longer. Vegetables should still be crisp. Add 1/4 cup water and chicken broth. Reduce heat to medium. Cover and simmer until water is almost all absorbed. Add cooked pork. Stir-fry 10 seconds. Serve hot. Makes 4 servings.

Roast Pork Coins

Cantonese

Stuffed pork discs are marinated, roasted and usually served with Steamed Flower Buns pages 154 and 155.

1-1/4 lb. lean boneless pork butt or
  loin
6 oz. pork fat
1 or 2 fresh carrots, cooked

Marinade:
  1/4 teaspoon five-spice powder
  3 slices fresh ginger root, page 16
  2 green onions, chopped
  4 teaspoons sugar
  1 tablespoon rice wine or dry sherry
  3 tablespoons soy sauce
  2 teaspoons sesame oil
  1/4 teaspoon pepper

1 teaspoon vegetable oil

Trim pork into a long sausage shape, 1-1/2 inches in diameter. Cutting only alternate slices all the way through, slice pork into 2/3 inch pieces. Each of the 20 to 22 double slices should resemble a hamburger bun. Slice pork fat into 20 to 22 round pieces, a little smaller than pork pieces. Slice carrot into 20 to 22 pieces. Combine marinade ingredients in a large bowl. Add pork slices, pork fat slices and carrot slices; mix well. Let stand 1 hour. Preheat oven to 350°F (175°C). Insert 1 carrot slice and 1 pork fat slice in the center of each piece of pork. Arrange pork coins on metal skewers, leaving 1/4 inch between each coin. Place skewers on a baking sheet. Bake 15 minutes. Remove from oven and brush coins with marinade. Return to oven and bake 12 to 15 minutes longer. Remove baking sheet from oven and let cool a few minutes. Remove skewers and arrange pork coins on a platter. Lightly brush with oil. Makes 4 to 6 servings.

Pork with Broccoli on Steamed Rice, page 151.

Pork Chop Suey

Cantonese

To see how rice noodles should look after they are deep-fried, see Mongolian Beef, page 116.

1/3 lb. pork butt

Marinade:
  1 teaspoon rice wine or dry sherry
  1/2 teaspoon minced fresh
    ginger root

4 cups oil for deep-frying
2 oz. rice noodles
**1/3 lb. squid, if desired, cleaned,
  shredded, page 11**

Seasoning sauce:
  1 tablespoon soy sauce
  1/2 teaspoon sugar
  1 teaspoon salt
  1 teaspoons sesame oil
  1/2 teaspoon pepper
  1/4 cup chicken broth
  1/4 teaspoon cornstarch

1/2 cup sliced fresh mushrooms
**1/2 cup shredded fresh carrot,
  page 11**
**1/2 cup shredded green pepper,
  page 11**
1/2 cup shredded celery, page 11
**1/2 cup shredded bamboo shoots,
  page 11, if desired**
1/4 cup fresh bean sprouts, if desired

Slice pork into thin strips with a cleaver. Cut strips into 1" x 1/2" shreds, page 11. Combine marinade ingredients in a small bowl. Add pork shreds; mix well. Let stand 30 minutes. Heat 4 cups oil in a wok over high heat to 350°F (175°C). Carefully drop in rice noodles. Press noodles under oil with a spatula and deep-fry 2 or 3 seconds until noodles puff. Remove with chopsticks or a slotted spatula, draining well over wok. Cool on a platter. Break cool noodles into small pieces. Combine seasoning sauce ingredients in a small bowl; mix well. Remove oil from wok except 1/2 cup. Heat oil remaining in wok 1 minute. Stir-fry pork and squid, if desired, over high heat about 2 minutes until pork is browned. Stir in mushrooms, carrot, green pepper and celery. Add bamboo shoots and bean sprouts, if desired. Stir-fry over medium heat 3 minutes. Pour seasoning sauce into wok and stir-fry 1 minute to coat vegetable mixture. Serve chop suey on cooked noodles. Makes 4 servings.

Variations

Beef Chop Suey: Substitute 1/3 pound flank steak for the pork.
Shrimp Chop Suey: Substitute 1/3 pound fresh shrimp, shelled and deveined, page 59, for the pork.

Pork Chow Mein

Cantonese

Substitute thin spaghetti if you can't find dry Chinese noodles.

1/2 lb. pork butt

Marinade:
 1/2 teaspoon rice wine or dry sherry
 1/2 teaspoon cornstarch
 2 green onions,
  chopped in 1-1/2-inch lengths
 1/2 egg white
 1/2 teaspoon minced fresh
  ginger root
 1/4 teaspoon salt
 1 tablespoon soy sauce

8 cups water
8 oz. dry Chinese noodles
1 tablespoon sesame oil
1/2 cup vegetable oil
1/2 lb. cooked fresh or
 frozen green beans, shredded,
 page 11
1/4 lb. fresh bean sprouts or
 shredded cabbage, page 11
1 cup sliced fresh or
 drained canned mushrooms
3 tablespoons chicken broth
1/2 teaspoon salt
3 tablespoons soy sauce
1/4 teaspoon pepper

Slice pork into thin strips with a cleaver. Cut strips into 1" x 1/4" shreds, page 11. Combine marinade ingredients in a medium bowl. Add pork; mix well. Let stand 30 minutes. Bring 8 cups water to a boil in a large pot. Cook noodles in boiling water about 5 minutes until tender. Rinse noodles with cold water; drain well. Add sesame oil to noodles. Mix well to coat; set aside. Heat 1/4 cup oil in wok over high heat 1 minute. Stir-fry marinated pork shreds about 2 minutes until no longer pink. Remove pork with a slotted spoon, draining well over wok; set aside. Add 1 tablespoon oil to wok. Stir-fry green beans, bean sprouts or cabbage and mushrooms over high heat 3 minutes. Add chicken broth and salt. If mixture is dry, add several more tablespoons chicken broth or water to moisten. Remove vegetables from wok; set aside. Reduce heat to medium. Add 3 tablespoons oil to wok. Stir-fry cooked noodles 3 or 4 minutes. Add salt, soy sauce, pepper and cooked vegetables. Stir-fry 2 minutes longer, mixing well. Serve hot. Makes 4 to 6 servings.

Szechuan Pork Strips

Szechuan

Yellow peppers make the crisp coating extra spicy.

1 lb. pork loin

Marinade:
 1 teaspoon rice wine or dry sherry
 1 teaspoon salt
 1/4 teaspoon pepper
 1 teaspoon sesame oil

Coating:
 2 eggs
 1/2 cup all-purpose flour
 1/4 cup minced yellow pepper
 1 teaspoon minced fresh ginger root
 1/2 teaspoon salt

6 cups oil for deep-frying

Slice pork into pieces 1/3 inch thick. Lightly pound with broad side of cleaver. Cut into strips 2 inches long. Combine marinade ingredients in a medium bowl. Add pork; mix well. Let stand 20 minutes. Mix coating ingredients in a large bowl. Heat 6 cups oil in a wok over high heat to 350°F (175°C). Reduce heat to medium. Use tongs to dip marinated pork strips one at a time into coating mixture. Carefully lower coated strips into hot oil. Deep-fry several at a time until golden brown, 2 to 3 minutes. Remove with tongs or a slotted spoon and drain on paper towels. Serve hot. Makes 4 servings.

Pork & Pickled Mustard Greens

Szechuan

Pickled mustard greens are sold in cans in Oriental food stores.

1/2 lb. pork butt or shoulder

Marinade:
  1 teaspoon rice wine or dry sherry
  1/4 teaspoon salt
  1 tablespoon water
  1-1/2 teaspoons cornstarch

Seasoning sauce:
  1/4 teaspoon sugar
  1/4 teaspoon pepper
  3 tablespoons chicken broth
  1 tablespoon water
  1 teaspoon cornstarch
  1 teaspoon sesame oil

1 cup vegetable oil
1/2 cup shredded pickled
  mustard greens, page 11
1/3 cup shredded bamboo shoots,
  page 11
1/2 cup fresh bean sprouts or
  shredded green pepper, page 11
1 tablespoon shredded green onion,
  page 11
1 tablespoon chopped fresh ginger root

Slice pork into thin strips with a cleaver. Cut strips into 1'' x 1/2'' shreds, page 11. Mix marinade ingredients in a medium bowl. Add pork shreds; mix well. Let stand 20 minutes. Mix ingredients for seasoning sauce in a small bowl; set aside. Heat oil in a wok over high heat 1 minute. Add marinated pork shreds. Stir-fry until pork is no longer pink, about 2 minutes. Remove pork shreds with a slotted spoon, draining well over wok; set aside. Remove oil from wok except 3 tablespoons. Heat oil remaining in wok over medium heat 30 seconds. Add pickled mustard greens, bamboo shoots, carrot, bean sprouts or green pepper, green onion and ginger root. Stir-fry until carrots are crisp-tender and ginger is fragrant, about 1 minute. Add seasoning sauce and pork. Stir-fry until sauce thickens slightly, about 1 minute. Serve hot. Makes 4 servings.

中國菜

For information on specific ingredients used in Chinese cooking, see pages 15 to 20.

Sizzling Rice Pork

Szechuan

When the sauce is poured over crisp rice squares, the rice crackles and pops.

1/2 lb. pork tenderloin

Marinade:
1 teaspoon rice wine or dry sherry
1/2 teaspoon soy sauce
1/2 teaspoon salt
1 tablespoon cornstarch
1 tablespoon sesame oil

Seasoning sauce:
1/4 cup chicken broth
1 cup water
1/2 teaspoon salt
2 teaspoons cornstarch
1/4 teaspoon pepper
1 teaspoon sesame oil

3 tablespoons vegetable oil
1/4 cup sliced bamboo shoots
2 tablespoons fresh or
   thawed frozen peas
1/4 cup sliced cooked carrot
4 cups oil for deep-frying
10 (2-inch) squares Crisp Rice,
   page 151

Slice pork into thin strips with a cleaver. Cut strips into 2-inch lengths. Combine marinade ingredients in a medium bowl. Add pork; mix well. Let stand 20 minutes. Combine ingredients for seasoning sauce in a small bowl. Mix well and set aside. Heat 3 tablespoons oil in a wok over high heat 1 minute. Stir-fry marinated pork until very lightly browned. Add bamboo shoots, peas, carrot and seasoning sauce. Stir-fry until sauce thickens slightly. Spoon into a heated serving bowl. Cover and keep hot. Heat 4 cups oil in another wok or a deep heavy skillet over high heat to 350°F (175°C). Test oil temperature by dropping a small piece broken from a rice square into hot oil. Oil is hot enough if rice puffs out in 3 seconds. Carefully lower rice squares into hot oil with a slotted metal spoon. Deep-fry over high heat until rice puffs out and turns golden. Quickly lift rice squares from oil with slotted spoon, drain well over wok and place on a rimmed platter. At the table, pour hot pork mixture over rice squares. The rice will pop and sizzle. Makes 4 servings.

Glazed Hunan Ham

Szechuan

Don't let the sandwich disguise fool you—this is an elegant main dish!

4 oz. red or black dates
4 cups water
1 (1-1/3-lb.) pkg. ham
1/2 cup crushed rock sugar
2 tablespoons rice wine or dry sherry
4-1/2 teaspoons lard or shortening
About 8 cups boiling water
1 teaspoon cornstarch
1 tablespoon water
6 slices white bread

Boil red dates in 4 cups water in a medium saucepan 20 minutes. Drain well; set aside. Cut ham into very thin 3" x 1-1/2" slices. Overlap slices in a small baking dish. Sprinkle half the rock sugar evenly on top of ham. Arrange boiled dates on top of rock sugar. Add wine, remaining rock sugar and lard or shortening. Cover baking dish. Pour 4 cups boiling water into a wok or a large pot. Place baking dish on a steamer rack over boiling water. Steam over high heat 2 hours, adding more boiling water as needed. Let cool. Remove glazed ham slices from baking dish. Arrange overlapping on a plate. Add water to cooking liquid to make 1 cup. Bring to a boil in a small saucepan. Dissolve cornstarch in 1 tablespoon water to make a paste. Add cornstarch paste to boiling cooking liquid. Stir until mixture thickens slightly. Pour slowly over ham slices. Cut crusts from bread. Cut bread slices in half. Place glazed ham slices between bread slices. Arrange on a platter. Serve hot. Makes 4 servings.

Shredded Pork with Fish Flavor

Szechuan

This sauce uses no fish or seafood, but it tastes like fish.

10 oz. pork tenderloin

Marinade:
  1 tablespoon soy sauce
  1 tablespoon cornstarch
  1 tablespoon water

3 wood ears
2 cups hot water
1 teaspoon baking soda

Seasoning sauce:
  1 tablespoon Worcestershire sauce
  1 tablespoon hot bean sauce
  1-1/2 teaspoons rice wine or
    dry sherry
  1/2 teaspoon salt
  1 teaspoon sugar
  1 tablespoon soy sauce
  1 teaspoon cornstarch
  1 teaspoon sesame oil
  1/4 teaspoon pepper
  1 tablespoon chopped green onion

1 cup vegetable oil
2 teaspoons minced fresh ginger root
1 teaspoon minced garlic
1/2 cup shredded water chestnuts,
  page 11

Slice pork into thin strips with a cleaver. Cut strips into 2" x 1/4" shreds, page 11. Combine marinade ingredients in a medium bowl. Add pork shreds; mix well. Let stand 20 minutes. Combine 2 cups hot water and baking soda. Add wood ears. Soak 20 minutes to soften. Remove hard stems from wood ears and shred wood ears with a cleaver, page 11. Combine ingredients for seasoning sauce; set aside. Heat 1 cup oil in a wok over medium heat 1 minute. Stir-fry pork shreds 1 minute or until pork is no longer pink. Remove pork with a slotted spoon, draining well over wok; set aside. Remove oil from wok except 3 tablespoons. Heat oil remaining in wok over medium heat 30 seconds. Stir-fry ginger root and garlic until garlic is golden, 30 seconds. Add shredded wood ears and water chestnuts. Stir-fry 1 minute. Add cooked pork and seasoning sauce. Stir-fry until sauce thickens slightly. Spoon into a heated serving dish and serve hot. Makes 4 servings.

Sliced Pork with Garlic Sauce

Szechuan

Sprinkling the finished dish with Chili Oil adds pungent flavor.

About 4 cups water
1/2 lb. pork shoulder
2 slices fresh ginger root, page 16
2 green onions, sliced
1 teaspoon rice wine or dry sherry
Garlic Sauce:
  2 tablespoons chicken broth
  2 tablespoons water
  2 tablespoons minced garlic
  1/4 teaspoon salt
  2 tablespoons soy sauce
  2 teaspoons sesame oil
  2 teaspoons sugar
About 1 tablespoon Chili Oil,
  page 85, or sesame oil

Bring 4 cups water to a boil in a medium saucepan. Add pork shoulder, ginger root, green onions and wine. Add more water to cover pork. Cook about 40 minutes, adding more boiling water if necessary. To test meat, pierce with a cooking fork or skewer. If juices are not red, meat is done. Remove pork from cooking liquid; cool and refrigerate for easier slicing. Reserve cooking liquid. Cut chilled pork across grain into thin slices. Cut slices into 2-inch squares. To make Garlic Sauce, bring chicken broth and water to a boil in a small saucepan. Remove from heat. Add remaining garlic sauce ingredients, mixing well. Bring pork cooking liquid to a boil. Place pork slices in boiling liquid about 10 seconds. Remove and drain. Pat dry with a paper towel. Arrange on a platter. Pour garlic sauce over pork slices. Sprinkle with Chili Oil or sesame oil to taste. Serve warm. Makes 4 servings.

Stir-Fried Bean Threads with Pork

Szechuan

Bean threads are thin noodles made from soybean flour.

1 teaspoon rice wine or dry sherry
1/4 lb. ground pork
3 oz. bean threads
4 cups warm water
1/4 cup vegetable oil
2 tablespoons chopped green onion
4-1/2 teaspoons minced fresh
  ginger root
1 tablespoon hot bean sauce
Seasoning sauce:
  1 teaspoon salt
  7 teaspoons soy sauce
  1/2 teaspoon sugar
  1 teaspoon cornstarch
  1/4 cup chicken broth
  1-1/4 cups water

Sprinkle wine over ground pork. Let stand 15 minutes. Combine bean threads and 4 cups warm water in a medium bowl. Let stand about 10 minutes to soften bean threads. Heat oil in a wok over medium heat. Stir-fry ground pork 2 minutes. Add green onion, ginger root and hot bean sauce. Stir-fry 2 minutes. Drain bean threads in a colander. Chop into 8-inch lengths and add to pork mixture. Combine ingredients for seasoning sauce in a small bowl; mix well. Add to pork mixture; stir-fry to mix well. Cover wok and reduce heat to low. Cook about 8 minutes until seasoning sauce is almost all absorbed. Spoon into a serving bowl and serve hot. Makes 4 servings.

Twice-Cooked Pork

Szechuan

Pork is boiled and then stir-fried.

1 lb. pork butt or shoulder
  (2/3 lean and 1/3 fat)
1 green onion
1 slice fresh ginger root, page 16
1 teaspoon rice wine or dry sherry
Seasoning sauce:
  1-1/2 teaspoons rice wine or
    dry sherry
  1 tablespoon sweet bean sauce
  1 tablespoon hot bean sauce
  2 tablespoons soy sauce
  1 teaspoon sugar
  1/4 cup vegetable oil

3 tablespoons vegetable oil
3 garlic cloves, sliced
1 green pepper,
  cut in 1-1/2-inch squares
3 cabbage leaves,
  cut in 1-1/2-inch squares
1 tablespoon vegetable oil

Place pork in a large saucepan; add water to cover. Add green onion, ginger root and wine. Bring to a boil over high heat. Reduce heat to medium and cook 30 minutes. Remove pork from cooking liquid and place on a platter to cool. Mix ingredients for seasoning sauce in a small bowl; set aside. Cut cooled pork into thin slices. Heat 3 tablespoons oil in a wok over high heat 30 seconds. Stir-fry pork slices 1 minute. Add garlic, green pepper and cabbage. Stir-fry 1 minute. Remove pork and vegetables with a slotted spoon, draining well over wok; set aside. Heat 1 tablespoon oil in wok over medium heat 30 seconds. Add seasoning sauce. Stir-fry 10 seconds. Return pork and vegetables to wok and mix well with sauce. Serve hot. Makes 4 servings.

Lion's Head Casserole

Shanghai

Meatballs and cabbage are arranged in a casserole to resemble the head of a lion.

3 slices fresh ginger root, page 16
2 green onions
1/3 cup water
1-1/2 lbs. ground pork
Marinade:
   1 tablespoon rice wine or dry sherry
   1-1/2 teaspoons salt
   4-1/2 teaspoons cornstarch
   1/4 teaspoon pepper
   1/2 teaspoon sugar
1 (1-1/4-lb.) Chinese cabbage
2 tablespoons vegetable oil
1 tablespoon cornstarch
2 tablespoons water
1 cup chicken broth
3 cups water
2 tablespoons soy sauce
1 tablespoon vegetable oil

Lightly crush ginger root and green onions with the broad side of a cleaver. Soak ginger root and green onions in 1/3 cup water 15 minutes. Chop ground pork with a cleaver 3 to 5 minutes to make a paste. Place in a large bowl. Combine marinade ingredients in a small bowl; mix well. Discard ginger slices and green onions and add liquid to marinade; mix well. Pour marinade over pork paste. Mix with your fingers and shape into a large ball. Lightly toss ball into the bowl 3 minutes until pork mixture is very sticky. Remove 3 large cabbage leaves and set aside. Chop remaining cabbage into 1-1/2-inch squares. Heat 2 tablespoons oil in a wok over high heat 30 seconds. Add cabbage squares. Stir-fry until soft. Remove with a slotted spatula, draining well over wok. Place cooked cabbage in the bottom of a large casserole or baking dish to make a nest for the meatballs. Heat 1/2 cup oil in wok over high heat 1 minute. Reduce heat to medium. Mix cornstarch with 2 tablespoons water to make a paste. Divide ground pork mixture into 4 portions. Put a little cornstarch paste in the palm of your hand then hold 1 pork portion in your palm and shape into a large ball. Carefully lower pork ball into hot oil with a slotted metal spoon. Fry on all sides until lightly browned. Remove with a slotted spoon, draining well over wok. Place on top of cabbage. Repeat with remaining pork portions. Cover the four balls with 3 reserved cabbage leaves. Add chicken broth and 3 cups water to casserole or baking dish. Cover and simmer over low heat 3 to 4 hours until only 1-1/2 cups sauce remains. Sprinkle with soy sauce and 1 tablespoon oil. Serve hot. Makes 4 servings.

Stewed Pork in Brown Sauce

Shanghai

After the pork mixture has cooked one hour, you can add diagonal slices of carrots, chopped cabbage or green beans.

1-1/2 lbs. pork butt
2 tablespoons vegetable oil
1 garlic clove, crushed
1 tablespoon rice wine or dry sherry
2/3 cup soy sauce
1 teaspoon sugar

Dice pork into 1-inch cubes. Heat oil in a large saucepan over medium heat 1 minute. Stir-fry garlic until golden, 30 seconds. Remove and discard. Stir-fry pork cubes 3 minutes. Add wine and soy sauce. Stir-fry until liquid begins to boil. Reduce heat to low and add sugar. Cover and simmer 1-1/2 hours. Add a little water if necessary. Serve on a heated platter. Makes 4 servings.

Pressed Shanghai Ham

Shanghai

One yard of food-grade cheesecloth will wrap around the ham.

1 (2- to 2-1/2-lb.) fresh boneless ham
   or pork butt
3 tablespoons Peppersalt, page 88
6 to 8 cups boiling water
2 slices fresh ginger root, page 16
2 green onions
1 tablespoon rice wine or dry sherry
Dipping sauce:
   4-1/2 teaspoons soy sauce
   1 teaspoon sugar
   1-1/2 teaspoons minced fresh
      ginger root
   1 teaspoon chopped green onion
      or 1 teaspoon Chinese parsley

Cut ham in half. Place in a large bowl and pat Peppersalt over entire surface. Refrigerate 3 days, turning once every day to keep surface coated. Place ham in a large pot with 6 to 8 cups boiling water. Add ginger root, green onions and wine. Cook 45 minutes to 1 hour over medium heat until juices are no longer red when meat is pierced with a cooking fork or skewer. Drain off water. Tightly wrap ham with strips of cheesecloth and place on a rack in a roasting pan. Place a brick or other large heavy object on top of the wrapped ham to press out juices. Let stand 1 hour at room temperature. Combine ingredients for dipping sauce in a small bowl; mix well. Remove cheesecloth from ham. Slice ham into thin pieces. Serve with dipping sauce. Makes 4 to 6 servings.

Ground Pork with Mushrooms

Shanghai

Green vegetables are good with this dish. Try it with Dry Cooked Green Beans, page 147.

1/2 lb. lean ground pork

Marinade:
   1 teaspoon rice wine or dry sherry
   1/2 teaspoon minced fresh
      ginger root
   2 tablespoons soy sauce
   1/4 teaspoon sugar
   1 teaspoon cornstarch
   1/4 teaspoon pepper
2 green onions, sliced
2 tablespoons vegetable oil
1 garlic clove, crushed
1/2 lb. fresh mushrooms, sliced
1 teaspoon salt
5 tablespoons water
1/2 teaspoon cornstarch

Chop ground pork with a cleaver. Combine marinade ingredients in a small bowl. Add chopped ground pork; mix well. Let stand 10 minutes. Arrange green onion slices on a platter. Heat 2 tablespoons oil in a wok over high heat 1 minute. Stir-fry garlic in wok about 1 minute until browned. Remove and discard. Add ground pork to wok. Stir-fry about 4 minutes until browned. Remove pork from wok with a slotted spoon and place on top of green onion slices to absorb oil. Reduce heat to medium. Stir-fry mushrooms in oil remaining in wok about 4 minutes until soft. Dissolve cornstarch in water to make a paste. Add salt, cornstarch paste, cooked pork and green onions to wok. Stir-fry 1 minute and serve hot. Makes 4 servings.

How to Make Pressed Shanghai Ham

1/Several days ahead, cut ham in half and pat with Peppersalt. Refrigerate 3 days, turning once every day.

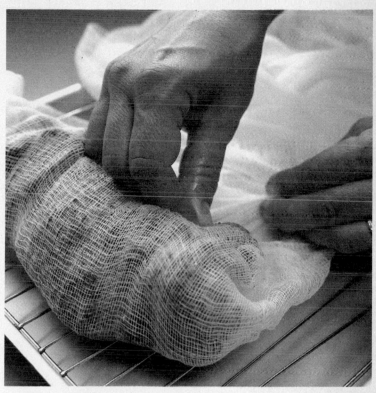

2/After cooking, wrap hot ham very tightly in several layers of cheesecloth.

Ground Pork with Peas

Shanghai

Fresh or frozen peas can be used, but frozen peas are faster and easier.

Marinade:
  1 teaspoon rice wine or dry sherry
  2 tablespoons soy sauce
  1/2 teaspoon chopped fresh
    ginger root
  1 teaspoon cornstarch
  1 tablespoon sesame oil

1/2 lb. ground pork
1/2 teaspoon cornstarch
1/4 cup water
1 tablespoon chicken broth
1/4 cup vegetable oil
1 garlic clove, crushed
1 (10-oz.) pkg. frozen peas,
  thawed (2 cups)
1/2 teaspoon salt
1 tablespoon soy sauce
1/4 teaspoon sugar

Mix marinade ingredients in a small bowl. Add ground pork; mix well. Let stand 20 minutes. Dissolve cornstarch in water and chicken broth to make a paste; set aside. Heat oil in a wok over medium-high heat 1 minute. Stir-fry garlic about 1 minute until browned; remove and discard. Add ground pork. Stir-fry until cooked, about 4 minutes. Remove ground pork from wok with a slotted spoon, draining well over wok; set aside. Reheat oil in wok over high heat 1 minute. Stir-fry peas 2 minutes. Add salt, soy sauce, sugar and cornstarch paste. Stir-fry 30 seconds. Add cooked pork; mix well. Serve hot. Makes 4 servings.

BEEF

牛肉

The farmers of China look at cattle as beasts of burden—not as food. Because of the small number of cattle raised, beef is expensive and used very sparingly. With a half pound of beef and a few handfuls of green vegetables, a Chinese cook can produce a dish that will amply feed four hungry people.

Use the appropriate cut of beef for each cooking technique. The best beef for stir-frying is tenderloin, sirloin or flank steak. For braising, use round, shank or shoulder cuts. Brisket and stew meat are suitable for stewing.

Beef for stir-frying is always sliced against the grain and any fat or muscle removed. The sliced beef is marinated for about 20 minutes in a mixture based on soy sauce and rice wine. A little vegetable oil is sometimes added to the marinade to make the meat more succulent. Sometimes beef slices are dusted with cornstarch before cooking. This keeps juice in so the beef is extra juicy after it is cooked.

Large cuts of beef are often stewed for several hours in a Dutch oven or heavy pot. Stewing is used as a cooking technique in Mandarin, Szechuan and Shanghai cuisines. Dried orange peel, peppercorns and star anise, which is a licorice-flavored spice, are used by Mandarin cooks to flavor Stewed Beef with Carrots.

Steaming is not a common method of cooking beef. An exception is Steamed Beef with Spicy Rice Powder, a Szechuan dish. Beef strips are marinated and coated with spicy rice powder. Then they are placed in a shallow baking dish and steamed.

Cold meats are a rarity in China, but the Cold Meat Platter is popular at large Shanghai banquets. It is surprisingly easy to prepare. Beef and pork tenderloins are first boiled and then simmered with seasonings such as star anise, green onions, dried orange peel and peppercorns. After the meat has cooled, it is sliced and arranged in rows on a large platter. When garnished with carrot and Chinese turnip, Cold Meat Platter is a colorful buffet dish.

Beef with Mushrooms & Bean Curd

Mandarin

Mushrooms, bean curd and oyster sauce combine with beef to make a mild but delicious dish.

**1/2 lb. beef flank steak or
other tender beef**

Marinade:
  1 teaspoon rice wine or dry sherry
  1/2 teaspoon minced fresh
    ginger root
  1 tablespoon soy sauce
  1 tablespoon oyster sauce
  1/4 teaspoon sugar
  1 teaspoon sesame oil
  1 teaspoon cornstarch
  1/2 teaspoon baking soda

Seasoning sauce:
  2 tablespoons oyster sauce
  1 tablespoon soy sauce
  1/4 cup water
  3 tablespoons chicken broth,
    if desired for added flavor
  1/2 teaspoon salt
  1/4 teaspoon sugar
  1/4 teaspoon pepper
  1/2 teaspoon cornstarch

1 cup vegetable oil
1 garlic clove, crushed
2 green onions,
  chopped in 1-inch lengths
1/2 lb. fresh mushrooms, cut in halves
3 (3-inch) squares Bean Curd,
  page 169, cut in 7/8-inch squares

Use a cleaver to slice beef across grain and at an angle into thin strips. Cut strips 2 inches long. Combine marinade ingredients in a medium bowl. Add beef strips; mix well. Let stand 20 minutes. Combine ingredients for seasoning sauce in a small bowl; set aside. Heat 1 cup oil in a wok over medium heat 1 minute. Stir-fry garlic until golden, 30 seconds. Add marinated beef; stir-fry until browned, about 1 minute. Remove beef with a slotted spoon, draining well over wok; set aside. Remove oil from wok except 5 tablespoons. Heat oil remaining in wok over high heat 30 seconds. Stir-fry green onions and mushrooms 3 to 5 minutes. Add bean curd and carefully stir-fry 2 minutes. Add seasoning sauce. Stir-fry until sauce thickens slightly. Add cooked beef. Mix well and serve hot. Makes 4 servings.

Mongolian Fire Pot

Mandarin

If you don't have a Mongolian fire pot, your fondue pot will work just as well.

1 (1-lb.) pork shoulder bone
6 to 8 cups water
1 teaspoon salt
1 lb. fresh shrimp
2 lbs. beef flank steak, partially frozen
2 (3-inch) squares Bean Curd,
  page 169
1 tomato
1/2 lb. fresh spinach
1 lb. Chinese cabbage
2 oz. bean noodles
3 cups hot water
6 tablespoons sha cha sauce
9 tablespoons soy sauce
1-1/2 teaspoons salt
6 green onions,
  chopped in 1-inch lengths
1 tablespoon lard or vegetable oil

Put pork shoulder bone in a saucepan half full of water. Cover and bring to a boil over medium-high heat. Reduce heat to low, add salt and simmer 2 hours. Shell and devein shrimp, page 59. Rinse and pat dry with a paper towel. Cut shrimp along outside curve without cutting all the way through. Open each shrimp to form a butterfly. Cut partially frozen steak across grain into paper-thin slices. Arrange shrimp and steak on a platter. Dice bean curd and tomato into 1-inch cubes. Arrange bean curd on a small platter. Set tomato aside. Wash spinach and Chinese cabbage and cut into bite-size pieces. Arrange on small platters. Soak bean noodles in 3 cups hot water 15 minutes. Drain and arrange softened noodles on a plate. Mix sha cha sauce and soy sauce. Spoon into 6 small bowls; set aside. Pour liquid from pork bone into fire pot, electric wok or fondue pot and bring to a boil. Add green onions, lard or oil and tomato cubes. Bring to a second boil. Reduce heat to medium. Arrange plates of raw flank steak, shrimp, Chinese cabbage, spinach, bean curd and bean noodles around fire pot. With chopsticks or a fondue fork each person drops several pieces of meat, shrimp or vegetables into simmering broth, removes each piece when done as desired, and dips it into the sauce. Makes 6 servings.

Stewed Beef with Carrots

Mandarin

Star anise and dried orange peel turn beef stew into a pungent, exotic dish.

2 lbs. beef brisket
2 star anise
1 teaspoon Szechuan peppercorns
1/4 cup vegetable oil
2 garlic cloves, crushed
4 slices fresh ginger root, page 16
2 tablespoons rice wine or dry sherry
2/3 cup soy sauce
2 tablespoons sugar
1 (2" x 1") piece dried orange peel,
  page 15
2/3 cup water
2 carrots, peeled, sliced diagonally

Use a cleaver to chop beef into 1-inch cubes. Place star anise and peppercorns on a 3-inch square of cheesecloth. Bring corners together and tie with kitchen twine. Heat oil in a large saucepan over high heat 1 minute. Stir-fry garlic and ginger root until garlic is golden, 30 seconds. Add beef cubes. Stir-fry until lightly browned, about 1 minute. Add cheesecloth bag, wine, soy sauce, sugar and dried orange peel; mix well. Cover and cook 5 minutes. Add 2/3 cup water. Reduce heat to low and cook 1-1/2 hours. Add carrots. Cook 45 minutes longer or until beef is very tender. Remove and discard cheesecloth bag. Serve stewed beef hot. Makes 6 to 8 servings.

Variation

Substitute 1/2 cup shredded bamboo shoots, page 11, for the carrots.

Mongolian Beef

Mandarin

Crisp noodles add texture to stir-fried beef and green onions.

2/3 lb. beef flank steak

Marinade:
   1 teaspoon rice wine or dry sherry
   1 tablespoon soy sauce
   1 tablespoon vegetable oil
   1 teaspoon sesame oil
   1/4 teaspoon baking soda
   1 teaspoon cornstarch
   1/2 teaspoon sugar

4 cups oil for deep-frying
1 oz. rice noodles
1 tablespoon hoisin sauce
1 tablespoon hot bean sauce
1 teaspoon cornstarch
1/2 cup water
8 to 10 green onions,
   chopped in 1-1/2-inch lengths

Use a cleaver to slice beef across grain and at an angle into thin strips. Combine marinade ingredients in a medium bowl. Add beef strips; mix well. Let stand at least 1 hour. Heat oil in a wok over high heat to 350°F (175°C). Gently loosen roll of rice noodles with your fingers and break into 2 portions. Carefully lower half the noodles into hot oil with a slotted metal spoon or in a large strainer and press under oil 2 seconds. Immediately remove puffed noodles from wok with slotted spoon or strainer; set aside to cool. Repeat with remaining half of rice noodle roll. Break cooled noodles into 2-inch lengths and arrange on a platter. Remove oil from wok except 5 tablespoons. Heat oil remaining in wok over high heat 30 seconds. Stir-fry marinated beef until very lightly browned. Remove with slotted spoon; set aside. Remove all but 2 tablespoons oil from wok. Add hoisin sauce, hot bean sauce, cornstarch and water to oil remaining in wok. Bring to a boil over medium heat. Add green onions and cooked beef. Stir-fry 30 seconds. Spoon over noodles. Makes 4 to 6 servings.

How to Make Mongolian Beef

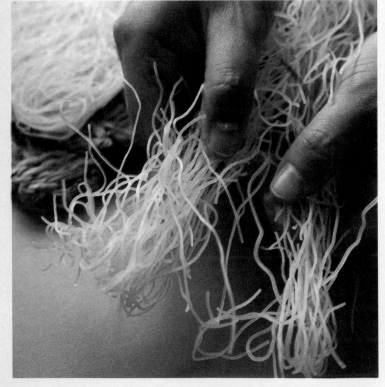

1/Loosen roll of rice noodles before breaking into 2 sections. Fry each section separately.

2/After stir-frying beef and green onions in seasoning sauce, spoon mixture over crisp noodles.

Beef with Snow Peas

Mandarin

Meat and vegetables to grace the Emperor's table with elegance.

2/3 lb. beef flank steak or other tender beef

Marinade:
1 tablespoon rice wine or dry sherry
1/2 teaspoon minced fresh ginger root
2 tablespoons soy sauce
1/4 teaspoon sugar
1 teaspoon cornstarch
2 tablespoons vegetable oil
1/2 teaspoon baking soda

Seasoning sauce:
1/4 cup chicken broth
1/2 teaspoon cornstarch
2 tablespoons water
1 tablespoon soy sauce
1/4 teaspoon sugar
1/4 teaspoon salt
1 teaspoon sesame oil

1/2 lb. fresh snow peas
2 cups boiling water
2 cups cold water
1 cup vegetable oil
1 garlic clove, crushed
1/4 teaspoon salt

Use a cleaver to slice beef across grain and at an angle into thin strips. Cut strips 2 inches long. Combine marinade ingredients in a medium bowl. Add beef strips; mix well. Let stand 30 minutes. Combine ingredients for seasoning sauce in a small bowl. Mix well and set aside. To blanch snow peas, plunge them into 2 cups boiling water 10 seconds, then into 2 cups cold water; drain well. Heat oil in a wok over medium heat about 2 minutes. Stir-fry marinated beef until very lightly browned. Remove beef with a slotted spoon, draining well over wok; set aside. Remove oil from wok except 2 tablespoons. Heat oil remaining in wok over high heat 30 seconds. Stir-fry garlic 10 seconds. Add blanched snow peas and salt. Stir-fry 10 seconds. Remove from wok with slotted spoon and arrange on a platter. Reduce heat to medium. Add 2 tablespoons oil and seasoning sauce to oil left in wok. Stir-fry until sauce thickens slightly. Add cooked beef. Mix well with sauce and spoon over snow peas. Serve hot. Makes 4 servings.

Beef & Vegetables

Mandarin

This hearty dish is the Chinese cousin of America's beef stew.

1 lb. beef brisket
2 small potatoes
1 medium, fresh carrot
1/2 lb. cabbage
2 medium tomatoes
1 medium onion
2 cups boiling water
8 cups water
1 tablespoon rice wine or dry sherry
4 green onions,
   chopped in 4-inch pieces
1 tablespoon soy sauce
1 tablespoon salt
1/4 cup vegetable oil

Use cleavers to chop beef, potatoes, carrot and cabbage into 1-inch cubes. Dice tomatoes and medium onion into 2/3-inch cubes. Pour 2 cups boiling water over beef cubes; drain well. In a large saucepan bring 8 cups water to a boil. Reduce heat to low. Add beef cubes. Cover and bring to a second boil. Add wine, green onions, soy sauce and salt. Cover and cook 2 hours over low heat. Heat 1/4 cup oil in a wok over medium heat 2 minutes. Stir-fry diced onion 1 minute. Add tomato. Stir-fry 30 seconds. Add cooked onion and tomato, potatoes, carrot and cabbage to beef. Cook over medium heat about 30 minutes until vegetables are tender. Serve hot. Makes 6 servings.

Beef with Broccoli

Cantonese

The broad side of a cleaver is often used to crush or flatten garlic, vegetables and meat.

2/3 lb. beef flank steak or
   other tender beef

Marinade:
   1 teaspoon rice wine or dry sherry
   1/2 teaspoon baking soda
   1 tablespoon soy sauce
   1 teaspoon cornstarch
   1 tablespoon sesame oil
   1/4 teaspoon sugar

1/2 lb. broccoli tops
1 teaspoon cornstarch
1/3 cup water
7 tablespoons vegetable oil
1 garlic clove, crushed
1 teaspoon salt
1/2 teaspoon soy sauce
3 tablespoons chicken broth
1/4 teaspoon pepper

Use a cleaver to slice beef across grain and at an angle into thin strips. Mix marinade ingredients in a medium bowl. Add beef strips; mix well. Let stand 30 minutes. Cut each broccoli top lengthwise into 2 or 3 pieces. Dissolve cornstarch in water to make a paste; set aside. Heat 6 tablespoons oil in a wok over high heat 1 minute. Stir-fry marinated beef until very lightly browned. Remove beef, draining well over wok; set aside. Add 1 tablespoon oil to oil left in wok. Heat 30 seconds. Stir-fry garlic 30 seconds. Add broccoli tops. Stir-fry 5 minutes. Add cornstarch paste, salt, soy sauce, chicken broth and pepper. Stir-fry until sauce thickens slightly. Add cooked beef; mix well. Remove from wok and arrange on a platter. Makes 6 servings.

Variation

After stir-frying broccoli, add beef. Stir-fry beef and broccoli 30 seconds to mix well. Mound on a plate or in a bowl to serve.

Beef with Oyster Sauce

Cantonese

Use lettuce, spinach, snow peas or celery alone or in any combination.

**1 lb. beef flank steak or
  other tender beef**

Marinade:
  1 tablespoon oyster sauce
  1 tablespoon soy sauce
  1 teaspoon sugar
  1 tablespoon cornstarch
  2 tablespoons vegetable oil

Seasoning sauce:
  2 tablespoons oyster sauce
  3 tablespoons water
  1/2 teaspoon sugar
  1/4 teaspoon salt
  1 tablespoon soy sauce
  1/2 teaspoon cornstarch
  1 teaspoon sesame oil
  **3 tablespoons chicken broth,
    if desired for added flavor**

**1/2 lb. fresh green vegetables such as
  lettuce, spinach, snow peas or celery**
2 cups boiling water
2 tablespoons vegetable oil
**1-1/2 teaspoons rice wine or
  dry sherry**
1/4 teaspoon salt
1/2 teaspoon sugar
1 cup vegetable oil
5 slices fresh ginger root, page 16

Use a cleaver to slice beef across grain and at an angle into thin strips. Cut strips 2 inches long. Combine marinade ingredients in a medium bowl. Add beef strips; mix well. Let stand 20 minutes. Combine ingredients for seasoning sauce in a small bowl. Mix well and set aside. Add green vegetables to 2 cups boiling water. Cook 10 seconds; drain well. Heat 2 tablespoons oil in a wok over medium heat 1 minute. Stir-fry cooked green vegetables 30 seconds. Add wine, salt and sugar. Stir-fry 10 seconds. Remove from wok and arrange on a platter. Heat 1 cup oil in wok over high heat 1 minute. Stir-fry ginger root 10 seconds. Add marinated beef and stir-fry until very lightly browned. Remove beef with a slotted spoon, draining well over wok; set aside. Remove oil from wok except 1 tablespoon. Heat oil remaining in wok over high heat 30 seconds. Add seasoning sauce. Stir-fry until sauce thickens slightly. Add cooked beef to wok, mixing well with sauce. Pour over green vegetables. Serve hot. Makes 4 servings.

Tomato Beef with Green Peppers

Cantonese

Tomatoes and green peppers combine with beef in a light sauce.

**2/3 lb. beef flank steak or
other tender beef**

Marinade:
   1 teaspoon rice wine or dry sherry
   1/2 teaspoon sugar
   2 tablespoons soy sauce
   1 teaspoon minced fresh ginger root
   1/4 teaspoon pepper
   1 teaspoon cornstarch
   2 tablespoons vegetable oil

Seasoning sauce:
   1/4 cup chicken broth
   1/4 cup water
   1 teaspoon cornstarch
   1 tablespoon soy sauce
   1 teaspoon sesame oil
   1 tablespoon sugar
   2 tablespoons ketchup

1 cup vegetable oil
**10 green onions,
   chopped in 1-inch lengths**
**1 green pepper,
   chopped in 1-inch pieces**
1 teaspoon salt
1 tomato, chopped in 1-inch pieces

Use a cleaver to slice beef across grain and at an angle into thin strips. Cut strips 2 inches long. Combine marinade ingredients in a medium bowl. Add beef strips; mix well. Let stand 20 minutes. Combine ingredients for seasoning sauce in a small bowl. Mix well and set aside. Heat oil in a wok over medium heat 1 minute. Stir-fry marinated beef until very lightly browned. Remove beef with a slotted spoon, draining well over wok; set aside. Remove oil from wok except 5 tablespoons. Heat oil remaining in wok over high heat 30 seconds. Stir-fry green onions 30 seconds. Add green pepper and salt. Stir-fry 1 minute. Add tomato and stir-fry 1 minute longer. Add seasoning sauce. Stir-fry until sauce thickens slightly. Add cooked beef. Mix well and serve hot. Makes 4 servings.

中國菜

If you use chopsticks as cooking utensils, they should be made of bamboo. Metal conducts heat. Plastic will melt. Ivory and laquer are too fine to expose to the rigors of cooking.

Tomato Beef with Green Peppers and Hot Mustard Sauce, page 23

Beef with Asparagus

Cantonese

For a different taste, substitute oyster sauce for soy sauce in this crunchy dish.

2/3 lb. beef flank steak or
  other tender beef

Marinade:
  1 tablespoon rice wine or dry sherry
  1/2 teaspoon sugar
  2 tablespoons soy sauce
  1 teaspoon minced fresh ginger root
  1 teaspoon cornstarch
  1/2 teaspoon baking soda

1 cup vegetable oil
2 tablespoons sesame oil or
  vegetable oil
1 garlic clove, crushed
10 (1-inch) pieces green onion
1 teaspoon salt
1/2 lb. fresh asparagus,
  chopped in 2-inch lengths
3 tablespoons chicken broth

Use a cleaver to slice beef across grain and at an angle into thin strips. Cut strips 2 inches long. Combine marinade ingredients in a medium bowl. Add beef strips; mix well. Let stand 20 minutes. Heat oil in a wok over medium heat 1 minute. Stir-fry marinated beef until very lightly browned. Remove beef with a slotted spoon, draining well over wok; set aside. Remove oil from wok, except 5 tablespoons. Heat oil remaining in wok over high heat 30 seconds. Stir-fry garlic and chopped green onion 30 seconds. Add salt and asparagus. Stir-fry 2 minutes. Add chicken broth and cooked beef; mix well with vegetables. Serve hot. Makes 4 servings.

Curried Beef

Cantonese

Tossing the meat and vegetables with sesame oil before serving gives the dish a glossy look.

2/3 lb. beef flank steak or
  other tender beef

Marinade:
  1 tablespoon soy sauce
  1 teaspoon sugar
  1 teaspoon cornstarch
  1 teaspoon sesame oil
  1 tablespoon vegetable oil
  1/2 teaspoon baking soda

1 fresh carrot, peeled
1 lb. potatoes, peeled
3 cups boiling water
5 tablespoons vegetable oil
1 medium onion,
  chopped in 2/3-inch cubes
1 tablespoon curry powder
1-1/4 cups water
1 teaspoon salt
1/2 teaspoon sugar
2 tablespoons sesame oil

Use a cleaver to slice beef across grain and at an angle into thin strips. Cut strips 2 inches long. Mix marinade ingredients in a small bowl. Add beef strips; mix well. Let stand 30 minutes. Cook whole carrot and whole potatoes 5 minutes in 3 cups boiling water; drain and let cool. Chop cooked carrot into thin slices and potato into diagonal slices 1/3 inch thick. Heat oil in a wok over medium heat 1 minute. Stir-fry onion 3 or 4 seconds. Add curry powder and chopped cooked carrot and potatoes. Stir-fry 30 seconds. Stir in 1-1/4 cups water, salt and sugar. Cover wok, reduce heat to low and simmer 10 minutes or until vegetables are tender. Place marinated beef on top of vegetables. Cover, turn heat up to high and cook 1 minute. Sprinkle sesame oil on top of beef; mix well. Serve hot. Makes 4 servings.

Beef Liver with Vegetables

Cantonese

Baking soda and egg white help tenderize the meat and improve the flavor.

2/3 lb. beef liver

Marinade:
    1 tablespoon rice wine or dry sherry
    1/2 teaspoon baking soda
    1 tablespoon soy sauce
    1/4 teaspoon sugar
    1 teaspoon cornstarch
    1/4 teaspoon pepper
    1 tablespoon sesame oil
    1 egg white

Seasoning sauce:
    1 tablespoon soy sauce
    3 tablespoons oyster sauce
    1/2 cup water
    1 teaspoon cornstarch
    3 tablespoons chicken broth
    1/4 teaspoon sugar
    1/4 teaspoon salt

1 cup vegetable oil
1 tablespoon sliced garlic
1 cup sliced celery
1 cup sliced fresh mushrooms
2 carrots, cooked, sliced

Use a cleaver to cut liver into thin slices. Combine marinade ingredients in a medium bowl. Add liver slices, mix well. Let stand 20 minutes. Combine ingredients for seasoning sauce in a small bowl. Mix well and set aside. Heat oil in a wok over medium heat 1 minute. Stir-fry garlic and marinated liver 2 minutes. Remove with a slotted spoon, draining well over wok; set aside. Remove oil from wok except 1/4 cup. Heat oil remaining in wok over high heat 30 seconds. Stir-fry celery and mushrooms 2 minutes. Add carrots and seasoning sauce. Stir-fry until sauce thickens slightly. Add cooked liver; mix well. Serve hot. Makes 4 servings.

中國菜

When stir-frying garlic to flavor oil, do not let the garlic burn or the oil will carry the burned flavor.

Steamed Beef with Spicy Rice Powder

Szechuan

You can use beef sirloin or tenderloin in place of the flank steak.

3/4 lb. beef flank steak or
   other tender beef

Marinade:
  3 slices fresh ginger root, page 16
  2 green onions
  1 star anise
  1 tablespoon rice wine or dry sherry
  2 tablespoons soy sauce
  1 teaspoon sugar
  1 teaspoon salt
  1 tablespoon hot bean sauce
  3 tablespoons sesame oil or
    vegetable oil
  1/2 teaspoon baking soda

1 cup Spicy Rice Powder, page 127
About 8 cups boiling water
1/2 teaspoon Peppersalt, page 88
1 tablespoon chopped green onion.

Use a cleaver to slice beef across grain and at an angle into thin strips. Cut strips 2 to 3 inches long. Combine marinade ingredients in a medium bowl. Add beef strips; mix well. Let stand 30 minutes. Put spicy rice powder in a plastic bag. Add marinated beef. Shake well to coat. Pour 4 cups boiling water into wok or large pot. Place beef in a baking dish in steamer over boiling water. Cover steamer. Steam over high heat 30 minutes, adding boiling water as needed. Remove from heat. Sprinkle steamed beef with Peppersalt and chopped green onion. Serve hot. Makes 4 servings.

Chungking Beef

Szechuan

This spicy dish originated in the city of Chungking on the Yangtze River in Southeastern Szechuan.

2/3 lb. beef flank steak or
   other tender beef

Marinade:
  1 teaspoon cornstarch
  1 teaspoon rice wine or dry sherry
  1/2 teaspoon baking soda

1 cup vegetable oil
2 teaspoons minced fresh ginger root
2 dried hot red peppers, chopped,
   more if desired
1 tablespoon hot bean sauce
1/2 lb. sliced fresh mushrooms or
  1 (4-oz.) can drained mushrooms
3 celery stalks,
  sliced diagonally in thin wedges
2 tablespoons soy sauce
1/2 teaspoon salt
1/2 teaspoon sugar

Use a cleaver to cut slice beef across grain and at an angle into thin strips. Cut strips into 1'' x 1/4'' shreds, page 11. Combine marinade ingredients in a small bowl. Add beef shreds; mix well. Let stand about 30 minutes. Heat oil in a wok over medium heat 1 minute. Stir-fry ginger root in hot oil until golden brown. Stir-fry marinated beef until very lightly browned. Remove beef, draining well over wok; set aside. Remove oil from wok except 1/4 cup. Stir-fry red peppers, hot bean sauce, mushrooms and celery 4 to 5 minutes. Add cooked beef; mix well. Add soy sauce, salt and sugar; Stir-fry to mix. Serve hot. Makes 4 servings.

Stewed Beef with Hot Sauce

Szechuan

Hot water is poured over the beef cubes to seal in juices and flavor.

2 lbs. beef loin
3 cups boiling water
1/4 cup vegetable oil
3 garlic cloves, crushed
2 slices fresh ginger root, page 16
3 tablespoons hot bean sauce
2 tablespoons rice wine or dry sherry
2/3 cup soy sauce
About 1-1/2 cups water
1 star anise
1 teaspoon sugar
1-1/2 teaspoons Szechuan
   peppercorns
1 (2" x 1") piece dried orange peel,
   page 15

Use a cleaver to chop beef into 1-1/2-inch cubes. Pour 3 cups boiling water over cubes; drain well. Heat 1/4 cup oil in a wok over medium heat 1 minute. Stir-fry garlic and ginger root until garlic is golden, 30 seconds. Turn heat up to high. Add hot bean sauce and beef cubes. Stir-fry 3 minutes. Add wine and soy sauce. Stir-fry 5 minutes. Add 1-1/2 cups water or more to cover beef. Bring to a boil, then reduce heat to low. Add star anise, sugar, peppercorns and dried orange peel. Cover and simmer about 2 hours until beef is tender. Serve hot. Makes 6 servings.

Sesame Seed Beef

Szechuan

Sesame oil in the meat marinade and sesame seeds in the sauce give this dish a nutty flavor.

2/3 lb. beef tenderloin or flank steak
Marinade:
   1 tablespoon rice wine or dry sherry
   1/2 teaspoon sugar
   1 teaspoon minced fresh ginger root
   2 teaspoons cornstarch
   1/2 teaspoon baking soda
   4-1/2 teaspoons sesame oil
   4-1/2 teaspoons soy sauce
3 or 4 large lettuce leaves
Seasoning sauce:
   1 tablespoon sesame seeds
   1-1/2 teaspoons hot bean sauce
   1-1/2 teaspoons hoisin sauce
   1-1/2 teaspoons oyster sauce
   1 teaspoon sugar
   1 teaspoon cornstarch
   2 tablespoons chicken broth
1 cup vegetable oil
1 garlic clove, crushed
1 tablespoon sesame oil

Use a cleaver to slice beef across grain and at an angle into thin 2-inch square pieces. Combine marinade ingredients in a medium bowl. Add beef squares; mix well. Let stand 30 minutes. Arrange lettuce on a platter. Combine ingredients for seasoning sauce in a small bowl. Mix well and set aside. Heat oil in a wok over high heat 1 minute. Stir-fry marinated beef in hot oil until very lightly browned. Remove from wok with a slotted spoon; set aside. Remove oil from wok except 2 tablespoons. Heat oil remaining in wok over high heat 1 minute. Stir-fry garlic until golden, 30 seconds. Add seasoning sauce. Stir-fry until sauce thickens slightly. Add cooked beef; mix well. Stir in sesame oil. Spoon mixture over lettuce leaves. Serve immediately. Makes 4 to 6 servings.

Stewed Beef Tongue

Szechuan

Dried orange peel is often used to sweeten stewed meats.

2 lbs. beef tongue
10 cups water
2 slices fresh ginger root, page 16
2 green onions, cut in half
1 tablespoon rice wine or dry sherry
1/2 cup soy sauce
1 star anise
2 teaspoons Szechuan peppercorns
1 (2" x 1") piece dried orange peel, page 15
1 teaspoon sugar
2 cups boiling water

Rinse beef tongue and slit the front of the skin. Bring 10 cups water to a rapid boil in a large pot. Add beef tongue, ginger root and green onions. Cook over medium-high heat 2 hours until skin can be removed easily. Remove tongue from pot; discard water. Slip the point of a knife through slit in tongue and remove skin. Rinse tongue with cold water and return to pot. Add wine and soy sauce. Bring to a boil over high heat. Add star anise, peppercorns, dried orange peel, sugar and 2 cups boiling water. Reduce heat to low and cook until 1/2 cup sauce remains, about 1-1/2 hours, turning tongue once. Remove tongue, slice very thin and serve on a platter. Makes 6 servings.

How to Make Stewed Beef Tongue

1/Slit the skin of the tongue at the front to make peeling after cooking easier.

2/After cooking, slip the point of a knife through the slit and remove skin.

Country-Style Shredded Beef

Szechuan

If you like spicy foods, add two chopped dried hot red peppers before stir-frying the vegetables.

2/3 lb. beef flank steak or
  other tender beef

Marinade:
  1 teaspoon rice wine or dry sherry
  2 tablespoons soy sauce
  1 teaspoon cornstarch
  1/2 teaspoon sugar
  1 teaspoon minced fresh ginger root
  1/2 teaspoon baking soda

Seasoning sauce:
  3 tablespoons chicken broth
  2 tablespoons water
  1/2 teaspoon cornstarch
  1 tablespoon soy sauce

1 cup vegetable oil
1 garlic clove, sliced
1 tablespoon hot bean sauce
1-1/2 teaspoons hoisin sauce
1 cup shredded cooked carrots,
  page 11
1/2 cup shredded celery, page 11
1/2 cup shredded bamboo shoots,
  page 11

Use a cleaver to slice beef across grain and at an angle into thin strips. Cut strips into shreds, page 11. Combine marinade ingredients in a medium bowl. Add beef shreds; mix well. Let stand 20 minutes. Combine ingredients for seasoning sauce in a small bowl. Mix well and set aside. Heat oil in a wok over medium heat 30 seconds. Stir-fry garlic and marinated beef about 2 minutes until beef is browned. Remove with a slotted spoon, draining well over wok; set aside. Remove oil from wok except 1/4 cup. Heat oil remaining in wok over medium heat. Add hot bean sauce and hoisin sauce. Heat 15 seconds. Add carrots, celery and bamboo shoots. Turn heat up to high and stir-fry 1 minute. Add seasoning sauce and stir-fry until sauce thickens slightly. Add cooked beef; mix well. Serve on a small platter. Makes 4 servings.

Spicy Rice Powder

Szechuan

Not always available in stores, spicy rice powder is easy to make.

1 cup rice
2 star anise
1/2 teaspoon Szechuan peppercorns
1 teaspoon five-spice powder

Heat a medium skillet 30 seconds to 1 minute over high heat. Add rice, star anise and peppercorns to hot skillet. Reduce heat to low. Stir-fry 6 to 8 minutes until rice is lightly browned. Remove skillet from heat and let cool. Put browned rice mixture in blender with five-spice powder and process until mixture resembles fine breadcrumbs. Makes 1 cup.

Beef with Assorted Vegetables

Szechuan

Marinated beef strips are stir-fried with mushrooms, sliced carrot and snow peas.

2/3 lb. beef flank steak

Marinade:
  1 teaspoon rice wine or dry sherry
  1/2 teaspoon minced fresh
    ginger root
  1/4 teaspoon sugar
  2 tablespoons soy sauce or
    oyster sauce
  1 teaspoon cornstarch
  1/2 teaspoon baking soda

Seasoning sauce:
  1/4 cup chicken broth
  1/4 cup water
  1 teaspoon cornstarch
  1/4 teaspoon sugar
  1/2 teaspoon sesame oil
  1 tablespoon soy sauce

1/4 teaspoon salt
1 carrot
2 cups boiling water
1 cup snow peas or sliced green beans
1 cup vegetable oil
1 cup sliced fresh mushrooms

Use a cleaver to slice beef across grain and at an angle into thin strips. Cut strips 2 inches long. Combine marinade ingredients in a medium bowl. Add beef strips; mix well. Let stand 20 minutes. Combine ingredients for seasoning sauce in a small bowl. Mix well and set aside. Add salt and carrot to boiling water in a small saucepan; boil 15 minutes. Add snow peas or green beans. Cook 1 minute. Remove from heat, rinse vegetables with cold water and drain. Slice carrot into thin slices. Heat oil in a wok over medium heat 1 minute. Stir-fry marinated beef until very lightly browned. Remove with a slotted spoon, draining well over wok; set aside. Remove oil from wok except 1/4 cup. Heat remaining oil in wok over high heat 30 seconds. Stir-fry mushrooms 3 minutes. Add seasoning sauce, cooked snow peas, carrots and cooked beef. Stir-fry until sauce thickens slightly. Serve hot. Makes 4 servings.

中國菜

When cornstarch paste is added to a hot mixture, it thickens almost immediately. After 1 to 2 minutes stirring over heat, do not expect the mixture to thicken further.

Shredded Beef with Green Peppers

Shanghai

Both beef shreds and green pepper shreds should be the size of matchsticks.

2/3 lb. beef flank steak or
  other tender beef

Marinade:
  1-1/2 teaspoons rice wine or
    dry sherry
  1/2 teaspoon salt
  1 tablespoon vegetable oil
  1 tablespoon sesame oil
  1/2 teaspoon baking soda

3 medium, green peppers
1/2 cup vegetable oil
1 tablespoon minced fresh ginger root
1/3 cup shredded green onions,
  page 11
1/4 teaspoon sugar
1 teaspoon salt

Use a cleaver to slice beef across grain and at an angle into thin strips. Chop strips into 1" x 1/4" shreds, page 11. Combine marinade ingredients in a medium bowl. Add beef shreds; mix well. Let stand about 1 hour. Cut green peppers in half. Remove and discard seeds and membranes. Cut green peppers into thin shreds, page 11. Heat 5 tablespoons oil in a wok over high heat 1 minute. Stir-fry marinated beef 10 seconds. Remove beef, draining well over wok; set aside. Add remaining 3 tablespoons oil to wok and reduce heat to medium. Stir-fry ginger root and green onions 1 minute. Add green pepper shreds, sugar and salt. Stir-fry 2 to 3 minutes. Add cooked beef. Mix well and serve immediately. Makes 4 servings.

Stewed Beef with Chinese Cabbage

Shanghai

Slices of fresh ginger root should be about 1 inch in diameter.

1 lb. beef brisket
6 cups boiling water
1 tablespoon rice wine or dry sherry
3 slices fresh ginger root, page 16
1 lb. Chinese cabbage
2 tablespoons vegetable oil
1-1/2 teaspoons salt
1/4 cup beef broth

Use a cleaver to cut beef into thin slices. Place in a large heavy pot. Pour 3 cups boiling water over beef slices; drain well. Add 3 more cups boiling water to beef and bring to a boil over low heat. Add wine and ginger root. Cover and cook 2 hours over low heat. Chop cabbage into 2-inch square pieces. Add chopped cabbage, oil, salt and beef broth to beef. Cook 30 minutes longer. Serve hot in a large bowl. Makes 4 servings.

Cold Meat Platter

Shanghai

Star anise gives cold meats a mild licorice flavor.

3 tablespoons vegetable oil or lard
3 slices fresh ginger root, page 16
1 tablespoon rice wine or dry sherry
2 green onions,
   cut in 2-inch long pieces
1 star anise
1 teaspoon Szechuan peppercorns
1/2 cup soy sauce
1 lb. pork tenderloin
1 lb. beef tenderloin
1-1/2 cups water
1 teaspoon sugar
1 (2" x 1") piece dried orange peel,
   page 15
1 fresh carrot, if desired
1 Chinese turnip, if desired

Heat oil or lard in a large saucepan over medium heat 1 minute. Add ginger root, wine, green onions, star anise and peppercorns. Stir-fry 1 minute or until fragrant. Stir in soy sauce. Bring to a boil and reduce heat to low. Add pork and beef. Cook 4 to 5 minutes, turning meat once. Add 1-1/2 cups water, sugar and dried orange peel. Cover and cook 2 hours over low heat until only 1/2 cup sauce remains. Refrigerate to cool. Slice chilled meat with a cleaver and arrange in rows on a large platter. Garnish with carrot and Chinese turnip. Serve cold. Makes 4 to 6 servings.

Ground Beef with Sweet Corn

Shanghai

Make this easy dish with either fresh or frozen sweet corn.

Marinade:
  1 teaspoon rice wine or dry sherry
  1/2 teaspoon minced fresh
    ginger root
  1 teaspoon cornstarch
  2 tablespoons soy sauce
  1 tablespoon sesame oil
  1/4 teaspoon sugar

1/2 lb. ground beef
1/4 cup vegetable oil
1 garlic clove, sliced
1/2 teaspoon cornstarch
1 teaspoon water
1/2 lb. fresh cut corn or
   thawed frozen cut corn
1/4 teaspoon salt

Combine marinade ingredients in a medium bowl. Add ground beef; mix well. Let stand 10 minutes. Heat oil in a wok over high heat 30 seconds. Stir-fry garlic 15 seconds. Add marinated beef. Stir-fry about 2 minutes over medium-high heat until browned. Remove from wok with a slotted spoon, draining well over wok; set aside. Dissolve cornstarch in water to make a paste. Heat oil remaining in wok over high heat 30 seconds. Stir-fry corn 3 minutes. Add salt and cornstarch paste. Stir-fry 1 minute. Return beef to wok and mix well. Place on a platter. Serve hot. Makes 4 servings.

Meatballs in Sour Sauce

Shanghai

Try this seasoning sauce as a change from Sweet & Sour Sauce.

1 lb. ground beef

2 tablespoons cold water

Marinade:

  1 tablespoon rice wine or dry sherry

  1 teaspoon salt

  1 teaspoon minced fresh ginger root

  1/4 cup chopped green onion

  1 tablespoon soy sauce

  1 tablespoon cornstarch

  1/4 teaspoon pepper

  1 egg

6 cups oil for deep-frying

1/2 teaspoon salt

3 cups boiling water

4 to 6 large cabbage leaves

Seasoning sauce:

  1/4 cup rice vinegar or white vinegar

  1/4 cup sugar

  1 tablespoon soy sauce

  1/2 teaspoon salt

  2 teaspoons cornstarch

  2/3 cup water

  2 tablespoons chicken broth, if desired for added flavor

  1 teaspoon sesame oil

1/4 cup shredded green onion, page 11

Mix ground beef with 2 tablespoons cold water 1 minute. Combine marinade ingredients in a medium bowl. Add ground beef. Mix until beef is sticky. Let stand 10 minutes. Use a teaspoon dipped in water and 2 teaspoons marinated beef mixture to make 1 meatball. Repeat with remaining beef mixture. Heat 6 cups oil in a wok over high heat to 325° to 350°F (165° to 175°C). Reduce heat to medium. Carefully lower meatballs into hot oil with a slotted metal spoon. Deep-fry several at a time 2 minutes or until crisp and golden. Remove meatballs with slotted spoon, draining well over wok; set aside. Turn heat up to high and reheat oil. Add half the meatballs and deep-fry again 30 seconds. Remove from wok and deep-fry remaining meatballs. Add salt to 3 cups boiling water in a large saucepan. Cook cabbage leaves 30 seconds; drain well and let cool before squeezing out excess water. Arrange on a platter. Combine ingredients for seasoning sauce in a small bowl. Mix well and set aside. Remove oil from wok except 1 tablespoon. Heat oil remaining in wok over medium heat 1 minute. Stir-fry green onion 30 seconds. Add seasoning sauce. Stir-fry until sauce thickens slightly. Add meatballs. Mix well and spoon over cabbage leaves. Serve hot. Makes 4 to 6 servings.

中國菜

For directions on saving and re-using cooking oil, turn to page 14.

VEGETABLES

Pickled cabbage, or *sauerkraut*, is usually credited to the Germans, but it was originally a Chinese dish. While the workers were building The Great Wall of China, they lived on cabbage and rice. In the winter, rice wine was added to cabbage to preserve it by fermentation. Pickled cabbage was both practical and delicious so it quickly became popular. Traders eventually carried the idea back to Central Europe. The Chinese still use rice wine and vinegar to pickle vegetables. Cantonese Pickled Vegetables and Szechuan Pickles are variations on that theme.

Stir-frying is the most common method of cooking vegetables. After they are sliced, chopped or diced, vegetables are stir-fried in a small amount of oil over high heat. Hot oil seals in the natural juices and preserves color, texture and flavor. A little chicken broth might be added when cooking hard vegetables such as carrots or broccoli. The wok is then covered and the vegetables simmer until they are crisp-tender. Vegetables cooked this way are higher in nutrients than vegetables boiled until they are limp and soggy.

Dried ingredients such as dried shrimp and dried mushrooms are often used to season vegetables—especially in Szechuan cooking. Dried foods must be soaked in hot water before using to restore moisture and bring out flavor. Dried shrimp have a much stronger flavor than fresh shrimp and should be used sparingly. Only about two ounces of dried shrimp are needed to season one vegetable dish.

Chinese cooks frequently prepare a cold vegetable dish or salad ahead of time so last-minute cooking preparations are minimal. These salads may seem different, but try them before you pass judgment—they are delicious. Cucumber Chicken Salad is made with shredded cucumbers, shredded chicken and agar agar which is a type of seaweed. A spicy mustard-sesame sauce is poured over the salad just before it is served.

Northern Mixed Vegetables

Mandarin

A marvelous winter dish because all the vegetables except the cabbage are canned.

1/2 (4-oz.) can baby corn, drained
1/2 lb. Chinese cabbage

Seasoning sauce:
  1 teaspoon salt
  1/4 teaspoon sugar
  1/4 cup chicken broth
  1/4 cup water
  1 teaspoon cornstarch
  1/4 teaspoon pepper

5 tablespoons vegetable oil
2 garlic cloves, crushed
1/2 (4-oz.) can sliced mushrooms, drained
1/2 (4-oz.) can sliced bamboo shoots, drained
1/2 (4-oz.) can sliced water chestnuts, drained
1 teaspoon sesame oil

Slice baby corn with a cleaver. Chop cabbage into 1-1/2-inch squares. Combine ingredients for seasoning sauce in a small bowl; mix well and set aside. Heat oil in a wok over high heat 1 minute. Stir-fry garlic until golden, 30 seconds. Add chopped cabbage. Stir-fry 1 minute. Add sliced baby corn, mushrooms, bamboo shoots and water chestnuts. Stir-fry 1 minute. Add seasoning sauce to vegetables. Stir-fry until sauce thickens slightly. Sprinkle with sesame oil. Serve hot. Makes 4 to 6 servings.

Stuffed Cucumbers

Mandarin

Serve these as a wholesome appetizer, a vegetable side dish or a main course.

3 tablespoons dried shrimp
1-1/2 cups hot water
1 teaspoon rice wine or dry sherry
1-1/2 teaspoons minced fresh ginger root
1/2 cup chopped green onions
2 tablespoons soy sauce
1 teaspoon cornstarch
2 tablespoons sesame oil
1/2 teaspoon salt
2/3 lb. ground pork
2 or 3 large cucumbers
About 1 teaspoon cornstarch
3 tablespoons vegetable oil
1 cup water

Soak dried shrimp in 1-1/2 cups hot water 10 to 15 minutes. Drain well; discard water. Chop softened shrimp into small pieces with a cleaver. Place shrimp in a medium bowl with wine, ginger root, green onions, soy sauce, 1 teaspoon cornstarch, sesame oil, salt and ground pork; mix well. Wash and peel cucumbers. Cut into 1-1/2-inch lengths. Scoop out seeds and sprinkle a little cornstarch on the inside of each piece. Stuff pork mixture into hollows. Heat vegetable oil in a large skillet over medium high heat 30 seconds to 1 minute. Carefully place each piece of stuffed cucumber in saucepan. Cover and cook 2 minutes until bottom of each piece is golden. Turn and cook the other side 1 minute. Reduce heat to low. Add 1 cup water. Cover and simmer until water is almost all absorbed by cucumbers. Serve hot. Makes 4 servings.

Vegetables with an Egg Hat

Mandarin

An omelet covers stir-fried vegetables. Then the vegetables and pieces of omelet are rolled up in pancakes.

1/3 lb. lean pork

Marinade:
   1 tablespoon soy sauce
   1 tablespoon cornstarch
   1 teaspoon sesame oil
   1 teaspoon water

2 oz. bean noodles
2 cups hot water
20 Mandarin Pancakes, page 153
3/4 cup vegetable oil
2 tablespoons soy sauce
2 teaspoons salt
1/2 lb. fresh bean sprouts
1 garlic clove, crushed
1/2 lb. fresh spinach, chopped
4 oz. frozen French-cut green beans or
   shredded asparagus, page 11
3 eggs
3 green onions, shredded, page 11
3 tablespoons Duck Sauce, page 71

Slice pork into thin strips with a cleaver. Cut strips into 2" x 1/4" shreds. Combine marinade ingredients. Add pork shreds; mix well. Let stand 15 minutes. Soak bean noodles in 2 cups hot water 5 minutes. Drain and chop into 2-inch lengths. Prepare Mandarin Pancakes; keep warm. Heat 3 tablespoons oil in a wok over medium heat 30 seconds. Add soy sauce, 1 teaspoon salt and chopped bean noodles. Stir-fry 1 minute. Turn heat up to high, add bean sprouts and stir-fry 10 seconds. Place bean sprouts and bean noodles on a platter. Heat 3 tablespoons oil in wok over high heat 30 seconds. Stir-fry garlic until golden, 30 seconds. Add spinach and 1/2 teaspoon salt; stir-fry 10 seconds. Place spinach on platter. Heat 1/4 cup oil in wok over medium heat. Stir-fry marinated pork 1 minute or until browned. Add green beans or asparagus and 1/2 teaspoon salt. Stir-fry 30 seconds. Place on platter. Beat eggs slightly. Heat 2 tablespoons oil in wok over medium heat. Add eggs, tilting wok so eggs cover entire bottom; do not stir. When eggs are almost set, turn with a spatula and cook other side. Both sides should be golden. Toss bean noodles and vegetables on platter to mix. Cover with cooked eggs. To eat: Spread Duck Sauce over pancake. Place green onion shreds in center. Separate some egg and 2 or 3 tablespoons vegetables from mixture on platter. Place on pancake; roll up and fold ends over. Makes 4 servings.

How to Make Vegetables with an Egg Hat

1/As eggs cook, tilt wok to make a thin sheet of egg on bottom of wok.

2/Toss bean noodles and cooked vegetables on a platter. Cover with hot cooked egg.

Chinese Cabbage with Dried Shrimp

Mandarin

Dried shrimp season this simple cabbage dish.

3 tablespoons dried shrimp
1-1/2 cups hot water
1-1/2 lbs. Chinese cabbage
1/4 cup vegetable oil
1-1/2 garlic cloves, crushed
1 teaspoon salt
2 tablespoons chicken broth

Soak dried shrimp in 1-1/2 cups hot water 10 to 15 minutes. Cut cabbage into 1-1/2-inch square pieces. Heat oil in a wok over medium-high heat 1 minute. Drain shrimp well; discard water. Stir-fry garlic and softened shrimp about until garlic is golden, 30 seconds. Add cabbage. Stir-fry 1 minute. Add salt and chicken broth. Stir-fry 3 minutes or until cabbage is soft. Serve hot. Makes 4 servings.

Garlic Cucumber Salad

Mandarin

This cold pickled dish will keep in your refrigerator up to one week.

1-1/4 lbs. fresh pickling cucumbers
1 teaspoon salt
2 tablespoons sugar
2 garlic cloves, chopped
2 tablespoons soy sauce
2 tablespoons rice vinegar or
  white vinegar

Lightly crush cucumbers with the broad side of a cleaver to release their flavor. Chop into bite-size pieces. Combine chopped cucumbers with salt in a medium bowl. Let stand 30 minutes. Lightly rinse with water and drain well. Add sugar, garlic, soy sauce and vinegar; mix well. Cover and refrigerate 4 hours before serving. Serve cold. Makes 4 servings.

Stir-Fried Bean Sprouts

Mandarin

Bean sprouts must be stir-fried quickly or they'll lose their crispness.

1 lb. fresh bean sprouts
3 tablespoons vegetable oil
1 teaspoon Szechuan peppercorns
4-1/2 teaspoons rice vinegar or
  white vinegar
1/2 teaspoon sugar
1 teaspoon salt

Rinse bean sprouts well with cold water. Remove any discolored ends. Place in a bowl of cold water to keep fresh. Heat oil in a wok over medium heat 1 minute. Stir-fry peppercorns about 1 minute until fragrant. Remove peppercorns with a spatula and discard. Reheat oil over high heat 30 seconds. Drain bean sprouts. Quickly stir-fry bean sprouts 5 to 10 seconds. Immediately add vinegar, sugar and salt. Stir-fry a few seconds longer. Remove from heat. Serve immediately. Makes 4 servings.

Three-Color Balls with Scallops   Photo on pages 72 and 73.

Mandarin

Carrots, turnips and cucumbers provide the three colors.

4 oz. fresh scallops
1/2 lb. fresh carrots
1/2 lb. Chinese turnips
1/2 lb. fresh pickling cucumbers

Seasoning sauce:
  1 teaspoon salt
  1/2 teaspoon sugar
  1/2 cup chicken broth
  2 cups boiling water
  1/4 teaspoon pepper

1-1/2 teaspoons cornstarch
1 tablespoon water

Rinse scallops with cold water, pat dry with a paper towel. Shred with a cleaver, page 11. Peel carrots, turnips and cucumbers. Cut into 1-inch cubes. Trim corners off cubes to make balls. Combine ingredients for seasoning sauce in a small bowl. Heat wok over medium heat 1 minute. Add seasoning sauce and vegetable balls. Cover and cook 20 minutes over low heat. Remove vegetable balls with a slotted spoon and place on a small platter. Dissolve cornstarch in 1 tablespoon water to make a paste. Add cornstarch paste to seasoning sauce. Cook over high heat until sauce thickens slightly. Add shredded scallops. Stir-fry 5 to 10 seconds. Pour over vegetable balls. Serve hot. Makes 4 servings.

Sweet & Sour Cabbage

Mandarin

Serve this spicy dish hot or cold.

1-1/4 lbs. Chinese cabbage
1/4 cup vegetable oil
1 garlic clove, sliced
1 teaspoon chopped dried
  hot red pepper
1 teaspoon salt
2 tablespoons vinegar
2 tablespoons sugar
2 tablespoons chicken broth

Chop cabbage into 3" x 1/2" pieces; set aside. Heat oil in a wok over high heat 30 seconds. Stir-fry garlic and red pepper until garlic is golden, 30 seconds. Add chopped cabbage and salt. Stir-fry 1 minute. Add vinegar, sugar and chicken broth. Stir-fry 5 minutes. Serve hot or cold. Makes 4 servings.

Stuffed Tomatoes

Cantonese

Tomatoes peel easily after they are blanched.

2/3 lb. ground beef or pork
1 onion, chopped
Marinade:
  1 tablespoon rice wine or dry sherry
  1 teaspoon salt
  1 tablespoon soy sauce
  1 egg white
  1/4 teaspoon pepper
  2 tablespoons cornstarch

8 firm tomatoes
4 cups boiling water
1 teaspoon cornstarch
7 tablespoons vegetable oil
1 tablespoon sugar
2 tablespoons soy sauce
2 tablespoons beef broth or
  chicken broth
1/2 cup water
About 8 cups boiling water
2 teaspoons cornstarch
2 teaspoons water

Mix ground meat and chopped onion. Combine marinade ingredients in a small bowl. Add meat mixture, mix well. Let stand 15 minutes. Use a paring knife to slit the skin of each tomato from top to bottom. To blanch tomatoes, submerge in 4 cups boiling water 10 seconds. Insert a paring knife under skin of 1 tomato. Peel off skin and cut tomato in half. Scoop out seeds and pulp with a spoon. Repeat with remaining tomatoes. Sprinkle cornstarch on the inside of each tomato half. Fill with ground meat mixture. Heat oil in a large skillet over high heat 30 seconds to 1 minute. Carefully place stuffed tomatoes meat-side down in skillet and fry 2 to 3 minutes until meat is browned. Remove tomatoes with a spatula. Arrange meat-side down in a baking dish. Mix sugar, soy sauce, broth and 1/2 cup water in a small cup. Pour over tomatoes. Cover baking dish. Pour 4 cups boiling water into a wok or large pot. Place baking dish on a steamer rack over boiling water. Steam over high heat 20 minutes, adding more boiling water as needed. Remove wok from heat and let cool slightly before removing tomatoes. Place tomatoes meat-side up on a platter. Pour liquid from baking dish into a small saucepan. Dissolve 2 teaspoons cornstarch in 2 teaspoons water to make a paste. Add cornstarch paste to liquid in saucepan. Stir over medium heat until thickened slightly. Pour over tomatoes. Serve hot. Makes 8 servings.

Stir-Fried Broccoli

Cantonese

Broccoli stems take longer to cook than flowerets, so stir-fry them first.

1 lb. broccoli
1/4 cup vegetable oil
1 garlic clove, crushed
1/2 teaspoon salt
1 teaspoon rice wine or dry sherry
1/4 teaspoon sugar
3 tablespoons chicken broth
1/4 cup water

Rinse broccoli with cold water. Cut into 2-inch flowerets and slice stems 1/4 inch thick. Heat oil in a wok over high heat 30 seconds. Stir-fry garlic until golden, 30 seconds. Add broccoli stems and salt. Stir-fry 30 seconds. Add flowerets. Stir-fry 1 minute. Add wine, sugar, chicken broth and water. Reduce heat to medium-low and continue to stir-fry until water is almost gone. Serve hot. Makes 4 servings.

Stuffed Green Peppers

Cantonese

Both fresh and dried shrimp give the pork filling its distinctive flavor.

1 tablespoon dried shrimp
1/2 cup hot water
2 oz. fresh shrimp
Marinade:
  1 teaspoon rice wine or dry sherry
  1/2 teaspoon salt
  1/2 teaspoon sugar
  1/4 teaspoon pepper
  1 tablespoon cornstarch
6 oz. finely ground pork
4 large green peppers
1 tablespoon cornstarch
Seasoning sauce:
  1 tablespoon soy sauce
  1/4 teaspoon salt
  1/4 teaspoon sugar
  1/4 cup water
  1/4 cup chicken broth
3 tablespoons vegetable oil
1 tablespoon chopped,
  rinsed salty black beans
2 garlic cloves, crushed
1 teaspoon minced fresh ginger root

Soak dried shrimp in 1/2 cup hot water 10 to 15 minutes. Drain well and discard water. Chop softened shrimp with a cleaver. Shell and devein shrimp, page 59. Rinse and pat dry with a paper towel. Chop with cleaver. Combine marinade ingredients in a small bowl. Add chopped dried shrimp, chopped fresh shrimp and ground pork. Stir with a spoon in one direction until mixed. Remove pork mixture from bowl with one hand and toss it back into the bowl. Repeat tossing 2 or 3 minutes until mixture is very sticky. Cut tops from green peppers; discard. Then cut off bottoms to make 4 shallow containers. Cut each remaining piece in half lengthwise to make 2 small containers. Each pepper will yield 3 small containers for stuffing. Remove seeds and membranes. Sprinkle cornstarch on the inside of each piece. Fill with pork mixture and smooth top. Mix ingredients for seasoning sauce in a small bowl; set aside. Heat oil in a large skillet over medium heat 30 seconds to 1 minute. Place stuffed peppers meat-side down in skillet; fry 1 minute. Push peppers to side of skillet. Combine black beans, garlic and ginger root in other side of skillet; stir-fry 30 seconds. Stir in seasoning sauce. Return peppers to center of skillet. Cover, reduce heat to low and simmer about 8 minutes until sauce is almost all absorbed. Place on a platter meat-side up. Serve immediately. Makes 4 to 6 servings.

Stir-Fried Asparagus

Cantonese

Stir-frying retains the natural flavor and color of asparagus.

2/3 lb. asparagus
1/4 cup vegetable oil
1 tablespoon sliced garlic
1/2 teaspoon salt

Rinse asparagus with cold water. Snap off tough ends. Slice asparagus diagonally into 1-inch pieces. Heat oil in a wok over high heat 30 seconds. Stir-fry garlic until golden, 30 seconds. Add asparagus and salt. Stir-fry 3 minutes or until asparagus is crisp-tender. Serve hot. Makes 4 servings.

Cantonese Pickled Vegetables

Cantonese

These are not as spicy as Szechuan Pickled Vegetables, page 141.

1 (2/3-lb.) turnip
1 medium, fresh carrot
3 pickling cucumbers or
   1/3 lb. cauliflower or cabbage
10 slices fresh ginger root, page 16
2 small dried hot red peppers,
   cut in small pieces, more if desired
2 teaspoons salt
1/4 cup sugar
1/4 cup rice vinegar or white vinegar

Cut turnip, carrot and cucumbers or other vegetables into bite-size pieces. Combine in a large bowl. Add ginger root, red peppers and salt; mix well. Cover and let stand about 6 hours. Lightly rinse vegetables with cold water. Drain well. Add sugar and vinegar; mix well. Cover and refrigerate 6 hours. Serve cold. May be refrigerated up to 1 week. Makes 6 to 8 servings.

Stir-Fried Snow Peas with Water Chestnuts

Cantonese

Softened dried shrimp are stir-fried with garlic and used to season the vegetables.

2 tablespoons dried shrimp
1 cup hot water
1/2 lb. fresh snow peas
2 cups water
1/2 teaspoon salt
1/4 cup vegetable oil
1 garlic clove, crushed
1/2 cup sliced water chestnuts
1/2 teaspoon salt
2 tablespoons chicken broth

Soak dried shrimp in 1 cup hot water 10 to 15 minutes. Drain well, discard water. Chop softened shrimp into 1/6-inch pieces with a cleaver. Snap off ends from snow peas; remove strings. Bring 2 cups water to a boil in a small saucepan. Add 1/2 teaspoon salt. To blanch snow peas, submerge 10 seconds in boiling water; drain and rinse with cold water. Heat oil in a wok over high heat 30 seconds. Stir-fry garlic and chopped shrimp 30 seconds. Add water chestnuts and salt. Stir-fry 1 minute. Add blanched snow peas and chicken broth. Stir-fry 10 seconds. Serve hot. Makes 4 servings.

Szechuan Pickled Vegetables

Szechuan

The traditional container for these pickles is a ceramic bowl.

8 cups boiling water
1/4 cup salt
2 tablespoons Szechuan peppercorns
1 tablespoon sugar
2 tablespoons rice wine or dry sherry
5 slices fresh ginger root, page 16
2 garlic cloves
5 fresh hot red peppers,
   halved lengthwise
1/2 lb. fresh carrots, peeled
1/2 lb. turnips, peeled
1/2 lb. fresh pickling cucumbers,
   unpeeled
1/2 lb. cabbage

Pour 8 cups boiling water into a large wide-mouth canning jar or crock. Combine salt and peppercorns in a small saucepan. Heat over medium heat 4 minutes. Let cool and add to water in jar. Add sugar, wine, ginger root, garlic and red peppers; mix well. Let stand 1 to 2 hours until water has cooled to room temperature. Cut carrots, turnips and cucumbers into 1-1/2" x 3/4" pieces. Dry with a paper towel and add to mixture in jar. Tear cabbage leaves into 4" x 2" pieces. Pat dry and add to mixture in jar, pushing pieces under liquid. Cover with a tight-fitting lid. Refrigerate 3 days before serving. Serve cold. Store in refrigerator. Makes about 1 quart.

Szechuan-Style Eggplant

Szechuan

If you don't have hot bean sauce, substitute 1 tablespoon Hot Chili Sauce, page 143, mixed with 1 teaspoon of salt.

1 (1-1/4-lb.) eggplant
1 teaspoon cornstarch
1/4 cup water
6 tablespoons vegetable oil
1 teaspoon minced garlic
1 tablespoon minced fresh ginger root
1 tablespoon hot bean sauce
1/2 teaspoon hoisin sauce
2 teaspoons rice vinegar or
   white vinegar
2 tablespoons soy sauce
1 teaspoon sugar
1/2 teaspoon salt
1/2 cup chicken broth
1-1/2 teaspoons sesame oil
1 tablespoon chopped green onion

Peel eggplant and cut into 3" x 1/2" pieces. Mix cornstarch with 1/4 cup water to make a sauce. Heat vegetable oil in a wok over high heat 1 minute. Stir-fry eggplant pieces 6 to 8 minutes until soft. Remove with a slotted spoon, draining well over wok; set aside. Remove oil from wok except 1 tablespoon. Add garlic, ginger root, hot bean sauce, hoisin sauce and vinegar to oil remaining in wok. Cook 30 seconds over high heat. Add soy sauce, sugar, salt, chicken broth and cornstarch paste. Bring to a boil, stirring occasionally. Add softened eggplant. Stir-fry about 1 minute until eggplant absorbs most of the sauce. Add sesame oil and green onion. Mix well and serve immediately. Makes 6 servings.

Spicy Sprout & Cucumber Salad

Szechuan

Salt draws excess water from bean sprouts and cucumbers, making them very crisp.

1/2 lb. fresh bean sprouts
1 cucumber
1 teaspoon salt
2 garlic cloves, minced
2 tablespoons soy sauce
1/2 teaspoon sugar
2 tablespoons rice vinegar or
white vinegar

Rinse bean sprouts with cold water. Place in a medium bowl. Peel cucumber, cut in half and remove seeds. Shred cucumber with a cleaver, page 11. Place cucumber shreds in another medium bowl. Sprinkle about 1/2 teaspoon salt on bean sprouts and another 1/2 teaspoon salt on cucumber shreds. Mix each vegetable well and let stand 30 minutes. Squeeze excess water and salt from each vegetable. Combine sprouts and cucumber. Add garlic, soy sauce, sugar and vinegar; mix well. Place in a shallow serving dish. Refrigerate at least 30 minutes before serving. Serve cold. Makes 4 servings.

Cucumber Slices with Dried Shrimp

Szechuan

Dried shrimp and garlic add intriguing flavor to cooked cucumbers.

2 medium cucumbers
3 tablespoons dried shrimp
1-1/2 cups hot water
6 tablespoons vegetable oil
2 garlic cloves, crushed
1 teaspoon salt

Peel cucumbers and cut in half lengthwise. Remove seeds and cut cucumber halves horizontally into 1/4-inch slices. Soak dried shrimp in 1-1/2 cups hot water 10 to 15 minutes. Drain well, reserving water. Heat oil in a wok over medium heat 1 minute. Stir-fry garlic until golden, 30 seconds. Add drained shrimp. Stir-fry 30 seconds. Add cucumber slices. Stir-fry 1 minute. Stir in salt and 1/2 cup reserved shrimp soak water. Cover and cook until water is absorbed by cucumber. If cucumber slices are not soft, add a little more water and simmer a few minutes longer. Serve hot. Makes 4 servings.

Szechuan Cucumber Rolls

Szechuan

Have all the ingredients ready before stir-frying so the cucumbers won't be overcooked.

1-1/2 lbs. fresh pickling cucumbers
1 teaspoon salt
5 tablespoons vegetable oil
4-1/2 teaspoons chopped garlic
6 dried hot red peppers, shredded,
page 11
2 tablespoons rice vinegar or
white vinegar
1 tablespoon sugar
2 tablespoons soy sauce

Peel cucumbers and cut in half crosswise. Use a paring knife to sharpen narrow end of each cucumber piece, as if sharpening a pencil. Combine cucumbers and salt in a small bowl; mix well. Let stand 2 hours. Rinse with cold water; drain well. Heat oil in a wok over high heat 30 seconds. Stir-fry garlic and dried hot peppers 15 seconds. Add drained cucumbers. Stir-fry 30 seconds. Add vinegar, sugar and soy sauce. Stir-fry 15 seconds. Spoon mixture into a bowl. Cover and refrigerate at least 2 hours before serving. Serve cold. Makes 4 servings.

Cucumber Salad with Spicy Dressing

Szechuan

Marinate shredded cucumbers for one hour before assembling the salad.

1-1/2 lbs. cucumbers
1 teaspoon salt
1 teaspoon sugar
1 tablespoon rice vinegar or
  white vinegar
1 tablespoon minced garlic, if desired
1 oz. bean noodles
3 cups boiling water
4-1/2 teaspoons soy sauce
1 teaspoon sesame oil
1 tablespoon Chili Oil, page 85

Peel cucumbers. Cut in half lengthwise. Scoop out seeds. Cut cucumber pieces in half and shred with a cleaver, page 11. Place in a large bowl. Add salt, sugar, vinegar and garlic, if desired. Mix well; let stand 1 hour. Place bean noodles in a bowl with 3 cups boiling water 2 minutes. Rinse with cold water; drain well. Chop into 2-inch lengths. Place on a platter. Arrange shredded cucumbers on top of bean noodles. Sprinkle with soy sauce, sesame oil and Chili Oil. Serve cold. Makes 4 servings.

Hot Chili Sauce

Spicy hot sauce goes well with dumplings, meat pastries and Shao Mai, pages 32 and 33.

1/2 cup chili powder

1 teaspoon minced garlic
1 teaspoon chopped,
  rinsed salty black beans, if desired
1 tablespoon sesame seeds
1/3 cup vegetable oil
1/3 cup sesame oil
1 teaspoon Szechuan peppercorns
2 thin slices fresh ginger root,
  page 16
2 green onions,
  chopped in 2-inch pieces

Mix chili powder and garlic in a small bowl. Stir in black beans, if desired; set aside. Heat a small saucepan over medium heat 1 minute. Add sesame seeds. Stir-fry 2 to 3 minutes until seeds become golden and oily. Add vegetable oil and sesame oil. Heat over high heat 2 minutes. Add sesame seeds, peppercorns, ginger root and green onions. Reduce heat to medium. Cook until ginger slices turn dark brown. Remove saucepan from heat and let cool 2 to 3 minutes. Strain mixture into a bowl to remove ginger root, peppercorns, sesame seed, and green onions. Add chili powder mixture. Mix well to dissolve lumps. Sauce may be covered and stored at room temperature about 6 months. Makes 2/3 cup.

Stuffed Eggplant

Shanghai

Eggplant is deep-fried twice—once, to cook it and again to make the coating crisp and golden.

Marinade:
  1 teaspoon rice wine or dry sherry
  1/2 teaspoon sugar
  1/2 teaspoon salt
  2 tablespoons soy sauce
  1/2 teaspoon minced fresh
    ginger root
  1 tablespoon sesame oil
  1/4 teaspoon pepper
  1 egg white
1/2 lb. ground pork or ground beef
1 (1-lb.) eggplant
Coating:
  1/4 cup all-purpose flour
  1/4 cup cornstarch
  1/4 teaspoon baking soda
  1 egg yolk
  1 tablespoon shortening
  1/4 teaspoon sugar
  1/2 teaspoon salt
  1/2 to 2/3 cup ice water
6 cups oil for deep-frying

Mix marinade ingredients in a small bowl. Add ground meat; mix well. Let stand about 20 minutes. Cut eggplant in half lengthwise. Cut each half into 3/4-inch slices. Cut each slice in half but not all the way through to make a pocket. Combine coating ingredients in a medium bowl. Mix well to dissolve lumps. Place 2 tablespoons marinated ground meat in an eggplant pocket; press together gently. Repeat with remaining meat mixture and pockets. Heat 6 cups oil in wok over high heat to 350°F (175°C). Reduce heat to medium. Dip each stuffed eggplant piece into coating and carefully lower into hot oil with a slotted metal spoon. Deep-fry several at a time 2 to 3 minutes. Remove from oil with slotted spoon and set aside. Repeat wth remaining pieces. When all have been fried once, turn heat up to high and reheat oil. Deep-fry eggplant pieces again 30 seconds to 1 minute until golden. Remove with a slotted spoon, drain on paper towels and serve hot. Makes 4 to 6 servings.

Celery & Dried Shrimp Salad

Shanghai

Dried hot red peppers may be used if you soak them in boiling water for five minutes before shredding.

1 lb. celery
1/2 to 1 small fresh hot red pepper
2 tablespoons dried shrimp
1 cup hot water
Seasoning sauce:
  1 tablespoon soy sauce
  1 tablespoon rice vinegar or
    white vinegar
  2 teaspoons sugar
  1/2 teaspoon salt
1 tablespoon minced garlic

Cut celery apart, rinse and pull off tough strings. Pound celery with the broad side of a cleaver a few times to release flavor. Shred with a cleaver, page 11. Place in a medium bowl. Shred red pepper, page 11, and mix with celery. Soak dried shrimp in 1 cup hot water 10 to 15 minutes. Drain well; discard water. Chop softened shrimp. Place celery mixture on a platter. Top with chopped shrimp. Mix ingredients for seasoning sauce in a small bowl. Sprinkle garlic and seasoning sauce on top of celery mixture. Mix well before serving. Serve cold. Makes 4 servings.

How to Make Stuffed Eggplant

1/Partially cut through middle of each eggplant slice to make a pocket.

2/Stuff the pocket of each eggplant piece with marinated meat filling.

Shanghai Vegetables

Shanghai

Buy whole bamboo shoots so all the vegetables can be chopped into finger-size pieces.

4 oz. fresh asparagus or green beans, cut 1-inch long
1 fresh carrot, peeled
3 cups boiling water
1 (8-oz.) can whole bamboo shoots, drained

Seasoning sauce:
  1/2 cup water
  1/4 cup chicken broth
  1 teaspoon cornstarch
  1 teaspoon sesame oil
  3 tablespoons milk
  1/4 teaspoon white pepper

6 tablespoons vegetable oil
1-1/2 garlic cloves, crushed
1 (4-oz.) can whole mushrooms, drained
1-1/4 teaspoons salt

Cook asparagus and carrot in 3 cups boiling water 3 minutes. Drain, then plunge cooked vegetables into cold water. Drain well. Chop drained vegetables and bamboo shoots into large matchsticks with a cleaver. Mix ingredients for seasoning sauce in a small bowl; set aside. Heat oil in a wok over high heat 30 seconds. Stir-fry garlic until golden, 30 seconds. Add chopped vegetables, mushrooms and salt. Stir-fry 2 to 3 minutes. Add seasoning sauce. Stir-fry until sauce thickens slightly. Mix well to coat vegetables with sauce. Serve hot. Makes 4 servings.

Snow Peas with Mushrooms & Bamboo Shoots

Shanghai

Blanching before stir-frying makes snow peas crisp and tender.

1/2 lb. fresh snow peas
2 cups water
1/2 teaspoon salt
5 medium dried black mushrooms
1 cup hot water

Seasoning sauce:
   2 tablespoons chicken broth
   1/4 teaspoon sugar
   1 teaspoon salt
   1 tablespoon soy sauce
   1/4 teaspoon cornstarch

6 tablespoons vegetable oil
3 slices fresh ginger root, page 16
1 garlic clove, crushed
1 cup sliced bamboo shoots

Snap off ends and pull off strings from snow peas. Bring 2 cups water to a boil in a small saucepan. Add salt. Blanch snow peas by submerging in salted boiling water 10 seconds; drain and rinse with cold water. Soak mushrooms in 1 cup hot water until soft, 15 to 30 minutes. Drain and remove hard stems. Mix ingredients for seasoning sauce in a small bowl; set aside. Slice softened mushrooms. Heat oil in a wok over high heat 30 seconds. Stir-fry ginger root and garlic 30 seconds. Add sliced mushrooms and bamboo shoots. Stir-fry 1 minute. Add seasoning sauce. Stir-fry 1 minute or until sauce is absorbed. Add blanched snow peas. Stir-fry 10 seconds. Serve hot. Makes 4 servings.

Creamed Chinese Cabbage

Shanghai

Any kind of green cabbage will work in this recipe.

1-1/2 lbs. Chinese cabbage
1 (4-oz.) can sliced mushrooms, drained

Seasoning sauce:
   1/2 cup chicken broth
   2/3 cup water
   5 tablespoons milk
   1 tablespoon cornstarch
   1/2 teaspoon salt

5 tablespoons vegetable oil
1 garlic clove, crushed
1/2 teaspoon salt
1 tablespoon vegetable oil
1/4 teaspoon white pepper

Chop cabbage into 1-1/2-inch squares with a cleaver. Slice mushrooms with cleaver. Combine ingredients for seasoning sauce in a small bowl. Mix well and set aside. Heat 5 tablespoons oil in a wok over high heat 1 minute. Stir-fry garlic until golden, 30 seconds. Add cabbage squares and mushroom slices. Stir-fry about 3 minutes until cabbage is crisp-tender. Add salt. Stir-fry 2 to 3 minutes longer. Remove cabbage mixture with a spatula and set aside. Heat 1 tablespoon oil in wok over high heat 30 seconds. Add seasoning sauce. Stir-fry until creamy. Add white pepper. Mix well and pour sauce over cabbage. Serve hot. Makes 4 servings.

Dry-Cooked Green Beans

Shanghai

Green beans will be wrinkled but tender.

1 lb. short tender green beans
2 tablespoons dried shrimp
1 cup hot water
1 tablespoon pickled mustard greens, rinsed
1/4 cup vegetable oil
2 oz. ground pork
2 teaspoons minced fresh ginger root
1 teaspoon minced garlic
1/2 teaspoon salt
2 tablespoons chopped green onion
1/2 teaspoon sugar
1 tablespoon soy sauce
1/4 cup chicken broth
1/4 cup water

Remove tips and strings from green beans, but do not cut. Soak dried shrimp in 1 cup hot water 10 to 15 minutes. Drain well; discard water. Remove and discard tails. Chop softened shrimp and pickled mustard greens into small pieces. Heat oil in a wok over medium heat 1 minute. Add ground pork, chopped shrimp, ginger root and garlic. Stir-fry 3 minutes. Add whole green beans, salt and green onion. Stir-fry 4 minutes longer. Add sugar, soy sauce, chicken broth and 1/4 cup water. Cover wok and cook 5 minutes over medium heat until green beans are soft. If necessary, add a little more water. When no liquid remains and green beans are wrinkled, stir-fry 1 minute. Serve hot. Makes 4 servings.

Three-Color Vegetable Salad

Shanghai

Chinese turnips, also called daikon, *resemble long horseradishes.*

1-1/2 cups shredded fresh carrot, page 11
1-1/2 cups shredded peeled cucumber, page 11
1-1/2 cups shredded Chinese turnip, page 11
1-1/2 teaspoons salt

Seasoning sauce:
  1/4 cup rice vinegar or white vinegar
  3 tablespoons sugar
  2 teaspoons sesame oil

Hot Chili Sauce, page 143, if desired

Place vegetables in separate small bowls and sprinkle each with 1/2 teaspoon salt. Let stand 2 hours. Rinse vegetables wth cold water and squeeze out excess water. Arrange in layers on a platter: turnip on bottom, cucumber in middle and carrot on top. Combine seasoning sauce ingredients in a small bowl. Pour over vegetables; toss to mix well. Salad can be refrigerated 2 or 3 days. Add a little Hot Chili Sauce before serving, if desired. Makes 4 servings.

Phoenix Tail Salad

Shanghai

Vegetables and hard-boiled eggs are arranged to resemble a phoenix's tail.

6 hard-cooked eggs
1/2 lb. lettuce
1/2 lb. Chinese turnip, shredded,
  page 11
1/2 lb. spinach
2 celery stalks, chopped in
  2-1/2-inch shreds, page 11
1 fresh carrot, shredded, page 11
1 large tomato
Sesame Soy Dip, page 26
Tomato rose for garnish, page 21

Peel eggs and cut lengthwise into 4 or 5 slices. Use a cleaver to chop lettuce into 1-1/2-inch squares. Spread chopped lettuce on one half of a large platter. Carefully arrange egg slices on lettuce. Arrange Chinese turnip on edge of platter around eggs. Chop spinach into 1-1/2-inch squares with cleaver. Spread spinach on empty half of platter. Arrange celery across spinach like a fan. Arrange carrot on spinach across celery following the fan pattern. Slice tomato with a sharp knife and cut each slice in half. Arrange tomato slices on each side of celery and carrot fan. Drizzle salad with Sesame Soy Dip before serving. Garnish with tomato rose. Makes 4 to 6 servings.

Variation

Substitute your favorite salad dressing for Sesame Soy Dip.

Sprinkle 1 tablespoon toasted sesame seeds, see below, over salad.

中國菜

To toast sesame seeds, heat a small saucepan over medium heat 30 seconds to 1 minute. Add sesame seeds and stir-fry until golden brown.

RICE, NOODLES & PASTRIES

飯麵

Warm weather and frequent rains make southern China an ideal climate for growing rice. In the cuisines of the south, rice is considered a staple. The wealthy enhance it with their favorite rich foods and the less fortunate consider it the mainstay of their meals.

Chinese cooks do not throw away leftover rice. They separate the grains with a chopstick and keep the rice covered in a cool place. It will keep in a refrigerator for three to four days. To reheat cold rice, put it in a heatproof bowl and steam it over boiling water for 12 to 15 minutes.

A more interesting use for leftover rice is fried rice. Chopped meat or vegetables are stir-fried in oil. Then cold cooked rice is added and the mixture is stir-fried with seasoning sauce until it's piping hot. Basic Fried Rice is just that—a basic recipe to give you the general idea so you can create your own versions.

Wheat, not rice, is the leading crop in northern China. Noodles are eaten at breakfast, lunch and dinner. They are popular among the poor because they are cheap and can be served in tasty and economical dishes. During the summer in the province of Szechuan, noodles are just as popular served cold as they are hot.

Most pastries originate from Mandarin cuisine because the North is the wheat cradle of China. Mandarin pastries tend to be more doughy and less sweet than other pastries and may even be heavy and seem underdone. If Chinese pastries are new to you, begin with Cantonese pastries which are lighter and sweeter than Mandarin.

To make buns, dough is wrapped around a filling and steamed. The result is a delicious sweet-savory treat. Buns are served with dumplings as *dim sum*, page 22, in tea houses.

Pancakes made from wheat flour are the sandwich breads of northern China. Stir-fried vegetables are rolled inside Mandarin Pancakes. Northern Pancakes are cupped around chopped vegetables. And Peking Lau Ping, like pocket bread, can be stuffed with meat or vegetable mixtures.

Steamed Rice   Photo on page 101.

Wait 15 minutes before removing the lid or steam will escape and the rice won't be cooked.

2 cups long-grain rice
4 cups cold water

Rinse rice in a bowl of water; drain well. Rinse and drain rice again. Repeat 2 or 3 times until water is clear. Combine rice and 4 cups cold water in a 3-quart saucepan with a tight-fitting lid. Bring to a boil. Cook over high heat about 5 minutes until almost all water is absorbed. Reduce heat. Cover and simmer 10 minutes. Remove from heat and let stand covered 15 minutes or longer. Remove cover and fluff rice with a spoon. Serve hot. Makes 6 servings.

Basic Fried Rice

After adding the rice, experiment and stir in your favorite diced cooked meat or vegetable.

2 eggs
1/2 teaspoon salt
5 tablespoons lard or peanut oil
1 cup chopped green onions
4 cups cold cooked rice
2 tablespoons chicken broth
3 tablespoons soy sauce
1/2 teaspoon pepper
2 teaspoons sesame oil

Beat eggs with 1/4 teaspoon salt in a small bowl. Heat 2 tablespoons lard or peanut oil in a wok over medium heat 1 minute. Pour in beaten eggs. Stir continuously until eggs are cooked dry and separated into small pieces. Remove cooked eggs from wok and set aside. Heat 3 tablespoons lard or peanut oil in wok over medium-high heat 1 minute. Add green onions and rice. Stir-fry 5 minutes. Add chicken broth, remaining salt and soy sauce. Stir to mix well. Stir in cooked eggs, pepper and sesame oil. Serve hot. Makes 4 to 6 servings.

Crisp Rice

You'll need these crisp squares to make Sizzling Rice Shrimp, page 64, and Sizzling Rice Soup, page 48.

1-1/2 teaspoons vegetable oil or
  sesame oil
1-1/2 cups cooked sweet rice or
  short-grain rice

Brush oil on the bottom of a large skillet. Spread rice in skillet and press with a spatula so rice covers bottom of skillet. Rice should be an even layer about 1/2 inch deep. Cook over low heat about 5 minutes until bottom of rice layer is crisp and golden brown. Carefully remove from skillet and cut into 2-inch-square pieces. Place an oven thermometer in the oven. Place rice squares on a baking sheet in oven at 120°F (50°C) 12 hours. The pilot light may keep your oven at this temperature or you may have to alternate between the lowest setting and turning off the oven. Rice squares are dry when a piece can be broken off with a crackling sound. Makes nine 2-inch squares.

Chicken Chow Mein

Mandarin

Chow mein means stir-fried noodles.

1/2 lb. skinned, boned chicken breast
Marinade:
   1/2 teaspoon rice wine or dry sherry.
   1/2 teaspoon cornstarch
   1/2 egg white
   1/2 teaspoon salt
   1 tablespoon vegetable oil

8 cups water
8 oz. dry Chinese noodles or
   thin spaghetti
1 tablespoon sesame oil
1/2 cup vegetable oil
1/2 cup shredded bamboo shoots,
   page 11
1 cup fresh bean sprouts or
   1 cup shredded cabbage, page 11
1 cup sliced mushrooms,
   fresh or drained canned
1/2 cup shredded onion, page 11
3 tablespoons chicken broth
1/2 teaspoon salt
3 tablespoons soy sauce
1/8 teaspoon pepper

Shred chicken with a cleaver, page 11. Combine marinade ingredients in a small bowl. Add shredded chicken; mix well. Let stand 30 minutes. Bring water to a boil in a large saucepan. Drop noodles or spaghetti into boiling water. Cook until tender, about 5 minutes. Rinse noodles with cold water. Drain well. Add sesame oil to noodles. Mix well to coat; set aside. Heat 1/4 cup vegetable oil in a wok over medium heat 1 minute. Stir-fry chicken until white, about 3 minutes. Remove chicken with slotted spoon, drain well over wok and set aside. Add 1 tablespoon vegetable oil to wok. Heat 30 seconds over high heat. Add bamboo shoots, bean sprouts or cabbage, mushrooms and onion to wok; stir-fry 3 minutes. Add chicken broth and salt to vegetables. If mixture seems too dry, add several tablespoons chicken broth or water. Remove vegetables from wok; set aside. Reduce heat to medium and add 3 tablespoons oil to wok. Stir-fry cooked noodles 3 or 4 minutes. Add soy sauce, pepper, vegetables and chicken to wok. Stir-fry 2 minutes longer, mixing well. Makes 4 to 6 servings.

Northern-Style Pancakes

Mandarin

Onion-flavored pancakes are delicious with stir-fried dishes.

1-1/2 cups all-purpose flour
1/2 teaspoon salt
1 egg
1-2/3 cups cold water
1/4 cup chopped green onion
3 tablespoons vegetable oil

Mix flour and salt in a large bowl. Add egg and half the cold water. Stir with a large spoon in one direction 2 minutes. Add remaining water and stir until lumps are dissolved. Add green onion; mix well. Heat a 10-inch skillet over medium heat 1 minute. Add 1-1/2 teaspoons oil. Heat 30 seconds. Pour about 1/6 of the batter into skillet, tilting so bottom of skillet is evenly covered. Cook 1 minute or until speckled with brown and edges are dry. Carefully turn pancake with a spatula and cook about 30 seconds until speckled with brown. Fold pancake in half, then in half again to keep warm. Place on a plate and serve immediately. Repeat with remaining dough and oil. Makes 6 pancakes.

Mandarin Pancakes   Photo on pages 72 and 73.

Mandarin

Cooking two pancakes back-to-back makes the pancakes thinner and the cooking time shorter.

1-1/2 cups all-purpose flour
1/2 teaspoon sesame oil
1/4 teaspoon salt
3/4 cup boiling water
About 1 tablespoon sesame oil

Place flour, 1/2 teaspoon sesame oil and salt in a medium bowl. Add 3/4 cup boiling water. Gradually mix flour and water with a wooden spoon to make a soft dough. On a lightly floured surface, gently knead dough until smooth. Cover with a damp cloth and let rest 15 minutes. Use your hands to shape dough into a long roll about 1 inch in diameter. Add more flour if necessary. Place the point of a sharp cleaver on cutting surface with middle of roll under cutting edge. Chop with a quick downward motion, cutting roll in half. Chop each half into 8 equal pieces. Roll each piece into a ball, then pat flat to make a circle. Brush top of 8 circles with sesame oil. Place an unoiled circle on top of each oiled circle. Use a rolling pin to flatten each pair of circles into one 5-inch circle. Roll both sides, changing directions frequently so flat pancake remains a circle. Cover pancakes with a dry towel. Heat an ungreased 8-inch skillet over high heat 30 seconds to 1 minute. Reduce heat to medium. Place 1 pancake in skillet. When pancake puffs and bubbles appear on the surface, turn and cook other side. Cook about 1 minute on one side until pancake is speckled with brown. Turn pancake and cook about 30 seconds until underside is speckled with brown. Remove from skillet, wrap in a clean, dry towel and place in a bread basket. Just before serving, separate each pancake into 2 pancakes, gently pulling apart from edges. Serve warm. Makes 16 pancakes.

How to Make Mandarin Pancakes

1/Brush sesame oil on 1 dough circle. Place another circle on top. Roll out together to one 5-inch circle.

2/To serve, separate each cooked pancake at edges and gently pull apart to make 2 pancakes.

Steamed Flower Buns

Mandarin

Deep-frying chopped shallots or green onions makes them very crisp.

Sweet Bun Dough or
  Mandarin Bun Dough, page 160
1 cup vegetable oil
1/4 cup chopped unpeeled shallots or
  green onions
3 tablespoons shortening or lard
1-1/2 teaspoons salt
About 6 cups boiling water

Prepare dough. Roll out to a thin 24" x 12" rectangle. Heat 1 cup oil in a wok over high heat 1 minute. Deep-fry shallots or green onions about 2 minutes until golden brown. Remove wok from heat then remove shallots or green onions from oil with a slotted spoon, draining well over wok; set aside. Spread shortening or lard evenly over dough to cover rectangle completely. Sprinkle with salt and browned shallots or green onions. Starting at a long side, roll up into a long roll. Place the point of a sharp cleaver on cutting surface with roll under cutting edge. Chop with a quick downward motion, making twelve 2-inch pieces. Press the middle of each piece with a chopstick so the ends curl up and each piece resembles a flower. Cover with a cloth and let rise 30 minutes in a warm place. Pour 4 cups boiling water into a wok or large pot. Arrange as many buns on a damp cloth in a steamer as will fit, leaving 1 inch between buns. Cover and place over boiling water. Steam over high heat 15 minutes, adding more boiling water as needed. Remove wok from heat. Let stand 5 minutes. Remove cover slowly as a quick cold draft may cause buns to collapse. Repeat with remaining buns. Serve hot. Makes 12 rolls.

Yu T'iau

Mandarin

Drugstores and Chinese food stores usually sell alum which makes a more elastic dough.

2 cups warm water
1 pkg. active dry yeast
1-1/2 teaspoons alum
2 teaspoons baking soda
2 teaspoons salt
4 cups bread flour
1/2 teaspoon vegetable oil
6 cups oil for deep-frying

Mix 2 cups warm water, yeast, alum, baking soda and salt in a large bowl. Add flour and mix well. Knead dough 3 to 5 minutes. Wet hands and knead 5 more minutes. Cover with a damp cloth and let stand 30 minutes. Punch down dough and knead 3 to 5 minutes. Let stand another 30 minutes. Knead dough again and shape into a long rectangle 3 inches wide. Rub surface with 1/2 teaspoon oil to prevent drying. Wrap loosely in waxed paper and let rise 4 hours in a warm place. Place dough on a floured surface. Heat 6 cups oil in a wok over high heat to 350°F (175°C). While oil is heating, stretch dough until it is 1/2 inch thick, keeping it 3 inches wide. Use a sharp knife to cut into 3" x 1" strips. Place 1 strip of dough on top of another. Press lengthwise with a chopstick to make a long indentation down the middle. Holding each end of the strip, twist once or twice, pulling each end until the twisted strip is 6 to 8 inches long. Carefully lower a twisted strip into hot oil. Fry 3 or 4 at a time until golden brown, turning continuously with long chopsticks or a long-handle spatula or spoon. Use chopsticks or spoon to remove yu t'iau from wok. Drain on paper towels. Makes 4 to 6 servings.

How to Make Steamed Flower Buns

1/Chop roll of dough into 2-inch pieces with a quick downward motion of the cleaver.

2/Press a chopstick or skewer along the middle of each piece of dough to make a flower shape.

Peking Lau Ping

Mandarin

Cut them in half and open as you would pocket bread. Then stuff them with stir-fried beef or pork dishes.

3 cups all-purpose flour
1 cup plus 3 tablespoons cold water
4 teaspoons lard or sesame oil
1/2 teaspoon salt

Sift flour into a large bowl. Make a well in the center and slowly add 1 cup cold water. Mix thoroughly with a spoon. Place dough on a floured surface and knead 3 minutes until smooth and soft. Return dough to bowl and cover with a damp cloth towel. Let rest 30 minutes in a warm place. Use a rolling pin to roll out half the dough to a circle about 16 inches in diameter and 1-1/16 inch thick. Brush 1 tablespoon lard or sesame oil on circle and sprinkle with 1/4 teaspoon salt. Roll up like a jelly roll and cut in half. Fold one end of each half over the opposite end to form a ball. Flatten with your palm and roll out each to a 7-inch circle. Repeat with remaining dough to make 4 lau ping. Heat an 8-inch skillet over medium heat 30 seconds to 1 minute. Place 1 lau ping in skillet. Cover and cook about 1 minute or until lau ping starts to puff. Turn with spatula or fingers, lightly tossing lau ping back into skillet and cooking 20 seconds. Repeat tossing and cooking 4 to 6 times until speckled with brown on both sides. Lau ping should be crisp outside with several soft layers inside. Repeat with remaining lau ping. Makes 4 servings.

Pork & Vegetable Buns   Photo on page 29.

Mandarin

Use two 12-ounce cans refrigerated buttermilk biscuit dough if you don't have time to make the bun dough.

Sweet Bun Dough or
  Mandarin Bun Dough, page 160
1/3 lb. Chinese cabbage
1/4 teaspoon salt
1 lb. ground pork
1 teaspoon minced fresh ginger root
1/4 teaspoon sugar
1/3 cup soy sauce
1/4 teaspoon pepper
2 tablespoons sesame oil
1 teaspoon cornstarch
1 cup chopped green onions
About 8 cups boiling water

Prepare dough. Chop cabbage into 1/8-inch pieces. Place chopped cabbage in a large bowl with salt. Let stand 5 minutes. Squeeze out excess liquid. Add ground pork, ginger root, sugar, soy sauce, pepper, sesame oil, cornstarch and green onions. Mix well. On a floured surface, use your hands to shape dough into a long roll 2 inches in diameter. Place the point of a sharp cleaver on cutting surface with middle of roll under cutting edge. Chop with a quick downward motion, cutting roll in half. Chop each half into 9 or 10 equal pieces. Roll each piece into a ball, then pat flat. Use a rolling pin to roll out each piece to a 4-inch circle, rolling from edges inward and making edges slightly thinner than centers. Cup a circle of dough in the palm of your hand. Place about 1-1/2 tablespoons of pork and vegetable filling in the center. Pleat edges of circle, lift sides over filling and twist together at the top. Repeat with remaining dough and filling. Arrange as many buns on a damp cloth in a steamer as will fit, leaving 1 inch between buns. Let stand about 30 minutes to rise. Pour 4 cups boiling water into a wok or large pot. Cover steamer and place over boiling water. Steam over high heat about 20 minutes, adding more boiling water as needed. Remove wok from heat. Let stand 5 minutes. Remove cover slowly as a quick cold draft may cause buns to collapse. Repeat with remaining buns. Serve hot. Makes 24 buns.

中國菜

After a wok with steamed buns has cooled slightly, lift the lid slowly to release steam a little at a time. Buns will be soggy if they are exposed to cold air all at once.

How to Make Pork & Vegetable Buns

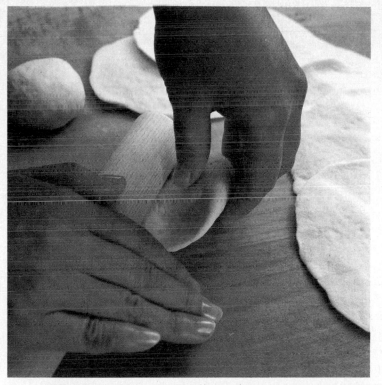

1/To make centers thicker than edges, roll out each ball of dough toward the center from the edges.

2/Place filling in center of circle. Pleat edges of circle and twist at top to seal.

Sweet Bean Buns

Mandarin

To reheat these buns for tomorrow's breakfast, steam them for five to ten minutes.

**Sweet Bun Dough or
   Mandarin Bun Dough, page 160**
1 (16-oz.) can red bean paste
About 8 cups boiling water

Prepare dough. On a floured surface, use your hands to shape dough into a long roll about 1-1/2 inches in diameter. Chop roll in half with a cleaver. Chop each half into 9 or 10 equal pieces. Roll each piece into a small ball, then pat flat. Use a rolling pin to roll out each piece to a 4-inch circle about 1/4 inch thick, rolling from edges inward and making edges slightly thinner than centers. Cup a circle of dough in the palm of your hand. Place about 1-1/2 teaspoons red bean paste in the center. Pleat edges of circle, lift sides up over filling and twist together at the top to seal. Gently shape each bun into a ball. Arrange as many buns twist-side up on a damp cloth in a steamer as will fit, leaving 1 inch between buns. Let stand 30 minutes to rise. Pour 4 cups boiling water into a wok or large pot. Cover steamer and place over boiling water. Steam over high heat 20 minutes, adding more boiling water as needed. Remove wok from heat. Let stand 5 minutes. Remove cover slowly as a quick cold draft may cause buns to collapse. Repeat with remaining buns. Serve hot. Makes 20 buns.

Variation

Sweet black bean paste or lotus paste may be used for the filling.

Shrimp Chow Mein

Cantonese

Although the variations call for different ingredients, the cooking methods remain the same.

1/2 lb. fresh shrimp

Marinade:
  1 teaspoon rice wine or dry sherry
  1/2 teaspoon salt
  1 egg white
  1 teaspoon cornstarch

6 dried black mushrooms
3 cups hot water

Seasoning sauce:
  3 cups water
  1/2 teaspoon salt
  1/2 teaspoon sugar
  2 tablespoons soy sauce
  1/4 teaspoon pepper

3 qts. water (12 cups)
1 teaspoon salt
1 teaspoon vegetable oil
1 lb. Chinese egg noodles
6 cups oil for deep-frying
1 tablespoon vegetable oil
3 green onions,
  chopped in 1-inch pieces
5 slices fresh ginger root, page 16
2/3 cup shredded bamboo shoots,
  page 11
1/2 cup shredded carrot, page 11
1 tablespoon cornstarch
2 tablespoons water
1/3 lb. fresh spinach, chopped

Shell and devein shrimp, page 59. Rinse and pat dry with a paper towel. Combine marinade ingredients in a medium bowl. Add shrimp; mix well. Let stand 15 minutes. Soak dried mushrooms in 3 cups hot water until soft, 15 to 30 minutes. Drain and remove hard stems. Shred softened mushrooms with a cleaver, page 11. Combine ingredients for seasoning sauce in a small bowl. Mix well and set aside. Bring 3 quarts water to a rapid boil in a 5-quart pot. Add salt, 1 teaspoon vegetable oil and noodles. Cook until noodles are tender; drain. Heat 6 cups oil in a wok over high heat to 350°F (175°C). Reduce heat to medium. Place half the cooked noodles in a large strainer with a long handle. Submerge noodles and strainer in hot oil and deep-fry about 1 minute until noodles are golden brown. Remove from oil, draining well over wok. Place fried noodles on a large platter. Repeat with remaining noodles. Heat 1 tablespoon vegetable oil in a large saucepan over medium heat 30 seconds to 1 minute. Stir-fry green onions and ginger root about 1 minute until fragrant. Add shredded mushrooms, bamboo shoots and carrot. Stir-fry 1 minute. Add seasoning sauce. Bring to a boil. Dissolve cornstarch in 2 tablespoons water to make a paste. Add spinach, marinated shrimp and cornstarch paste to mixture in saucepan. Stir until sauce thickens slightly. Spoon over deep-fried noodles. Serve hot. Makes 4 servings.

Variations

Pork Chow Mein: Omit dried black mushrooms and 3 cups hot water. Substitute 1/2 lb. shredded pork butt, page 11, for the shrimp. Stir-fry pork in 3 tablespoons oil before cooking vegetables. Substitute 1/3 cup fresh bean sprouts for the shredded bamboo shoots.

Chicken Chow Mein: Omit dried black mushrooms and 3 cups hot water. Substitute 1/2 lb. shredded chicken breast, page 11, for the shrimp. Stir-fry shredded chicken in 3 tablespoons oil before cooking vegetables. Substitute 1/3 cup fresh bean sprouts for the bamboo shoots.

Beef Chow Mein: Omit dried black mushrooms and 3 cups hot water. Substitute 1/2 lb. shredded flank steak, page 11, for the shrimp. Stir-fry beef in 3 tablespoons oil before cooking vegetables. Substitute 1/3 cup fresh bean sprouts for the bamboo shoots.

Vegetable Chow Mein: Omit fresh shrimp and marinade. Soak 1/4 cup dried shrimp in 2 cups hot water 10 to 15 minutes; drain well. Add shrimp to sauce with spinach. Use only 4 dried black mushrooms.

Barbecued Pork Buns

Cantonese

A delectable dim sum treat!

Sweet Bun Dough, page 160
1/2 Barbecued Pork recipe, page 35
4-1/2 teaspoons soy sauce
1-1/2 teaspoons sugar
1 cup water
4-1/2 teaspoons oyster sauce,
   if desired
2 tablespoons cornstarch
2 tablespoons water
1/4 cup chicken broth
2 tablespoons pork fat, lard or
   vegetable oil
2 teaspoons sesame oil
1/4 teaspoon pepper
About 8 cups boiling water

Prepare dough. Dice Barbecued Pork into 1/2-inch cubes. Combine soy sauce, sugar, 1 cup water and oyster sauce, if desired, in a small saucepan. Bring to a boil over medium heat. If using pork fat, cut into 1/4-inch dice. Dissolve cornstarch in 2 tablespoons water. Add to soy sauce mixture with chicken broth. When mixture thickens slightly, add pork fat, lard or vegetable oil, sesame oil and pepper; mix well. Let cool 5 minutes. Add pork cubes; mix well. On a floured surface, use your hands to shape dough into a long roll about 2 inches in diameter. Place the point of a sharp cleaver on cutting surface with middle of roll under cutting edge. Chop with a quick downward motion, cutting roll in half. Chop each half into 8 to 10 equal pieces. Roll each piece into a small ball, then pat flat. Use a rolling pin to roll out each piece to a 4-inch circle, rolling from edges inward and making edges slightly thinner than centers. Cup a circle of dough in the palm of your hand. Place about 1-1/2 tablespoons pork filling in the center. Pleat edges of circle, lift sides over filling and twist together at the top, page 157. Repeat with remaining dough and filling. Let buns stand about 30 minutes to rise. Pour 4 cups boiling water into a wok or large pot. Fold a damp cloth 2 or 3 times. Place in the bottom of a steamer. Arrange as many buns on cloth as will fit, leaving about 1 inch between buns. Cover steamer and place over boiling water. Steam 20 minutes over high heat, adding more boiling water as needed. Remove wok from heat. Let stand 5 minutes. Remove cover slowly as a quick cold draft may cause buns to collapse. Repeat with remaining buns. Makes about 20 buns.

Sweet Soy Sauce

Delicious with steamed buns and deep-fried appetizers!

1 cup soy sauce
1/2 cup sugar
1/2 teaspoon ground cinnamon
1 star anise

Combine soy sauce, sugar, cinnamon and star anise in a small saucepan; mix well. Cook over low heat 30 minutes, stirring occasionally. Remove and discard star anise. Set sauce aside to cool. Pour cooled sauce into a sterilized jar with a tight-fitting lid. Sauce may be refrigerated about 6 months. Makes about 1 cup.

Sweet Bun Dough

Cantonese

If you've never sampled Chinese pastries before, begin with this sweet tasty dough.

1/4 cup sugar
1-1/3 cups warm water
1 pkg. active dry yeast
4 cups all-purpose flour
1 teaspoon shortening

Mix sugar and warm water in a small bowl. Sprinkle yeast over sugar water. Stir to dissolve. Place flour in a large bowl. Make a well in the center. Slowly pour in yeast mixture. Add shortening. Mix thoroughly with a wooden spoon. Turn out onto a floured surface. Knead about 5 minutes until dough is smooth and elastic. Dough will be firm. Place in a large bowl and cover with a damp cloth and a lid. Let rise in a warm place about 3 hours until doubled in bulk. Turn out onto a floured surface. Cover with a cloth and let stand 3 to 5 minutes. Dough is ready to use. Makes enough dough for 20 to 24 buns.

Variation

Mandarin Bun Dough: Decrease sugar to 2 tablespoons.

Szechuan Noodles

Szechuan

Hot bean sauce, a typical Szechuan seasoning, gives these noodles a special flavor.

Seasoning sauce:
  1/2 (4-oz.) can hot bean sauce
  1/2 (4-oz.) can red bean paste
  1 tablespoon rice wine or dry sherry
  2 teaspoons sugar
  1/4 cup soy sauce
  1 tablespoon sesame oil

5 tablespoons vegetable oil
2/3 lb. ground pork or ground beef
2 cups chopped green onions
3 qts. water (12 cups)
1 lb. fresh noodles or
  1/2 lb. dry egg noodles
2 cups shredded cooked carrots,
  page 11
2 cups sliced or shredded
  peeled cucumber, page 11
2 cups fresh bean sprouts
4 garlic cloves, minced

Combine ingredients for seasoning sauce in a small bowl. Mix until smooth. Heat 5 tablespoons oil in a wok over medium-high heat 1 minute. Stir-fry ground meat about 5 minutes until browned. Add green onions and seasoning sauce. Stir-fry until sauce comes to a boil. Carefully pour into a large bowl; set aside. Bring 3 quarts water to a boil in a heavy 5-quart pot. Add noodles. Cook until tender; drain. Divide noodles into 6 portions in 6 small bowls. Spoon meat sauce on top of noodles. Garnish with carrots, cucumber and bean sprouts. Sprinkle with minced garlic. Toss lightly and serve. Makes 6 servings.

Cold Noodles with Hot Sauce

Szechuan

Roasted peanuts and sesame oil add a nutty flavor to cold noodles.

3 qts. water (12 cups)
1 lb. fresh noodles or
  1/2 lb. dry noodles
1/2 cup cold water
6 cups ice water
2 tablespoons sesame oil
2 cups fresh bean sprouts
4 cups boiling water
Cold water

Seasoning sauce:
  2 tablespoons sesame seed paste
  6 tablespoons soy sauce
  1 tablespoon vegetable oil
  3 tablespoons sesame oil
  1 tablespoon rice vinegar or
    white vinegar
  1 teaspoon sugar
  3 tablespoons chopped green onion
  2 teaspoons minced fresh ginger root
  2 teaspoons minced garlic
  1 tablespoon Chili Oil, page 85
  2 teaspoons Peppersalt, page 88

2 cups shredded peeled cucumber,
  page 11
1 cup shredded, cooked chicken breast,
  page 11
1 tablespoon chopped roasted peanuts

Bring 3 quarts water to a rapid boil in a heavy 5-quart pot. Add noodles and bring to a second boil over high heat. Add 1/2 cup cold water, reduce heat to medium and cook noodles until tender. Drain. Soak cooked noodles in 6 cups ice water 30 seconds; drain. Add sesame oil and mix thoroughly to coat noodles. Cover and refrigerate. Submerge bean sprouts in 4 cups boiling water 10 seconds. Remove and plunge into a large bowl of cold water. Drain, let cool and squeeze out excess water. Place bean sprouts and cold noodles on a large platter. Mix ingredients for seasoning sauce in a small bowl. Spoon over cold noodles. Place shredded cucumber around edges of platter. Sprinkle with shredded chicken and peanuts. Mix just before serving. Serve cold. Makes 6 servings.

中國菜

To chop nuts, place them between paper towels on a cutting board and crush them with the flat side of a cleaver. After that, they'll need only brief chopping with the cleaver's sharp edge.

Tossed Noodles   Photo on page 87.

Szechuan

Egg noodles are deliciously different when tossed with shredded vegetables, pork and a sweet seasoning sauce.

1/2 lb. pork tenderloin

Marinade:
  1 teaspoon rice wine or dry sherry
  1 tablespoon water
  2 teaspoons cornstarch

Seasoning sauce:
  1/4 cup red bean paste
  1 tablespoon sesame oil
  2 tablespoons sugar
  1/4 cup soy sauce
  1 teaspoon rice wine or dry sherry

1 cup vegetable oil
1 large onion, diced
4 garlic cloves, crushed
3 qts. water (12 cups)
2 cups fresh bean sprouts
Cold water
1 teaspoon salt
1 teaspoon vegetable oil
1 lb. fresh noodles or
  1/2 lb. dry noodles
2 cups shredded cooked carrots,
  page 11
2 cups shredded peeled cucumber,
  page 11

Chop pork with a cleaver into 1/2-inch cubes. Combine marinade ingredients in a small bowl; mix well. Add pork cubes. Let stand 20 minutes. Combine ingredients for seasoning sauce in a small bowl; mix until smooth. Heat 1 cup oil in a wok over medium heat 1 minute. Stir-fry marinated pork 2 minutes until very lightly browned. Remove pork with a slotted spoon, draining well over wok; set aside. Remove oil from wok except 6 tablespoons. Heat oil in wok over medium heat 30 seconds. Stir-fry onion until tender. Add seasoning sauce and bring to a boil. Add pork and garlic. Stir-fry to mix well. Remove and place in a large bowl. Bring 3 quarts water to a rapid boil in a heavy 5-quart pot. To blanch bean sprouts, place in a strainer and submerge in the boiling water 5 seconds, then plunge strainer with sprouts into cold water, remove and drain well. Add 1 teaspoon salt and 1 teaspoon vegetable oil to the boiling water. Add noodles; cook until tender. Drain. Divide noodles into 6 portions and place in 6 small bowls. Spoon pork and sauce on top. Garnish with carrots, cucumber and blanched bean sprouts. Toss lightly before eating. Makes 6 servings.

웃웃웃웃웃 中國菜 웃웃웃웃웃웃웃웃웃웃웃웃웃웃웃웃웃웃웃웃웃웃웃웃웃웃웃웃웃웃웃웃웃웃웃웃웃웃

Sesame seeds brown quickly and burn easily. Watch them carefully while they are being toasted.

Sesame Seed Buns

Shanghai

Although two doughs are needed, canned biscuit dough is used for one.

1/4 cup chopped green onions
4 slices bacon, choppped
1/4 teaspoon pepper
1/4 teaspoon sugar
1 teaspoon soy sauce
1/4 cup lard or shortening
1 cup all-purpose flour
1 (8-oz.) can refrigerated biscuit dough
1 egg yolk
1/4 cup sesame seeds

Cut ten 1-1/2-inch squares of waxed paper; set aside. Heat a small skillet over medium-low heat 30 seconds to 1 minute. Stir-fry green onions and bacon until bacon is golden brown. Add pepper, sugar and soy sauce; mix well. Remove from heat and set aside. Melt lard or shortening. Combine flour and hot melted lard or shortening in a medium bowl. Mix thoroughly. Dough will be moist and sticky. Divide dough into 10 equal balls. Separate canned biscuit dough into 10 equal pieces. Place 1 dough ball in the center of each piece of biscuit dough. Wrap edges around ball. Flatten with the palm of your hand. Roll out each biscuit to a 3-1/2" x 2-1/2" rectangle 1/4 inch thick. Roll up jelly-roll fashion, stopping halfway. Spread 2/3 teaspoon bacon mixture on unrolled section and continue rolling. Use a rolling pin to roll out to a 4" x 2" rectangle. Brush egg yolk on top and dip coated top in sesame seeds. Repeat with remaining buns. Preheat oven to 375°F (190°C). Place buns on waxed paper on a baking sheet and bake about 15 minutes until golden brown. Serve hot. Makes 10 buns.

Green Onion Pancakes

Shanghai

Popular pan-fried bread is sold by street vendors in Peking.

4 cups all-purpose flour
1 cup boiling water
2/3 to 1 cup cold water
1/4 cup minced pork fat
2 teaspoons salt
1 cup minced green onions
1 cup vegetable oil
2 tablespoons soy sauce

Place flour in a large bowl. Pour 1 cup boiling water over flour and immediately stir with chopsticks or a wooden spoon to mix well. Let flour mixture stand 2 minutes. Add 2/3 cup cold water. Knead dough about 5 minutes until smooth; add more water if needed. Cover with a damp cloth and let stand 15 minutes. Turn out onto a lightly floured surface. Divide dough into 8 equal pieces. Use your hands to roll each piece into a ball. Use a rolling pin to roll out each ball to a 10-inch circle. Spread 1-1/2 teaspoons pork fat on each circle, then sprinkle with 1/4 teaspoon salt and 2 tablespoons green onions. Roll up each circle like a jelly roll, then coil like a snail. Press coil flat with the palm of your hand. Use a rolling pin to roll out about 1/4 inch thick. Heat a medium skillet over medium heat. Add 2 tablespoons oil. Fry 1 pancake about 2 minutes; turn and fry other side 1 to 2 minutes, adding more oil if necessary and jiggling skillet so pancake doesn't stick and crust is flaky. When both sides are crisp and golden, remove from skillet and keep warm. Repeat with remaining pancakes and oil. Serve pancakes hot with soy sauce as a dipping sauce. Makes 8 pancakes.

Yangchou Fried Rice

Shanghai

Combining shrimp and Chinese sausage, or la ch'ang, *sets this fried rice apart.*

1/2 cup small fresh shrimp
2 eggs
1/4 teaspoon salt
6 tablespoons vegetable oil
1 cup frozen mixed peas and carrots
1 cup boiling water
1/2 teaspoon salt
1 garlic clove, crushed
2 Chinese sausages, if desired,
　diced in 1/16-inch cubes or
　sliced diagonally
4 cups cold cooked rice
2 tablespoons minced green onion
2 tablespoons soy sauce
2 tablespoons chicken broth,
　if desired, for flavor

Shell and devein shrimp, page 59. Rinse and pat dry with a paper towel; set aside. Beat eggs slightly with 1/4 teaspoon salt in a small bowl. Heat 2 tablespoons oil in a wok over medium heat 1 minute. Rotate wok to coat sides with oil. Pour in beaten eggs. Slowly rotate wok several times to spread eggs thinly over surface. When eggs are lightly browned on bottom, turn with a spatula and cook other side. Remove from wok. Chop cooked eggs with a cleaver in 1/2-inch square pieces or shred into strips and set aside. Put frozen peas and carrots in a saucepan with 1 cup boiling water and 1/2 teaspoon salt. Cook 5 minutes; drain. Heat 2 tablespoons oil in wok over high heat 30 seconds. Stir-fry garlic until golden, 30 seconds. Add sausages and shrimp. Stir-fry 5 minutes. Add cooked peas and carrots; mix well. Remove mixture from wok. Reduce heat to medium. Add 2 tablespoons oil and heat 30 seconds. Break up any lumps in cooked rice. Add rice to oil in wok. Stir-fry 3 to 4 minutes. Add soy sauce and chicken broth, if desired. Stir-fry 2 minutes. Add cooked vegetable mixture, chopped eggs and green onions. Stir-fry until thoroughly heated, about 3 minutes. Serve hot. Makes 4 to 6 servings.

Variation

Substitute 1/2 cup frozen green beans and 1/2 cup thinly sliced carrots for the mixed peas and carrots.

Crush garlic cloves on a flat surface with the flat side of a cleaver or large knife.

Yangchou Fried Rice

EGGS & BEAN CURD

Picturesque street vendors carry large buckets suspended from bamboo poles balanced on their shoulders. These buckets contain Tea Eggs being kept warm until a hungry customer approaches the vendor. Eggs are hard-cooked, left in the shell and soaked in black tea. The shells absorb the color of the tea and when an egg is peeled, it resembles brown marble.

Eggs are an important source of protein in China. In addition to being eaten as snacks, they are served as main dishes such as Shrimp Egg Fu Yung and Minced Pork Omelet.

With China's large population and short meat supply, soybeans are indispensable. They are a source of protein and are plentiful and inexpensive. Soybeans grow best in northern China, particularly Manchuria, but they are also cultivated farther south.

Soybean milk is more digestible than cow's milk and, in many cultures, is often used as a milk substitute for infants. When sugar and almonds are added and the soybean milk is heated, it provides a delightful snack—especially when served with Yu T'iau, page 154, or Sesame Seed Buns, page 163.

Bean curd is made from soybean milk. The Chinese call it *dofu;* the Japanese call it *tofu.* Bean curd has a smooth creamy texture. Because it is very bland, it easily absorbs the flavor of seasoning sauces and can be used in a variety of dishes. Ma Po's Bean Curd is a spicy Szechuan dish. Peking-Style Bean Curd is flavored with ginger, sesame oil and green onions.

You can buy bean curd in some health food stores and most Oriental markets. It is sold in 3-inch square cakes. For most recipes, allow about one cake for each serving. Fresh bean curd spoils easily, so use it within two or three days. Store it in a container of water in the refrigerator and change the water daily. Bean curd is a very inexpensive protein source and is quite easy to make. See Bean Curd, page 169.

Shredded Egg Balls

Mandarin

Pork and shrimp balls are rolled in shredded egg, then steamed and garnished with a ring of spinach.

2 oz. fresh shrimp
2 dried black mushrooms
1 cup hot water
4 oz. ground pork
Marinade:
  1/2 teaspoon salt
  1/4 teaspoon sugar
  1/4 teaspoon pepper
  1 teaspoon sesame oil
  1 teaspoon cornstarch
  1 tablespoon water
  1/2 teaspoon rice wine or dry sherry

3 eggs
3 tablespoons vegetable oil
About 6 cups boiling water
1/3 lb. fresh spinach
1/2 teaspoon salt

Shell and devein shrimp, page 59. Rinse and pat dry with a paper towel. Mince with a cleaver. Soak dried black mushrooms in 1 cup hot water until soft, 15 to 30 minutes. Drain and remove hard stems. Mince softened mushrooms with a cleaver. Combine marinade ingredients in a small bowl. Add chopped shrimp, chopped mushrooms and ground pork; mix well. Divide pork mixture into 12 pieces and roll each piece into a ball; set aside. Beat eggs well. Brush an 8-inch skillet with 1 teaspoon oil. Heat over medium heat 30 seconds to 1 minute. Pour half the beaten eggs into oiled skillet. Rotate skillet to spread eggs thinly over bottom. When egg is almost set, turn carefully with a spatula and lightly cook other side. Place on a cutting board and shred with cleaver, page 11. Repeat with 1 teaspoon oil and remaining beaten eggs. Roll pork balls in shredded egg to coat. Place in a deep baking dish. Cover baking dish. Pour 4 cups boiling water into a wok or large pot. Place baking dish in steamer or on a rack over boiling water. Steam over high heat 12 minutes, adding more boiling water as needed. Remove wok from heat. Let cool slightly. Heat 1 tablespoon oil in a small saucepan. Combine ingredients for seasoning sauce in a small bowl; mix well. Add to oil in saucepan. Cook until sauce thickens slightly. Remove cooked egg balls from baking dish and place on a small platter. Pour seasoning sauce over egg balls. Chop spinach into 2-inch lengths. Heat 4 teaspoons oil in a large skillet over medium heat 30 seconds to 1 minute. Add salt and spinach. Stir-fry until spinach is limp. Arrange spinach in a ring around egg balls and serve. Makes 4 servings.

Steamed Eggs

Mandarin

If you don't have dried black mushrooms, use 8 fresh mushrooms but don't soak them.

2 tablespoons dried shrimp
3 dried black mushrooms
2-1/2 cups hot water
4-1/2 teaspoons vegetable oil
1/2 teaspoon minced fresh ginger root
2 oz. ground pork
2 tablespoons shredded green onion,
  page 11
1 tablespoon soy sauce
1-1/2 cups water
1-1/4 teaspoons salt
5 eggs
About 6 cups boiling water

Soak dried shrimp and dried black mushrooms in 3 cups hot water until soft, 15 to 30 minutes. Drain well; discard water. Remove hard stems from softened mushrooms. Shred mushrooms with a cleaver, page 11. Chop shrimp with a cleaver. Heat oil in a medium skillet 30 seconds to 1 minute. Stir-fry ginger root, chopped shrimp and ground pork 2 minutes until pork is very lightly browned. Add green onion, shredded mushrooms, soy sauce, 2-1/2 cups water and salt. Stir-fry until water boils. Remove skillet from heat and let sauce cool. Grease a large deep baking dish. Beat eggs in a small bowl. Add cooled sauce; mix well. Pour egg mixture into prepared baking dish; cover. Pour 4 cups boiling water into a wok or large pot. Place bowl in a steamer or on a steamer rack over boiling water. Steam over high heat 15 to 20 minutes until eggs are set, adding more boiling water as needed. Remove wok from heat. Let cool slightly before removing eggs. Serve eggs hot. Makes 4 servings.

Scrambled Eggs with Beef

Mandarin

Eggs are easy to scramble in a wok. Try them for brunch this Sunday.

1/3 lb. beef flank steak or
other tender beef

Marinade:
2 teaspoons rice wine or dry sherry
1/4 teaspoon minced ginger root
1/4 teaspoon sugar
1 tablespoon cornstarch
1 tablespoon soy sauce
1 tablespoon vegetable oil or
sesame oil
1/4 teaspoon baking soda

5 eggs
1/2 teaspoon salt
1 cup vegetable oil
2 tablespoons shredded green onion,
page 11

Use a cleaver to cut beef across grain into thin strips. Combine marinade ingredients in a small bowl. Add beef strips; mix well. Let stand 20 minutes. Beat eggs until frothy. Stir in salt. Heat oil in a wok over high heat 1 minute. Stir-fry marinated beef strips until browned. Remove from oil with a slotted spoon, draining well over wok. Mix with beaten eggs. Remove oil from wok except 5 tablespoons. Reduce heat to medium. Stir-fry green onion shreds 10 seconds. Pour egg mixture into wok and stir-fry until cooked as desired. Remove from wok and serve hot. Makes 4 servings.

Cold Bean Curd with Dried Shrimp

Mandarin

This simple cold dish is packed with protein—perfect for lunch on a hot summer day.

4 (3-inch) squares Bean Curd,
see opposite page
3 cups boiling water
1 tablespoon chopped dried shrimp
1/2 cup hot water

Seasoning sauce:
3 tablespoons chopped green onion
2 tablespoons soy sauce
1/2 teaspoon sugar
1/2 teaspoon salt
1 tablespoon oyster sauce
1 tablespoon sesame oil
1/4 teaspoon pepper

Place bean curd in a large bowl. Add 3 cups boiling water and let stand 10 minutes. Soak dried shrimp in 1/2 cup hot water 5 minutes. Drain well; discard water. Combine ingredients for seasoning sauce in a small bowl. Add softened shrimp; mix well. Drain bean curd and pat dry with a paper towel. Arrange bean curd on a small platter. Spoon seasoning sauce over bean curd. Mix well. Serve at room temperature or cold. Makes 4 servings.

Bean Curd

Mandarin

To make a very smooth and tender bean curd, use gypsum which is available in most Oriental food stores.

2 cups soybeans
6 cups water for soaking
11 cups water
1/4 cup white vinegar or
    1-1/2 teaspoons gypsum
2/3 cup water

Rinse soybeans well. Place in a large bowl. Add 6 cups water and soak 10 to 12 hours until soybeans have doubled in size. Drain well and discard water. Place half the beans in a blender. Add 3 cups water and blend to a fine paste. Empty blender. Repeat with remaining soybeans and 3 more cups water. Line a large saucepan with 3 layers of cheesecloth. Pour soybean paste into cheesecloth. Gather corners and ends of cheesecloth together to make a bag containing soybean paste. Squeeze bag to obtain all milk from paste. Add remaining 5 cups water to paste. Squeeze cheesecloth again, adding it to soybean milk in large saucepan. Discard paste. For a more pure curd, strain and squeeze the milk again through clean cheesecloth. Combine vinegar or gypsum with 1 cup water; set aside. Bring soybean milk in large saucepan to a vigorous boil over medium heat. Let foam rise to top of saucepan. Remove from heat immediately. Pour vinegar or gypsum mixture into hot soybean milk. Quickly stir 3 or 4 times in one direction. Do not continue to stir. Let stand 15 minutes to form soft bean curd jelly. Line a 13" x 9" baking dish with 3 layers of cheesecloth. Add bean curd jelly. Fold cheesecloth over bean curd jelly and place a piece of wood slightly smaller than container or another baking dish of the same size on top of bean curd. Place a gallon jug full of water on top of wood to press bean curd. Let stand 15 minutes, removing liquid that drains from jelly with a basting bulb or by pouring it off. Remove jug, wooden cover and cloth. Slice bean curd into pieces about 3 inches square. Refrigerate in a covered container of cold water. Change water daily and bean curd will keep 2 weeks. Makes 8 squares.

Peking-Style Fried Bean Curd

Mandarin

Bean curd simmered in a spicy broth absorbs flavor from the broth.

4 (3-inch) squares Bean Curd,
    see above
1/3 cup all-purpose flour
1 egg, beaten
6 tablespoons vegetable oil
1 tablespoon rice wine or dry sherry
2 teaspoons minced fresh ginger root
2 tablespoons chopped green onion
1-1/2 teaspoons salt
1 teaspoon sugar
3 tablespoons chicken broth
1/3 cup water

Cut bean curd into 3" x 1" x 1/2" pieces. Coat pieces with flour and dip into beaten egg. Heat 3 tablespoons oil in a large skillet over medium heat 1 to 2 minutes. Carefully place bean curd pieces in oil and fry 1 minute until bottoms turn golden. Turn pieces over, add 3 tablespoons oil and fry other side until golden. In a small bowl, combine wine, ginger root, green onion, salt, sugar, chicken broth and water; mix well. Pour over bean curd. Reduce heat to low. Pierce each bean curd piece with a fork and simmer uncovered until all liquid is absorbed. Serve hot. Makes 4 servings.

Bean Curd with Crab Sauce

Mandarin

A flavorful dish with interesting texture contrasts.

6 (3-inch) squares Bean Curd,
  page 169
4 cups boiling water
Seasoning sauce:
  1/2 cup chicken broth
  2 cups water
  1 teaspoon salt
3 tablespoons vegetable oil
4-1/2 teaspoons minced fresh
  ginger root
1 (4-oz.) can crab meat without salt
1 teaspoon rice wine or dry sherry
7 teaspoons cornstarch
1/4 cup water
1 egg white, beaten
2 tablespoons chopped green onion
1 teaspoon sesame oil

Chop bean curd into 3/4-inch cubes. Cook bean curd cubes in 4 cups boiling water in a medium saucepan 1 minute. Remove cooked cubes with a small strainer. Drain well and set aside. Combine ingredients for seasoning sauce in a small bowl. Mix well and set aside. Drain crab meat and set aside. Heat vegetable oil in a wok over medium heat 1 minute. Stir-fry ginger root and crab meat 15 seconds. Add wine and seasoning sauce; mix well. Stir in bean curd cubes. Reduce heat to low and cook 3 to 4 minutes. Dissolve cornstarch in 1/4 cup water to make a paste. Slowly add cornstarch paste to crab mixture. Stir gently until sauce thickens slightly. Slowly add egg white, stirring in one direction. Remove from heat and sprinkle with chopped green onion and sesame oil. Serve hot. Makes 4 to 6 servings.

Shrimp Egg Fu Yung

Cantonese

You'll enjoy all the variations of this Chinese-style omelet.

1/2 lb. fresh shrimp
4 dried black mushrooms
1 cup hot water
6 eggs
1/2 teaspoon salt
1/4 cup water
1/4 cup chicken broth
1/2 cup vegetable oil
1/4 cup shredded fresh carrot,
  page 11
1/2 cup shredded bamboo shoots,
  page 11, or fresh bean sprouts
1/2 cup shredded mushrooms,
  page 11
1/3 cup shredded onion, page 11
1 teaspoon salt
1 teaspoon soy sauce

Shell and devein shrimp, page 59. Rinse and pat dry with a paper towel and dice into 1/8-inch pieces. Soak dried mushrooms in 1 cup hot water until soft, 15 to 30 minutes. Drain and remove hard stems. Shred softened mushrooms with a cleaver, page 11. Beat eggs in a medium bowl until frothy. Add 1/2 teaspoon salt, water and chicken broth; beat again. Heat 6 tablespoons oil in a large skillet over high heat, 30 seconds to 1 minute. Add diced shrimp, softened black mushrooms, carrot, bamboo shoots, or bean sprouts, mushrooms, onion, 1 teaspoon salt and soy sauce. Stir-fry about 3 minutes. Reduce heat to medium. Add 2 tablespoons oil to skillet. Add egg mixture, tilting pan to cover entire bottom—do not stir. When egg is almost set and bottom is golden, turn with a spatula and cook other side until golden. Serve hot. Makes 4 to 6 servings.

Variations

Pork Egg Fu Yung: Substitute 1/2 lb. uncooked pork butt or shoulder, shredded, page 11, for the diced shrimp.

Beef Egg Fu Yung: Substitute 1/2 lb. uncooked flank steak or other tender beef, shredded, page 11, for the diced shrimp.

Chicken Egg Fu Yung: Substitute 1/2 lb. uncooked chicken breast, shredded, page 11, for the diced shrimp.

Spicy Eggs with Pork

Cantonese

Five-spice powder adds an intriguing new flavor to eggs.

3 tablespoons vegetable oil
4 shallots or garlic cloves, minced
1/2 lb. ground pork
1 tablespoon rice wine or dry sherry
1/2 cup soy sauce
1 cup water
1-1/2 teaspoons sugar
1/4 teaspoon five-spice powder
6 hard-cooked eggs, peeled

Heat oil in a wok over medium heat 1 minute. Stir-fry shallots or garlic until golden. Add ground pork. Stir-fry until pork is no longer pink. Stir in wine and soy sauce. Stir-fry 4 to 5 minutes. Add water, sugar and five-spice powder. Reduce heat to low and simmer uncovered 30 minutes. Add whole hard-cooked eggs. Cook 30 minutes, turning eggs once. Serve hot. Makes 6 servings.

Stuffed Bean Curd

Cantonese

Any kind of white fish can be used for the stuffing.

4-1/2 teaspoons dried shrimp
1 cup hot water
1 (2-oz.) fish fillet such as
　sole or red snapper
4 oz. ground pork

Marinade:
　1 teaspoon rice wine or dry sherry
　1/2 teaspoon minced fresh
　　ginger root
　1/4 teaspoon pepper
　2 teaspoons cornstarch

4 (3-inch) squares Bean Curd,
　page 169
1 teaspoon cornstarch
6 tablespoons vegetable oil

Seasoning sauce:
　1/3 cup chicken broth
　2/3 cup water
　1/4 teaspoon salt
　1/2 teaspoon sugar

1 teaspoon cornstarch
1 teaspoon water
4-1/2 teaspoons soy sauce
1 tablespoon vegetable oil

Soak dried shrimp in 1 cup hot water 5 minutes to soften. Drain well; discard water. Use a cleaver to chop fish and softened shrimp together. Mix with ground pork. Combine marinade ingredients in a small bowl. Add pork mixture; mix well. Let stand 15 minutes. Cut each bean curd square into 4 small equal squares. Use a teaspoon or paring knife to make a deep indentation 1 inch in diameter in the center of each square; do not cut all the way through bean curd. Sprinkle 1/4 teaspoon cornstarch in each indentation, then stuff with pork filling. Heat 6 tablespoons oil in a large skillet over high heat 30 seconds to 1 minute. Reduce heat to medium. Carefully arrange bean curd meat-side down in skillet. Fry until bottom is golden brown. Turn and cook until other side is golden. Combine ingredients for seasoning sauce in a small bowl; mix well. Pour over stuffed bean curd. Cover and cook until 1/3 cup seasoning sauce remains in skillet. Dissolve 1 teaspoon cornstarch in 1 teaspoon water to make a paste. Add cornstarch paste and soy sauce to remaining sauce. Cook until sauce thickens slightly. Sprinkle 1 tablespoon oil over bean curd. Remove bean curd from skillet with a spatula and place on a small platter. Spoon seasoning sauce over bean curd. Serve hot. Makes 4 servings.

Tea Eggs

Cantonese

Flavor and color seeps through the cracked shells to the egg.

12 eggs
4 qts. water (16 cups)
1/4 cup black tea leaves
2 star anise
1-inch piece cinnamon stick
1 tablespoon salt
1/2 teaspoon five-spice powder

Place eggs in a large saucepan. Cover with 2 quarts water and bring to a boil over high heat. Reduce heat to medium and cook 7 minutes. Drain; let stand until cool. Lightly tap eggs to crack shells, but do not peel. Bring 2 quarts water to a boil in a large saucepan. Add tea leaves, star anise, cinnamon stick, salt and five-spice powder. Carefully add cracked eggs. Reduce heat to low. Cover and simmer 1 hour. Let cool; drain. Peel while still warm or thoroughly cooled. Serve whole as a snack to eat with your fingers. Makes 12 eggs.

Bean Curd with Soybean Milk

Szechuan

Ground pork and chopped shrimp in a spicy sauce enhance bean curd.

5 (3-inch) squares Bean Curd,
  page 169
1-1/2 cups Soybean Milk, page 186,
  without sugar
3 tablespoons dried shrimp
1-1/2 cups hot water
1 tablespoon vegetable oil
3 oz. ground pork
1/4 cup soy sauce

Seasoning sauce:
  1 teaspoon salt
  1/4 cup soy sauce
  1/2 teaspoon sugar
  3 tablespoons chopped
    Chinese parsley
  1 tablespoon Hot Chili Sauce,
    page 143
  1 tablespoon sesame oil

Place bean curd in a medium saucepan. Add Soybean Milk. Bring to a boil over medium heat. Reduce heat to low. Cover and simmer 20 minutes. Soak dried shrimp in 1-1/2 cups hot water 10 to 15 minutes. Drain well; discard water. Chop softened shrimp with a cleaver. Heat oil in a wok over high heat 30 seconds. Add ground pork and chopped shrimp. Stir-fry until pork is very lightly browned, about 2 minutes. Add soy sauce. Bring to a boil; remove from heat. Combine ingredients for seasoning sauce in a large bowl; mix well. Add shrimp and pork mixture. Mix well and set aside. Place cooked bean curd and soybean milk in a large serving bowl. Spoon sauce over bean curd. Serve hot. Add more Hot Chili Sauce, if desired. Makes 5 servings.

Ma Po's Bean Curd

Szechuan

Hot bean sauce and marinated ground pork make all the difference!

Marinade:
  1 teaspoon rice wine or dry sherry
  1 teaspoon minced fresh ginger root

1/3 lb. ground pork

Seasoning sauce:
  2 tablespoons soy sauce
  1 teaspoon salt
  1/3 cup chicken broth
  2/3 cup water
  2 teaspoons cornstarch

6 tablespoons vegetable oil
2 garlic cloves, minced
1 tablespoon hot bean sauce
5 (3-inch) squares Bean Curd,
  page 169, cut in 1/2-inch cubes
5 chopped dried red peppers, if desired
2 tablespoons chopped green onion
1 teaspoon sesame oil
1 teaspoon Peppersalt, page 88

Combine marinade ingredients in a small bowl. Add ground pork; mix well. Let stand 10 minutes. Combine ingredients for seasoning sauce in a small bowl. Mix well and set aside. Heat vegetable oil in a wok over medium heat 1 minute. Stir-fry marinated ground pork 2 minutes until browned. Add garlic, hot bean sauce, bean curd and red peppers, if desired. Stir-fry 1 minute. Pour seasoning sauce into wok. Stir-fry until sauce thickens slightly. Sprinkle with green onion and sesame oil; stir to mix. Spoon bean curd mixture on a plate. Sprinkle with Peppersalt and serve hot. Makes 4 servings.

Minced Pork Omelet

Szechuan

Omelets are foolproof when you cook them in a wok.

Marinade:
  1 teaspoon minced fresh ginger root
  1 teaspoon rice wine or dry sherry
  1/4 teaspoon pepper
  1/2 teaspoon cornstarch
  1 tablespoon soy sauce
1/3 lb. ground pork
4 eggs
1/4 teaspoon salt
5 tablespoons vegetable oil
2 tablespoons chopped green onion

Combine marinade ingredients in a medium bowl. Add ground pork. Mix well and set aside. Beat eggs until pale. Beat in salt. Heat oil in a wok over medium-high heat 1 minute. Stir-fry pork mixture about 2 minutes until pork is browned. Add green onion. Stir-fry 1 minute longer. Rotate wok to coat evenly with oil and add eggs all at once. Stir once to mix pork with eggs, then let eggs set. Cook 2 to 3 minutes until bottom of omelet is golden. Turn with a spatula. If necessary for easy turning, sprinkle 1 tablespoon oil on wok around edges of omelet. Cook 2 minutes longer until eggs are set and both sides are golden. Serve hot. Makes 4 servings.

Salty Eggs

Shanghai

Eggs are pickled in a large glass jar or crock with a tight lid.

12 eggs
6 cups boiling water
1 cup salt
3 tablespoons rice wine or dry sherry
1 tablespoon Szechuan peppercorns

Gently wash eggs and pat dry with a paper towel. Place eggs in a baking pan and let stand outdoors in the warm sun 30 minutes or at room temperature 1 hour. Pour 6 cups boiling water into a large crock or jar. Add salt, wine and peppercorns. Mix until salt is completely dissolved. Let mixture cool 20 minutes. Carefully add eggs, cover and let stand 30 to 40 days in a cool place; do not refrigerate. Before serving, cook eggs 10 minutes in boiling water over medium heat. Cool under cold water or at room temperature. Peel eggs and cut into quarters. Serve warm as a snack. Makes 12 servings.

Scrambled Eggs with Shrimp

Shanghai

Scrambled eggs are easy to make in a well-seasoned wok. To season your wok, see page 13.

1/2 lb. fresh shrimp
Marinade:
  1/2 teaspoon rice wine or dry sherry
  1/4 teaspoon salt
  1/2 teaspoon minced fresh
    ginger root
  1 teaspoon cornstarch
  1 teaspoon sesame oil
5 eggs
1/2 teaspoon salt
1 cup vegetable oil

Shell and devein shrimp, page 59. Rinse and pat dry with a paper towel. Combine marinade ingredients in a small bowl. Add shrimp; mix well. Let stand 10 minutes. Beat eggs slightly in a medium bowl. Beat in salt. Heat oil in a wok over high heat 1 minute. Stir-fry shrimp 30 seconds. Remove shrimp from oil with a slotted spoon, draining well over wok. Set shrimp aside. Remove oil from wok except 5 tablespoons. Reduce heat to medium. Pour egg mixture into wok. Add cooked shrimp. Stir-fry 1 to 2 minutes until eggs are set. Remove from wok and place on a small platter. Makes 4 servings.

Sweet Rice Omelet

Shanghai

Golden omelets are rolled around a divine filling of sweet rice, shrimp and ham.

1-1/4-cups sweet rice, uncooked
3 cups cold water
2 dried black mushrooms
2 cups hot water
2 tablespoons dried shrimp
9 tablespoons vegetable oil
1 garlic clove, crushed
1/4 cup diced ham
2 tablespoons diced green pepper
1 tablespoon rice wine or dry sherry
1 teaspoon salt
1/2 teaspoon sugar
1/4 cup chicken broth
1/4 cup water
1 tablespoon cornstarch
2 tablespoons water
4 eggs

Rinse rice with cold water. Soak rice in 3 cups cold water 2 hours. Drain well. Soak dried black mushrooms in 1 cup hot water until soft, 15 to 30 minutes. Drain and remove hard stems. Chop softened mushrooms with a cleaver. Soak dried shrimp in 1 cup hot water 10 to 15 minutes to soften. Drain well; discard water. Chop softened shrimp with cleaver. Heat 4 tablespoons oil and garlic in a wok over medium heat. Add chopped shrimp and mushrooms, ham and green pepper. Stir-fry 30 seconds. Add wine, salt and sugar; mix well. Remove mixture from wok with a slotted spoon; set aside. Heat 2 tablespoons oil in wok over medium heat 30 seconds. Add soaked rice. Stir-fry 1 minute over medium-high heat. Slowly add chicken broth and 1/4 cup water. Stir-fry 10 to 15 minutes until rice is tender. Add cooked shrimp mixture; mix well. Remove wok from heat; set aside. In a medium bowl, dissolve cornstarch in 2 tablespoons water to make a paste. Add eggs to cornstarch paste and beat well. Heat 1-1/2 teaspoons oil in a small skillet over medium heat 30 seconds to 1 minute. Pour half the egg mixture into skillet, tilting so egg mixture covers bottom of skillet. Cook without stirring until egg is almost set. Carefully remove omelet from skillet and place cooked side down on cutting board. Repeat with another 1/2 teaspoon oil and remaining egg mixture. Place half the rice mixture in center of omelet, spreading evenly hortizontally. Fold bottom edge over rice mixture and roll up towards top. Repeat with remaining omelet and rice mixture. Heat 2 tablespoons oil in skillet over medium heat 30 seconds to 1 minute. Carefully place rolled omelets in skillet. Fry 2 minutes or until golden, turning once. Place on cutting board and chop into 1-inch pieces. Arrange omelet pieces on a platter. Makes 4 to 6 servings.

How to Make Sweet Rice Omelet

1/Spread half the rice mixture on one omelet. Fold one side over and roll up.

2/After frying rolled omelets, cut into 1-inch pieces and serve.

Bean Curd Sandwiches

Shanghai

Little pork-filled sandwiches resemble ravioli.

1/4 lb. ground pork

Marinade:
  1 teaspoon rice wine or dry sherry
  1/4 teaspoon salt
  1 teaspoon cornstarch

2 (3-inch) squares Bean Curd,
  page 169
About 1/3 cup all-purpose flour

Seasoning sauce:
  2 tablespoons soy sauce
  1/2 teaspoon salt
  1/4 cup chicken broth
  1 teaspoon cornstarch
  1/4 cup water

1/4 cup vegetable oil
2 tablespoons chopped green onion
1-1/2 teaspoons minced fresh
  ginger root
2 teaspoons sesame oil

Lightly chop ground pork with a cleaver. Combine marinade ingredients in a small bowl. Add ground pork; mix well. Let stand 10 minutes. Cut each bean curd cake into four 1-1/4-inch squares. Cut each square into 3 slices. Sprinkle each slice with flour. Spread about 1-1/2 tablespoons pork mixture on 12 slices of bean curd. Top with remaining bean curd slices to make 12 sandwiches. Combine ingredients for seasoning sauce in a small bowl. Mix well and set aside. Sprinkle each sandwich with flour. Heat vegetable oil in a large skillet over medium heat 30 seconds to 1 minute. Fry bean curd sandwiches until lightly browned on one side. Turn with a spatula and fry until other side is golden brown. Add green onion and ginger root. Carefully stir-fry 15 seconds. Stir in seasoning sauce. Reduce heat to low. Cover and simmer 5 minutes. Stir in sesame oil. Serve hot. Makes 4 to 6 servings.

DESSERTS & SWEETS

A sweet dish to eat at the end of a meal is not something the Chinese are enthusiastic about. On rare occasions, fresh fruits such as watermelon, pineapple or oranges are served at home after dinner. Most Chinese are content to sip tea after a big meal. Desserts are reserved mainly for banquets and feasts. Sweet nut soups, light puddings and pastries filled with red bean paste sometimes appear at the end of a family dinner. They are more often served as a change of pace in the middle of a formal banquet.

Sweet snacks are very popular. Fresh and dried fruits as well as pastries frequently appear between meals.

Because Chinese kitchens are not usually equipped with ovens, many pastries are deep-fried. Slits are made in the dough so it curls and opens in the hot oil. Directions for this procedure are in Pastry Flowers and Sesame Bows.

Bakeries in China use lard instead of butter so many pastries are not as irresistible as they may look. In fact, most are not very sweet. Some pastries are filled with sweet bean paste but others contain a salty filling.

Many sweets are part of festivals. Sesame Bows and Steamed Layer Cakes or Steamed Cake are served for Chinese New Year. Moon cakes, a round moon-shape pastry, are served at the Moon Festival. Cantonese Moon Cakes go one step farther with a salty egg yolk tucked in their centers to symbolize the moon. Fruits with many seeds such as pomegranates or watermelons are symbols of fertility and are served at festivals.

Sweet soups are sometimes served as a bedtime snack. Nuts such as peanuts or almonds are cooked with sugar and water until the nuts are soft. Sometimes a little milk is added. Sweet nourishing soup can be served hot or cold.

Because no one cuisine has developed its own particular desserts, it's difficult to identify the recipes in this section as originating from a particular region. For the most part, these sweets are common throughout China.

Steamed Layer Cakes

Canned sweet cucumbers are sold in Oriental food stores.

1 pkg. active dry yeast
1-1/2 cups warm water
3-1/2 cups all-purpose flour
Filling:
   1 cup sugar
   1 cup shredded coconut
   3 tablespoons chopped dates
   1/2 cup lard or margarine, melted
3 tablespoons canned shredded
   sweet cucumber
About 8 cups boiling water

Sprinkle dry yeast into 1-1/2 cups warm water; stir to dissolve. Set aside until mixture begins to foam, 5 to 10 minutes. Sift flour into a large bowl. Make a well in the sifted flour and slowly add yeast mixture. Mix thoroughly with a spoon. Place dough on a floured surface and knead about 3 minutes until smooth and elastic. Place dough in large bowl and cover with a damp cloth. Let stand in a warm place 3 or 4 hours until doubled in bulk. Combine filling ingredients in a medium bowl, mixing well; set aside. Place dough on a floured surface and knead again until smooth and elastic. Use a rolling pin to roll out to a very thin 30" x 12" rectangle. Spread 1/6 of the filling over center third of dough. Fold one side over filling. Spread 1/3 of the remaining filling on top of folded section. Fold remaining side over filling. Turn dough so the last folded edge faces you. Roll out again into a 18" x 12" rectangle. Repeat folding steps with remaining filling. Then fold dough in half and in half again to make a 6-inch square. Spread shredded sweet cucumber on an 8-inch square of greased waxed paper. Place dough on cucumber. Let stand 30 minutes. Pour 4 cups boiling water into a wok or large pot. Place cake in a steamer. Cover steamer and place over boiling water. Steam over high heat 35 to 40 minutes, adding more boiling water as needed. Remove from heat and let cool 3 to 5 minutes. Remove cover slowly as a quick cold draft may cause cakes to collapse. Cut into slices and serve warm. Makes 4 to 6 servings.

Steamed Cake

This is a very moist soft cake. Serve it either warm or cold.

2 eggs
1-1/2 cups brown sugar
1-1/3 cups all-purpose flour
1/4 cup sweet rice powder
2 teaspoons baking powder
1/2 teaspoon baking soda
1/2 cup corn oil
About 8 cups boiling water

Grease a round 9-inch cake pan. Mix eggs, brown sugar, flour, rice powder, baking powder, baking soda and corn oil in a large bowl. Beat about 1 minute with electric mixer until smooth. Pour into the prepared pan. Pour 4 cups boiling water into a wok or large pot. Place cake in steamer. Cover steamer and place over boiling water. Steam 35 minutes, adding more boiling water if necessary. Remove from heat and let cake cool in steamer about 5 minutes. Invert cake over a plate; remove pan. Makes 1 cake.

Variation

Stir 1/2 cup raisins into batter before pouring into baking pan.

Cantonese Moon Cakes

It's a Chinese tradition to give moon cakes to celebrate the autumn moon.

10 uncooked Salty Egg yolks, page 175
2 cups red bean paste
2 cups all-purpose flour
1/2 tablespoon baking powder
1/4 cup dry milk powder
3 eggs
2/3 cup sugar
1/3 cup melted butter
1/4 teaspoon salt
1 egg yolk, beaten

Preheat oven to 325°F (165°C). Bake Salty Egg yokes on a baking sheet 10 to 12 minutes. Divide bean paste into 10 portions. Roll each portion between your palms into a ball. Make a hole in each ball with your thumb and place a baked egg yolk in each ball. Press bean paste around yolk to cover. Roll again to reshape into balls. Sift together flour, baking powder and dry milk powder into a large bowl. Repeat sifting 2 more times. Beat eggs and sugar in another large bowl until sugar has dissolved, about 2 minutes with an electric mixer. Add melted butter and salt. Add flour mixture; mix to a soft dough. Divide dough into 10 pieces and roll each piece into a ball. Flatten each ball into a 4-inch circle between your palms. Place a bean paste ball in the center of a circle and gather edges together to enclose filling. Lightly flatten the top to make a round cake 2 inches wide and 1/2 inch high. Repeat with remaining dough balls and bean paste balls. If using a mold, press cake into mold, then tap inverted mold to remove cake. Place cakes on a baking sheet. Brush each cake with beaten egg yolk. Preheat oven to 375°F (190°C). Place a small pan of water in the oven to provide moisture and prevent the cakes from cracking. Bake cakes 20 to 25 minutes until browned. Remove from baking sheet with a spatula. Cool on a rack. Serve immediately or wrap cooled cakes in waxed paper or aluminum foil until ready to serve. Makes 10 servings.

Variation

Salty Egg yolks may be omitted.

Candied Banana Fritters

For crisp fritters, quickly dip syrup-coated banana pieces in a bowl of water containing several ice cubes.

1 egg
3 tablespoons all-purpose flour
3 tablespoons cornstarch
1/8 teaspoon salt
1 tablespoon ice water
3 bananas
6 cups oil for deep-frying
2 tablespoons vegetable oil
1/2 cup sugar

Beat egg slightly in a small bowl. Add flour, cornstarch, salt and ice water. Mix to a smooth batter and set aside. Peel bananas and slice each one diagonally into 5 or 6 pieces. Heat 6 cups oil in a wok over high heat to 350°F (175°C). Reduce heat to medium. Dip banana pieces in batter and carefully lower into hot oil with a slotted metal spoon. Fry 15 to 30 seconds until lightly browned. Remove with slotted spoon, draining well over wok; set aside. Heat 2 tablespoons oil in a small saucepan over medium heat 30 seconds to 1 minute. Add sugar; mix well. Cook until thickened to a syrup. Remove from heat. Add fried bananas and mix lightly to coat. Place on a lightly greased platter and serve immediately. Makes 4 to 6 servings.

How to Make Cantonese Moon Cakes

1/Press a Salty Egg yolk into each ball of bean paste and mold bean paste around egg yolk.

2/Wrap bean paste ball in dough and press it into a mold or flatten between your palms.

3/Brush each moon cake with egg yolk before baking.

Mango Pudding

Agar agar is a seaweed-based gelatin and is available in both white and red.

1/4 oz. agar agar
2 cups warm water
4 cups water
1 large fresh mango
2/3 cup sugar
1/4 cup evaporated milk
Maraschino cherries

Soak agar agar stick in a medium bowl with 2 cups warm water 30 minutes. Transfer agar agar and water to a large saucepan. Add 4 cups water. Bring to a boil over medium heat and cook until agar agar is completly dissolved. Peel mango and chop into small pieces. Remove saucepan from heat and add sugar, milk and chopped mango. Stir until sugar is totally dissolved. Pour into a 12" x 8" cake pan. Let stand until cool. Refrigerate until pudding is firm, about 15 minutes. Cut into diamond shapes. Garnish with maraschino cherries. Serve chilled. Makes 6 to 8 servings.

Variation

Mandarin Orange Pudding: Substitute 1 segmented peeled mandarin orange for the mango pieces.

Almond Cookies

Crisp nutty cookies are delicious with a pot of Chinese tea, page 20.

1 cup lard or shortening
1 cup sugar
1 egg, beaten
1/2 cup ground blanched almonds
1 teaspoon almond extract
2-1/2 cups all-purpose flour
1-1/2 teaspoons baking powder
1/2 teaspoon salt
36 blanched almond halves
1 egg yolk
1 tablespoon water

Grease baking sheets; set aside. Mix lard or shortening and sugar in a large bowl until smooth. Add egg, ground almonds and almond extract; mix well. Sift together flour, baking powder and salt, gradually adding to egg mixture and mixing well. Dough will be stiff. Preheat oven to 350°F (175°C). Shape dough into 36 small balls. Place balls 2 inches apart on prepared baking sheets. Press an almond half on each ball and flatten with the palm of your hand to a 2-inch cookie. Mix egg yolk and water in a small cup to make a glaze. Brush each cookie with glaze and bake about 20 minutes until golden. Makes 36 cookies.

Crisp Rice with Sesame Seeds

Squares of Crisp Rice must be made at least one day in advance.

6 cups oil for deep-frying
10 squares Crisp Rice, page 151
2 tablespoons sesame seeds
7 teaspoons sugar

Heat 6 cups oil in a wok over high heat to 375°F (190°C). Test oil by dropping in a small piece of crisp rice. The oil is hot enough if the rice puffs out in 3 seconds. Reduce heat to medium. Carefully lower a few rice squares at a time into hot oil with a slotted metal spoon. Deep-fry until golden brown. Remove with slotted spoon, drain on paper towels and place on a plate. Heat a small saucepan over medium heat 30 seconds to 1 minute. Add sesame seeds and stir-fry until golden brown. Remove from heat and let cool. Add sugar; mix well. Pour sesame seed mixture over fried rice squares. Makes 4 to 6 servings.

Sweet Pastry Flowers

When these pastries are deep-fried, they blossom into flowers.

1 cup red bean paste
3 uncooked Salty Egg yolks,
   page 175, if desired

Dough 1:
   1 cup all-purpose flour
   1/4 cup lard or shortening

Dough 2:
   2 cups all-purpose flour
   1/4 cup lard or shortening
   1/2 cup ice water
   1-1/2 teaspoons sugar
   1/4 teaspoon salt

6 cups oil for deep-frying

Divide bean paste into 20 pieces and roll into round balls. If desired, crumble Salty Egg Yolks until fine and divide into 5 equal portions. Combine ingredients for Dough 1 in a large bowl; mix well. Place dough on a floured surface. Use your hands to shape into a roll 1 inch in diameter. Chop the roll into 20 pieces with a cleaver. Combine ingredients for Dough 2 in a large bowl; mix well. Use your hands to shape into a long roll about 1-1/2 inches in diameter. Chop roll into 20 pieces with a cleaver. Flatten each piece of Dough 2 between your palms. Place a piece of Dough 1 on top of a piece of Dough 2. Gather up edges of Dough 2 to make a larger ball. Flatten ball with the palm of your hand. Use a rolling pin to roll out to a rectangle 1/4 inch thick. Roll up jelly-roll fashion. Roll between your palms into a ball then flatten to a 2-inch circle. In the center of each circle place 1 ball of bean paste and 1/4 portion of Salty Egg Yolk, if desired. Gather up edges of dough around filling and twist together on top to seal. With a sharp paring knife, make 3 diagonal cuts on the bottom of each pastry without cutting all the way through the dough. Repeat with remaining pieces of dough and filling. Heat 6 cups oil in a wok over high heat to 350°F (175°C). Place pastries in a large strainer. Reduce heat to low. Carefully submerge pastries in hot oil, remove strainer and deep-fry pastries 12 to 15 minutes until pastry flowers blossom. Turn heat up to high and cook 1 minute longer. Remove pastries from oil with strainer, draining well over wok. Cool and serve. Makes 20 pastries.

Sesame Bows

Store crisp sesame bows in a covered container and they will stay fresh for several weeks.

2 cups all-purpose flour
1/3 cup sugar
Pinch of salt
1/4 cup black sesame seeds,
   or regular sesame seeds
1 egg
1/2 (3-inch) square Bean Curd,
   page 169
1 to 2 teaspoons milk, if needed
3 cups vegetable oil for deep-frying

Sift together flour, sugar and salt into a large bowl. Add sesame seeds; mix well. Beat egg slightly in a small bowl. Use a spoon to break up bean curd. Add to egg; mix well. Add egg mixture to flour mixture. Knead to mix well. Dough should be soft. If too dry, knead in 1 to 2 teaspoons milk. Cover with a damp towel and let stand 30 minutes. Place dough on a floured surface. Use a rolling pin to roll out dough to a long 1/8-inch thick sheet. Use a sharp knife to cut dough into 3" X 1-1/2" strips. Make three 1-1/2-inch slits lengthwise in the middle of each strip. To make a bow, pull one end through the middle slit. Heat 3 cups oil in a wok over medium-high heat to 350°F (175°C). Reduce heat to low and carefully lower several bows into hot oil with a slotted metal spoon. Fry several at a time 3 minutes. Increase heat to high and fry 1 minute longer until golden brown. Remove with slotted spoon, drain and cool on paper towels. Makes 4 to 6 servings.

Open-Mouth Laughs

Roll balls of sweet dough in sesame seeds, then deep-fry and watch them pop open.

2 cups all-purpose flour
1 teaspoon baking powder
2 eggs, lightly beaten
2/3 cup sugar
1 tablespoon water
1 tablespoon lard or shortening
1/2 cup water
1/2 cup sesame seeds
8 cups oil for deep-frying

Sift flour and baking powder together twice. Combine eggs, sugar, 1 tablespoon water and lard or shortening in a medium bowl; mix well. Slowly stir in flour mixture. Knead 1 to 2 minutes to a soft dough. Shape into a roll 1 inch in diameter. Chop roll into 16 pieces with a sharp knife. Roll each piece into a ball in the palms of your hands. Dip each ball in 1/2 cup water and roll in sesame seeds. Heat 8 cups oil in a wok over medium heat to 350°F (175°C). Reduce heat to low and carefully lower 8 sesame balls into hot oil with a slotted metal spoon. Deep-fry until balls expand and open, about 2 minutes. Carefully remove fried balls with slotted spoon, draining well over wok; set aside. Repeat with remaining 8 balls. Reheat oil over high heat, return 8 balls to oil and fry until golden brown. Remove with slotted spoon, drain on paper towels and let cool. Repeat with remaining 8 balls. Makes 16 sesame balls.

Sajima

Deep-fried noodles are coated with syrup and pressed together to make a crunchy sweet.

3 cups all-purpose flour
1 tablespoon baking powder
1/8 teaspoon salt
4 eggs
6 cups vegetable oil for deep-frying

Seasoning sauce:
  1 cup sugar
  3/4 cup maltose or 1-1/4 cups honey
  1/4 cup water
  1-1/2 teaspoons lemon juice

2 tablespoons sesame seeds
1/4 cup raisins

Lightly grease an 8- or 9-inch square cake pan; set aside. Sift together flour, baking powder and salt into a large bowl. Add eggs; mix thoroughly with a spoon. Knead 2 minutes to make a smooth dough. Cover with a damp cloth and let stand 20 minutes. Divide dough in half and place one half on a floured surface. Use a rolling pin to roll out dough to a thin rectangle about 1/4 inch thick. Slice into strips 1-inch long. Shred strips widthwise with a cleaver to make thin noodles 1 inch long, page 11. Heat oil in a wok over high heat to 375°F (190°C). Reduce heat to medium. Carefully lower noodles into hot oil with a slotted metal spoon. Deep-fry 45 to 60 seconds until noodles are puffed and golden brown. Remove with slotted spoon, drain on paper towels and place in a large bowl. Repeat with remaining dough. Combine ingredients for seasoning sauce in a small saucepan. Cook sauce without boiling over medium heat about 2 minutes until thickened to a syrup. Pour syrup over fried noodles and mix thoroughly to coat. Pour mixture into prepared cake pan. Stir-fry sesame seeds in a small saucepan until golden. Add browned sesame seeds and raisins to noodles. Press mixture firmly into cake pan and let cool. Cut into squares. Makes 12 to 15 squares.

Soybean Milk

Serve this for breakfast or for a morning snack with Yu T'iau, page 154.

2 cups soybeans
6 cups water for soaking
12 cups water
Sugar

Rinse soybeans well. Place in a large bowl with 6 cups water. Soak 8 to 10 hours until soybeans have doubled in size. Drain well and discard water. Place half the beans in blender with 3 cups water. Blend to a fine paste. Empty blender. Repeat with remaining soybeans and 3 more cups of water. Spread 3 layers of cheesecloth over a large saucepan. Pour soybean paste into cheesecloth. Bring corners of cheesecloth together and twist, squeezing milk from soybean paste. Add remaining 6 cups water to paste. Squeeze cheesecloth again, adding it to soybean milk in large saucepan. Discard paste and cheesecloth. Bring soy milk almost to a boil over medium heat, stirring frequently. Remove from heat. Serve hot or cold. Add sugar to taste to each serving. Makes 6 servings.

Creamy Peanut Soup

Enjoy this dish as a dessert or as a bedtime snack.

1/2 cup sesame seeds
1 cup unsalted roasted shelled peanuts
8 cups water
2/3 cup sugar
3 tablespoons cornstarch
3 tablespoons water
1/2 cup evaporated milk

Stir-fry sesame seeds and peanuts in a wok over low heat until golden. Remove from wok with a large spoon and place in blender. Add 2 cups water. Blend at high speed until smooth. Strain mixture through a double thickness of cheesecloth into a large saucepan. Add 6 cups water and sugar. Bring to a boil over medium heat. Dissolve cornstarch and 3 tablespoons water to make a paste. Stir cornstarch paste into boiling soup. Stir often over medium heat. When soup begins to thicken, remove from heat. Add evaporated milk; mix well. Serve hot or cold. Makes 6 servings.

Creamy Almond Soup

Look for canned almond paste in Oriental grocery stores.

1/2 cup sesame seeds
7 cups water
4-oz. almond paste
3/4 cup sugar
3 tablespoons cornstarch
3 tablespoons water
1/2 cup evaporated milk
2 teaspoons almond extract

Stir-fry sesame seeds in a small saucepan over medium heat until golden. Place toasted sesame seeds in blender with 1 cup water. Blend at high speed until smooth. Place sesame seed mixture in a large saucepan. Add almond paste and sugar; mix well. Add 6 cups water. Bring to a boil over medium heat. Dissolve cornstarch in water to make a paste. Stir cornstarch paste into boiling soup. Remove saucepan from heat. Add evaporated milk and almond extract; mix well. Serve hot. Makes 6 servings.

How to Make Soybean Milk

1/Blend soaked soybeans with water to a fine paste.

2/Twist top of cheesecloth to squeeze milk from soybean paste.

Sweet Peanut Soup

Be sure to use raw peanuts, not roasted peanuts.

2/3 lb. shelled raw peanuts
10 cups water
2/3 cup to 1 cup sugar

Rinse peanuts in cold water. Place rinsed peanuts and 10 cups water in a large saucepan. Bring to a boil. Cover and reduce heat. Simmer 3 to 4 hours until peanuts are very tender. Stir in sugar. Bring to a boil uncovered over medium heat. When sugar has dissolved, pour soup into small bowls. Serve hot. Makes 6 servings.

Sweet Almond Jelly

Canned lichee nuts or pineapple slices go well with this pudding-like dessert.

1/4 oz. agar agar, page 15
6 cups water
1/3 cup sugar
1/2 cup milk
1 tablespoon almond extract
6 maraschino cherry halves

Quickly rinse agar agar. Place in a large bowl with 3 cups water. Let soak 30 minutes. Drain well, discarding water. Place drained agar agar in a medium saucepan. Add remaining 3 cups water. Stir constantly over medium heat until agar agar dissolves. Add sugar, milk and almond extract; mix well. Pour into 6 individual dishes. Refrigerate about 1 hour until firm. Garnish with maraschino cherry halves. Makes 6 servings.

Coconut Rice Balls

Sweet rice powder, or glutinous rice powder, resembles powdered sugar.

1 cup red bean paste
2 cups sweet rice powder
1 cup water
6 cups boiling water
3 maraschino cherries, quartered
1/2 cup shredded coconut

Cut twelve 2-1/2 inch squares of waxed paper; set aside. Divide bean paste into 12 portions. Shape each portion into a ball. Mix sweet rice powder and 1 cup water in a large bowl to make a smooth dough. Divide dough into 4 portions. Use the palm of your hand to flatten each portion into a 5" x 4" rectangle 1/4-inch thick. Place rectangles in 6 cups boiling water and cook over medium heat 5 minutes. They will rise to the surface of the water and become almost transparent. Remove with a large strainer and drain well. Place cooked dough in a large bowl and beat vigorously with a wooden spoon 3 to 5 minutes until very sticky. Wet your hands and divide beaten dough into 12 portions. Shape each portion into a ball and flatten to a circle with the palm of your hand. Place 1 ball of bean paste in the center of a circle and gather edges together to enclose filling. Pinch edges to seal. Roll between your palms to shape into a smooth ball. Place each ball on a piece of waxed paper. Repeat with remaining dough portions and filling. Top each ball with a cherry piece and sprinkle with shredded coconut. Makes 12 balls.

Sweet Rice Balls

Red bean paste is also called sweet bean paste.

1 cup red bean paste
2 cups sweet rice powder
1/3 cup sugar
3/4 cup water
1 cup water
1 cup sesame seeds
6 cups oil for deep-frying

Divide bean paste into 16 portions. Mix rice powder, sugar and 2/3 cup water in a large bowl to make a smooth dough. Lightly grease a flat surface. Knead dough on greased surface until smooth. Use your hands to shape dough into a long roll about 1 inch in diameter. Chop dough into 16 pieces with a cleaver. Flatten each piece into a 2-inch circle with the palm of your hand. Place 1 portion of bean paste in the center of a dough circle and gather edges around filling. Roll into a ball. Dip ball in 1 cup water and roll in sesame seeds to coat. Repeat with remaining dough and bean paste. Heat 6 cups oil in a wok over high heat to 350°F (175°C). Reduce heat to medium. Carefully lower balls into hot oil with a slotted metal spoon. Deep-fry 5 minutes until golden; balls will expand. Remove from oil with slotted spoon and drain on paper towels. Serve warm. Makes 16 balls.

Sweet Bean Soup

As a winter dessert, it should be hot. Serve it cold in the summer.

1 lb. dried mung beans or
  dried red beans
7 cups water
1 cup sugar

Rinse beans in cold water. Place rinsed beans and 7 cups water in a large saucepan. Bring to a boil. Cover and reduce heat. Simmer 3 to 4 hours until beans are tender. Stir in sugar. Serve soup hot or cold in small bowls. Makes 6 servings.

INDEX

INDEX

A-9.302912902